LEAN HIGHER EDUCATION

Increasing the Value and
Performance of University Processes

LEAN HIGHER EDUCATION

*Increasing the Value and
Performance of University Processes*

William K. Balzer

CRC Press
Taylor & Francis Group
Boca Raton   London   New York

CRC Press is an imprint of the
Taylor & Francis Group, an **informa** business

A PRODUCTIVITY PRESS BOOK

Productivity Press
Taylor & Francis Group
270 Madison Avenue
New York, NY 10016

© 2010 by Taylor and Francis Group, LLC
Productivity Press is an imprint of Taylor & Francis Group, an Informa business

No claim to original U.S. Government works

Printed in the United States of America on acid-free paper
10 9 8 7 6 5 4 3 2 1

International Standard Book Number: 978-1-4398-1465-9 (Paperback)

Library of Congress Cataloging-in-Publication Data

Balzer, William K.
    Lean higher education : increasing the value and performance of university processes / William K. Balzer.
        p. cm.
    Includes bibliographical references and index.
    ISBN 978-1-4398-1465-9 (pbk. : alk. paper)
    1. Universities and colleges--United States--Administration. 2. Organizational effectiveness--United States. 3. Organizational change--United States. I. Title.

LB2341.B273 2010
378.1'01--dc22   2010006507

Visit the Taylor & Francis Web site at
http://www.taylorandfrancis.com

and the Productivity Press Web site at
http://www.productivitypress.com

This book is dedicated to

My parents, my wife Margaret, and our children,
Kate, Anna, Matthew, and Julia.

You have enriched my life and made every day special.

Contents

Preface

The idea for this book began in 2004 as areas of professional interest began to converge. As an industrial-organizational psychologist, I maintained a strong interest in, and healthy skepticism of, large-scale change programs designed to improve organizational performance and the quality of work life among employees. As a university administrator, I saw opportunities for improving the way we do the work essential to the goals of higher education, convinced that there were alternative ways to meet the needs of students and faculty that would be more efficient for the university and provide more satisfying and fulfilling work for university employees. At about this time, several of my colleagues at Bowling Green State University were offering professional development workshops on a topic of great interest among area organizations, that of Lean manufacturing, which proposed a radical new philosophy and set of operational practices to improve performance and effectiveness. Intrigued, I attended several of these weeklong workshops, which included a "hands-on" component to apply the principles and practices of Lean in nearby organizations. I began to understand how Toyota, the originator and champion of Lean thinking, developed its comprehensive philosophy by building on two important pillars—an unswerving commitment to meeting the needs of customers (external and internal) and a parallel commitment to developing the capabilities of a motivated and satisfied workforce required to implement the Lean philosophy. Based on its successful application in manufacturing processes, the application of Toyota's Lean principles and practices expanded to other business functions (e.g., research and product development, customer sales and service, etc.). This led me to read more broadly on Lean, although most of the published work focused on applications in manufacturing, which seemed less directly applicable to higher education than the few books that addressed other functions within an organization (e.g., back office operations).

During an administrative leave in the Fall of 2005, I began a more focused research effort exploring whether the adoption of a Lean philosophy and the application of Lean principles and practices would be an appropriate large-scale change program that could benefit the important work of colleges and universities. Fortuitously, James Womack and Daniel Jones published their second co-authored book that year, *Lean Solutions: How Companies and Customers Can Create Value and Wealth Together* (2005, New York: Free Press). Their book articulately demonstrated and promoted applications of Lean in the service industry, and offered a useful framework for understanding and improving workplace processes from both the perspectives of the company that provides them and the customer who benefits from them. This was my epiphany, which further stimulated my thinking about how Lean could work in higher education settings. It also led to a series of Lean projects at my university that provided practical experience in applying Lean and demonstrated the potential of Lean for making colleges and universities more competitive and successful. Eventually, the idea for this book took form. Standing on the shoulders of Lean authors before me—Womack, Jones, Imai, Liker, Rother, Shook, Laraia, Monden, Keyte, Tapping, and many others—this first book on Lean Higher Education (LHE)—the application of Lean principles and practices in colleges and universities—was written. I hope my enthusiasm for the potential of LHE comes across in the writing. LHE holds great promise for helping colleges and universities do a better job of meeting the needs of those they serve, improving the efficiency and effectiveness of the critical processes and services that allow them to achieve their mission and goals, and providing faculty and staff with more enriching and rewarding experiences at work.

Acknowledgments

Many friends and colleagues at Bowling Green State University (BGSU) made this book possible and deserve recognition for their guidance and support. Linda Dobb, Executive Vice President, provided me with the time and strong encouragement to pursue this project; I could not have written this without her. Sidney Ribeau, President, pledged his personal support for the LHE demonstration projects at BGSU included in this book. Ed Whipple, Vice President for Student Affairs, opened up his division and actively recruited areas to participate in LHE projects. I am deeply indebted to these three visionary university leaders for their confidence, support, and friendship.

Tom Andrews, a faculty colleague, Lean black belt, and Shingo Prize winning co-author, provided exceptional mentoring. Tom also co-led several of the LHE projects at BGSU described in this book along with Wil Roudebush. Many colleagues at the BGSU Counseling Center, Student Health Services, and Continuing and Extended Education unit contributed to the success of the LHE projects: Craig Vickio, Becky Davenport, Garrett Gilmer, Cathy Kocarek, Stefani Hathaway, Amy Lanning, Arena Mueller, Glenn Egelman, Dick Sipp, Marcia Salazar-Valentine, Ann Light, Lisé Konecny, Pat Bruielly, Gentry Green, Teresa McLove, and Pat Wise. Dick See (University of Iowa) and Baha Inosu (formerly with the University of New Orleans) generously shared their wealth of knowledge and information on the successful Lean projects at their campuses. Two wonderful graduate students, Erin Smith and Katherine Alexander, collaborated on research investigating the effectiveness of Lean programs; in addition, Erin made significant contributions to the LHE project completed at the BGSU Counseling Center. Jim Smith, a colleague at BGSU's Firelands College, provided helpful input on Chapter 8. Mike Doherty, Distinguished University Professor Emeritus and one of my most esteemed colleagues in the Department of Psychology, provided excellent editorial feedback on the first three chapters, which subsequently influenced the later chapters. Dave LaHote of the Lean Enterprise Institute provided both direction and feedback on ideas included in this book. Scott Withrow, my hardworking graduate assistant, provided formatting and organizational support. Together these individuals helped shape the ideas, organization, and writing. Their contributions are acknowledged; all errors and shortcomings are mine alone.

Other individuals provided unflagging support during the writing process. Chris Mruk, Ken Pargament, Bruce Edwards and Steve Jex, faculty colleagues and noted book authors themselves, helped me navigate the book authoring and publishing process. Dick Smith, a former advisory board member at BGSU, business leader, and friend, constantly encouraged my efforts with his enthusiasm and belief in the benefits of LHE. Michael Sinocchi and Lara Zoble, Senior Acquisitions Editor and Assistant Editor and Project Coordinator, respectively, at Productivity Press, were especially helpful in turning rough manuscript pages into a finished book. Finally, my family provided the time, support, and encouragement I needed throughout this long process. To Margaret, Kate, Anna, Matthew, and Julia: thanks for your patience and love.

Introduction

This book is written to appeal to a broad audience: individuals interested in learning how to apply Lean principles and practices to higher education (i.e., referred to as Lean Higher Education or LHE), university administrators interested in learning more about LHE and how it can help achieve academic and operational excellence, graduate students in higher education interested in improving university processes and introducing large-scale institutional change programs, and constituent leaders (e.g., university trustees seeking a competitive advantage over other higher education institutions, elected and appointed government officials balancing institutional support versus institutional outcomes, business leaders dependent on college graduates and the intellectual output of universities). Practical examples are provided throughout the book, and the endnotes for each chapter reference additional readings for those interested in learning more about the specific topics covered.

Chapter 1 provides a contextual overview of the need for LHE. The challenges of declining support for higher education, and an increased call for accountability, underscore the importance of new models for delivering the complex set of processes that make up a university. The chapter introduces the success of Lean principles and practices outside higher education and LHE's potential for creating low-cost, high-quality, and "just-in-time" processes valued by those served by institutions of higher education.

Chapter 2 provides a detailed overview of the application of LHE using a typical scenario at a residential university: the new freshman move-in process, which provides parents and students with an early impression of their new university and its concern for their needs. This example walks through the key steps involved in applying LHE principles and practices, and culminates in the identification and implementation of solutions that remove waste and improve the flow of the move-in process. Chapter 3 presents a number of successful examples of the application of LHE principles and practices across a variety of institutions in higher education. These examples, while small in number because of the relatively recent application of Lean principles and practices in higher education, show the dramatic improvements in critical university processes that are possible whether introduced university-wide or "locally" in specific divisions or areas of the institution.

Chapters 4 through 8 each focus on the key steps followed when adopting LHE as an intentional and disciplined approach to improve critical processes at a university. Chapter 4 discusses initial considerations that should be taken into account prior to launching an LHE initiative: confirming the institution's readiness for introducing LHE, creating an organizational structure to support LHE, choosing the university process that will be the target of the LHE project, and selecting and training the LHE project team. Chapter 5 underscores the importance of identifying the needs and expectations of the beneficiaries of the process, and provides practical advice for translating these needs and expectations into specific metrics designed to assess the effectiveness of the process before and after introducing LHE solutions. Chapter 6 demonstrates how to create visual maps that provide a comprehensive understanding of all the steps and activities that are part of the process targeted for improvement through LHE. The visual map also identifies current levels of performance on the established metrics for assessing the process. Chapter 7 identifies numerous examples of waste and impediments to flow in university processes that add cost for both the university and the beneficiary of the process but add no value. The chapter catalogs a number of recommended techniques to eliminate different forms of waste and make the process flow more smoothly.

Chapter 8 discusses how to choose and implement specific LHE solutions to improve the process, and offers a number of strategies to help ensure that the gains achieved through the application of LHE are sustained (and enhanced through LHE's commitment to continuous improvement). Throughout these chapters, the process for receiving approval to offer a new academic course is used as a running example to demonstrate and reinforce the LHE principles and practices discussed.

The final chapter of the book looks to the future, discussing a number of current challenges facing the introduction of LHE as well as the many opportunities possible for extending the application of LHE today and in the future.

Like most books, this one is designed to be read from beginning to end in a linear fashion. However, given the broad audience for which this book is intended, different groupings of the chapters can be read independently of the others. For those audiences interested in a more general overview of LHE, readers may choose to skim or exclude Chapters 4 through 8. For those interested in seeing a complete example of "LHE at work," Chapter 2 can be read separately. For audiences wishing to see for themselves (or show others) the "bottom-line" contributions of LHE, readers can focus on the successful examples of LHE included as Chapter 3. Finally, for those wishing to roll up their sleeves and begin using LHE principles and practices to improve their university's critical processes, Chapters 4 through 8 provide step-by-step guidance and can be used as a reference guide in the workplace for introducing, implementing, and sustaining LHE.

Chapter 1

The Case for Lean Higher Education

For most American colleges and universities, the pendulum has swung from the heyday of growth, prosperity, and public favor to new times that call for institutions to adapt themselves to current, harsher realities…. The challenges of institutional change presented by the new environment are daunting. For institutions to be successful, change must be both intentional and continuous.[1]

This book offers colleges and universities a new alternative to address the challenge of fundamental change facing higher education. *Lean Higher Education* (LHE) extends the application of the "Lean Systems" philosophy from manufacturing, service, professional, and government organizations to the vital sector of higher education. LHE is a comprehensive approach to systematic change that can help colleges and universities fundamentally rethink how they respond to the needs and expectations of those served by higher education. LHE principles and practices become part of the culture of the institution, engaging faculty and staff in analyzing and improving the underlying processes of higher education to make them more efficient and effective.

1.1 The Need for Change in Higher Education

The case for LHE is compelling. Consider the following three scenarios that may reflect similar experiences on many university campuses.

1.1.1 Scenario 1: Approval of a New or Modified Course

Professor Chippen prides himself in maintaining a strong relationship with program alumni and past employers of successful graduates from the applied psychology program. He is also involved with recruiting new students to the college, and scans the professional and disciplinary environment for new trends and enhancements to the program. In response to the growing popularity of *CSI (Crime Scene Investigation)* and other police-related dramas on television, Professor Chippen feels there would be strong interest in revamping the existing forensic psychology course, modifying some of the course's content and creating a second, more advanced level course for students wishing to specialize in this area in graduate school. The second course may also be of great interest to working professionals who desire to expand or update their knowledge and skills. Knowing that those in the course approval process at the university like to see if there is student interest in new or revised courses, Professor Chippen was careful to pilot the new course twice over two semesters to demonstrate student demand for both courses.

The university uses a standardized form and process for requests to modify and create new courses, with ultimate approval by the Office of the Provost. The process allows other academic units affected by the course change to weigh in early before any decision is made. Professor Chippen completes the course change request form, which includes six major sections with a total of 23 open-ended responses and eleven closed-ended responses (depending on the closed-ended responses, he may be asked to provide additional supporting open-ended responses). Professor Chippen then routes this completed document with the required cover sheet (which contains a number of "check off" responses and fill-in items completed during the routing process) to his department chair. The chair routes the proposal to the department's curriculum committee for review prior to his endorsing, and Professor Chippen makes minor changes to the proposal in response to the committee's questions and concerns. With the department chair's signature, the university library reviews the course request to ensure that library holdings are adequate to support this new course. The routing form notes that the library review is a time-consuming step, so Professor Chippen waits patiently. When the form returns with the library's endorsement, it is next forwarded to the college curriculum committee, which reviews the request at its next bimonthly meeting. Some questions are raised, requiring some small modifications and a 2-week wait for a second review and approval.

The form is then forwarded to the college dean for her endorsement (which is based on a review and recommendation by the associate dean who oversees academic issues for the college).

Eleven copies of the signed routing document and request form are sent to the Office of the Provost, which distributes them to each of the colleges for their review. This review ensures that there is no curriculum encroachment by the proposed course (e.g., the dean of the business college could register his concern regarding curriculum infringement if the word "management" appeared in the course title or description). The deans invariably take the full 14 days they have to respond. Because the new course could have a "substantial impact" on students in other programs, 32 paper copies of the proposal are forwarded to the Office of the Provost to distribute to members of the university-wide Undergraduate Curriculum Committee. Unfortunately, an accumulation of agenda items prevented the committee from holding a first reading of the proposal at their next meeting. Two weeks later, the Undergraduate Curriculum Committee raised a few concerns when they met that required a written response and additional revision from Professor Chippen (fortunately, the level of concerns did not require that the revised proposal be sent back to the beginning of the review process). At the next bimonthly meeting, the curriculum committee endorsed the proposal.

Finally, the Office of the Provost receives the fully reviewed proposal for final endorsement. Following a positive review and recommendation from the associate provost who oversees academic issues for the university, the provost approves the new course. Approximately 10 months after beginning the process to update an existing course and create an advanced course in forensic psychology in response to student interest and disciplinary changes, Professor Chippen finally sees the fruit of his labors.

1.1.2 Scenario 2: Installing a Door in a Faculty Research Laboratory

Dr. Teahan, Chair of the Department of Biology, is delighted that Dr. Annat has accepted her offer to join the faculty. Dr. Annat was very pleased with his employment contract and the generous startup package provided by the university. This was accomplished thanks to the chair's strong advocacy for Dr. Annat, particularly because he was bringing 2 years of funding that remained on a large federal grant (with the likelihood of an additional 3-year renewal). Laboratory space is available, with the only accommodation required by the funding agency being the installation of an interior connecting doorway between two adjacent spaces. (This doorway minimizes exposure of his laboratory animals to uncontrollable noise and lighting conditions as well as limiting exposure to potential germs and viruses in the existing animal colony.) Given that Dr. Annat was not set to arrive (with external grant and laboratory animals) for almost 7 months, there was plenty of time to have the door installed and grant funds would pay for this modest remodeling.

Dr. Teahan left her first voicemail message in February, requesting assistance in having a door installed. Given the workload in the Office of Design and Construction (ODC; the staff was stretched thin due to two major building projects on campus), the call was returned 2 weeks later to inform Dr. Teahan that the call had been received and an application would be put in campus mail later that day. Dr. Teahan completed the short application, identifying where the door should be installed and which budget should be charged for the remodeling. After waiting 6 weeks, Dr. Teahan called to follow up on her request. She learned that the office hired an outside architect to draw up plans for the door to keep the project moving because the university architect was already overextended with a backlog of current and planned construction projects. The consulting architect, already familiar with university building codes and campus standards, visited the laboratory and determined the best location for the new door. He then needed to contact the ODC for existing building plans to determine whether there were pipes or wires in the wall that required rerouting (and included as part of the bid request prepared for outside contractors).

Approximately 6 weeks later, another call from Dr. Teahan discovered that the drawings were reviewed by the university architect just last week (things have been very hectic with new projects starting now that the residence halls have been emptied), and a few small changes will be needed prior to sending the project out for bid. The ODC believes that the revised drawings and remodeling specs for the RFP should be back within 2 weeks. Schedules permitting, the Business Office should advertise the project and review bids in a period of 30 days. Now Dr. Teahan is beginning to worry. Almost 5 months will have passed before a contractor is even hired. Fortunately, it is only an interior door.

At exactly the end of the 30-day period, Dr. Teahan again follows up with the ODC. The good news is that the university accepted a bid for the door installation. The ODC reports that it needs to finalize some paperwork and get the final contract approved by the Office of General Counsel before signing. However, the ODC also acknowledges that several residence hall projects have taken priority, given that the fall semester begins within the month. Without a final contract prepared by the ODC, the construction contractor will not put it on his schedule (and order the door). Given the late time frame, the ODC is pessimistic that the door will be installed prior to the beginning of the fall semester. Dr. Teahan has the uncomfortable task of calling Dr. Annat and relaying the news. And Dr. Annat, upset that this simple laboratory modification—that his grant would cover—has not been completed, questions the university's commitment to research and his new chair's ability to get things done. Dr. Annat calls back later in the day to report that the grant agency will not allow the research to be relocated until the laboratory improvements are made, thus jeopardizing Dr. Annat's ongoing studies. Dr. Annat wonders if it would be more prudent for him to delay his start at the university until the spring semester, allowing him to continue his funded research without interruption at his current institution, especially given that the vice president for research there (i.e., his current institution) is keenly interested in keeping him and the balance of the $2.5M grant at that institution.

1.1.3 Scenario 3: Thank-You Notes to Donors

Danielle Leemer, Vice President for University Advancement, has been heavily involved in preparing the campaign groundwork for an impending $200 million comprehensive campaign with the help of an outside consultant. At focus group meetings with significant donors and university friends, she is pleased that there appears to be widespread support for the campaign theme and its targeted focus on scholarships and endowed professorships. One concern, however, is that in almost every focus group held around the country, a donor mentions an example of not receiving a thank-you note after making a donation. When probed by the consultant, the donors cannot provide specific details about their own experience or those about which they have heard indirectly. Given the number of times the issue has been raised, Leemer and the consultant agree that she (Leemer) should follow up on the concern when she returns to campus.

Leemer shared this concern with members of the office staff, who were upset and offended to hear that there were questions about thank-you acknowledgments. Their records indicate that the office sent thank-you notes to all donors who made a gift, regardless of the size of the gift. "Stale" addresses might account for some individuals not receiving these notes, but this would certainly not be the case for the donors who were involved in the focus groups. Leemer assures the staff that she was not questioning the staff's ability or commitment. Although she is ready to let the issue drop given what was learned, she continues to hear the same concern raised in subsequent focus groups.

Leemer decides to call a good friend and important donor to eliminate any nagging doubts that this is a real issue with donors. Much to her chagrin, the donor confides that she does not remember receiving thank-you notes after each gift, attributing the lack of response to the heavy staff workload. Additionally, she receives other thank-yous throughout the year for her support to the university. This further puzzles Leemer because her records do not indicate mailing additional thank-you notes to donors. As she pores over this donor's records, she notices that while the office sent a thank-you note after each gift, it is unclear when the office actually sent the note.

Leemer once again brings the concern to the attention of staff. With some indignation, the staff reports that they send the note out as soon as possible according to the acknowledgment process that has been in place for years (and predates Leemer). As she inquires about the acknowledgment process, Leemer begins to see the problem. Acknowledgments to key donors at the university have their own "special process," independent of the standard acknowledgment process in place. Immediately after depositing the check or credit card payment, a special handling process sets aside the names of these key donors. When enough of them have accumulated, the Associate VP for Advancement receives a printout of these gifts for personalized thank-you notes (especially significant donations would eventually make their way to the VP's desk for her own personalized note). Given that the associate VP is out of the office frequently, he writes the thank-you notes when he can find the time, with a self-imposed deadline of mailing notes within 2 weeks of arriving at his desk. His secretary photocopies the notes for the files, prepares envelopes, and mails the thank-you notes.

A clear picture is starting to emerge. Donors do not remember receiving thank-you recognition for their gifts for good reason—the university's process of recognition for special donors takes approximately 5 weeks from start to finish. This means that a month and a half may transpire between the mailing of the gift and receipt of a thank-you by the donor. This explains why the records indicate that every donor was sent a thank-you as well as why the donors do not remember being thanked. What puzzles Leemer is why a system designed to treat individuals in a special and personalized manner took so long. Contrary to its intention, the process was not providing enhanced recognition and thanks to key donors to the university.

These three scenarios, representing three different areas at a university (academic affairs, operations, and development; in the next chapter, a fourth example from student services will be provided), typify the challenges faced on many campuses. An informal survey on any campus would likely turn up numerous additional examples of a well-intentioned university whose processes fail to meet expectations.[2] Together they highlight a number of common concerns within the higher education community:

■ Many university processes are failing to meet the needs of those they serve (e.g., parents, students, faculty, department chairs, campus offices, donors, employers, and alumni).

■ Many university processes are perceived to be extremely slow, and individuals and offices involved in these processes are often seen as adding more time but little additional value.

■ Many university processes involve multiple vice presidential areas that each work on their part of the process, with no single "owner" responsible for ensuring that the process works efficiently and effectively.

■ Typical responses to complaints of failures of university processes require an individual with authority (but little contact with the process) to intervene and handle the complaint outside of the official process. Staff time spent helping administrators resolve these complaints delays help for those who are in the standard process queue and waiting patiently.

■ Documentation is poor for many university processes, with no standardized written instructions or employee training programs that establish clear expectations for each of the steps and activities contributed by employees to each process.

■ Many university processes fail to benefit from the insights and recommendations of the employees who are intimately involved in the process but have no formal mechanism to share their concerns and suggestions.

■ Many universities have not established a climate that helps transform the institution into a learning organization that regularly improves itself to serve the individuals and organizations that are the beneficiaries of their work.

In an environment of plentiful resources and strong support, these shortcomings might be embarrassing but tolerable. It is not possible to design an organization so perfectly that it satisfies everyone all the time. Senior leaders, administrators, and faculty recognize many of their institution's shortcomings and frustrations, with some regular efforts made to change the status quo. Institutions are reorganized, new leaders are appointed, task forces are created, inspirational addresses are given, external consultants are retained, new initiatives are introduced, and mandates from on high are delivered, all in an effort to make the university more successful—better students, higher retention and graduation rates, higher-ranked academic programs, increased levels of giving by alumni and friends, etc.

1.2 Implementing Improvement and Change in Higher Education

In reading the scenarios that introduced this chapter, immediate solutions may have come to mind. Using an online routing system with electronic signatures would save both time and trees. Stipulating that externally funded research requests require a priority response from the Office of Design and Construction would ensure timely responses to those construction requests. Thank-you notes will flow to donors in a timely fashion when an expectation is established requiring all gifts be acknowledged within 72 hours of receipt. Most organizational leaders who have a stake in the process, however, rarely have the opportunity to step back and view a complete process, discovering its inherent problems, delays, and activities that add no value. They need to ensure that the process, despite its deficiencies, continues to operate, because the "crash" of a process would be ten times more disastrous than simply continuing a process that all acknowledge is inefficient. For good or bad, the institution cannot stop operating. Even when there is time to examine a university process, there is often no common, overarching framework that guides how a process should be studied, diagnosed, and changed. Instead, individuals rely on what they think will be best, and fail to recognize that a change in one part of a process may have unintended consequences for the upstream and downstream steps and activities.

Most universities[3] are committed to improvement, whether the improvement reflects a small and incremental change to how it works or whether it embraces radical change in response to a current or imminent crisis. However well-intentioned these efforts, many (if not most) have fallen short, and in some cases have been deleterious to the university. The university makes improvements, but certainly not to the fullest extent possible. The university does not monitor many of the improvements to see if they are successful, and limited understanding of the extent to which real improvement is possible makes it difficult to judge just what they have achieved. The improvements may work in the short run but fail in the end. Given the attention span of oversight agencies and the average tenure of university leaders and board members, this might satisfice. Working toward a small gain may improve both the process and its outcome, even if the immediate gain is small relative to the investment of resources required to make these improvements. Nevertheless, institutions will rarely have a sense of the true gains possible but never reached. While institutions of higher education put forth their best effort to be more efficient and effective, the real problem is that this best effort is no longer good enough.

A thoughtful examination of the challenges facing higher education in the United States raises a number concerns about the future:

■ Many states have cut support, or significantly slowed the growth of support, for public higher education. As enrollment has grown, universities have struggled with a declining level of support per student.[4] While state support for higher education has often fluctuated with the strength of a state's economy, competing demands for K–12 education, Medicaid, and prisons suggest that the future funding for public higher education will remain a significant challenge. Some have argued that taxpayer support for public higher education is a poor investment with minimal payoff.[5]

■ Higher education is a labor-intensive process with faculty and staff deserving equitable compensation for the education, skills, and experiences they bring to their institutions. The use of non-tenure track and part-time faculty helps to maintain a low student-to-faculty ratio, but the growth of support staff in response to meeting state and federal compliance requirements and serving the needs of underprepared students continues to strain institutions' personnel budgets.

■ There is a growing trend to view public higher education as a personal good rather than a societal good. Because students are viewed as the key beneficiaries of higher education (i.e., higher starting salaries and lifetime earnings), it is argued that an increasing proportion of the costs of the education should be borne by the students and their families. Shifting the burden to lower-income students and families without a concomitant offsetting increase in financial aid threatens access to the higher level of education for its citizens that states desire to advance.

■ Business and political leaders with short-term interests see higher education as jobs training. Private support for research has focused on areas that have an immediate impact on technology transfer or commercially viable patents. Public support has shifted away from general student support toward competitive programs that increase student enrollment and graduation rates in high-need employment areas. The shift from "higher" education to "hire" education disrupts an institution's ability to support basic research and academic majors that do not directly translate into technological, biomedical, etc. jobs.

■ Those outside higher education (and some within) correctly perceive it as expensive and inefficient. Faculty members are confronted about their high salaries and limited time in the classroom. News reports on presidential compensation rarely conclude that increases are reflective of the comparability between their jobs and those of CEOs in the private sector. Many faculty members view the administration as a bloated bureaucracy that adds little value to higher education. Legislators' perceptions of waste are affirmed as colleges and universities enroll greater numbers of students despite cuts in public funding (even though these cuts are typically absorbed in large part by tuition increases and not increases in efficiency).

■ Many demand greater public accountability of higher education. Students and parents want assurances that their tuition is being used toward their personal education rather than subsidizing other students, the research activities of faculty, or student athletics. The organization of State Higher Education Executive Officers has established the National Commission on Accountability in Higher Education to propose policy recommendations to measure whether public appropriations for higher education are serving the economic and social goals of the states. During the 2005 reauthorization of the Higher Education Act, U.S. lawmakers tried and failed to establish national standards of accountability for the country's more than 4,000 colleges and universities. The National Center for Public Policy and Higher Education, and the National Center for Higher Education and Management Systems are leading a grant-funded effort to reexamine the basic assumptions of how to achieve the public purposes of higher education, but clear accountability continues to be elusive.[6]

These and other challenges to the future of higher education confront senior administrators and board trustees as they seek to preserve the distinct missions of their institutions. Discussions take place at every campus regarding the balance of tuition increases and financial aid awards that impact access. The university's leadership makes decisions about the size, composition, and compensation of faculty, and how these decisions impact the resources needed for the nonacademic staff and physical plant. The increasing costs of support for academic services and student support programs may necessitate the reduction or elimination of these efforts despite their potential impact on student success. Overall, the future of higher education faces significant challenges in its efforts to promote student access and success.

The responses to these challenges by universities are as diverse as the types and missions of these institutions. Some institutions hope these challenges are transitory, believing that strong public and financial support for higher education will return over time. Given the historically cyclical nature of public support for higher education, this might seem reasonable or risky, because it assumes that future conditions are not very different from those in the past. The president may recommend short-term decisions to shore up the institution until the golden days return. Some institutions might react to challenges by implementing plans of action that offer a reasonable response for the near future. For example, a university may offer an early retirement program that quickly vacates a number of senior faculty lines to reduce personnel costs. On the other hand, a university may continue to operate on a "cost-plus" basis, increasing tuition as necessary to meet the costs of a good education and hope that it does not price itself out of its market. Programs and initiatives might be introduced (e.g., energy savings, limits of travel, etc.) that end when funding levels increase. This reactive approach is probably the most common, seeking to strike a balance between short- and long-term interests of the institution.

Other institutions proactively address the challenges they face through strong leadership and a formally developed strategic plan reflecting perhaps a change in mission, a new focus for academic programs, a change in emphasis on research, and recruiting students in anticipation of national trends. The leaders of these institutions might introduce university-wide initiatives and programs to change their climates and operations in an effort to maintain and enhance their quality and effectiveness. These universities consider university-wide input and participation in their responses to these challenges, support the new directions with training and other resources required for success, and motivate faculty and staff participation with statements and actions by campus leaders as well as the institution's reward system. The American Council on Education's Project on Leadership and Institutional Transformation[7] studied 26 institutions as they implemented a wide variety of change initiatives. There were significant challenges in implementing both the university-wide initiatives and creating the necessary preconditions to help the initiatives take root and grow. But the project recognized that intentional university-wide change efforts are needed to transform higher education in this new century so that it can achieve its aspirations while holding on to its important values.[8]

Universities have had mixed success with institution-wide initiatives to maintain their quality and effectiveness. Over the years they have embraced "top-down" programs originally introduced in the private sector, including management by objectives, total quality management, responsibility centered budgeting, Six Sigma, and process re-engineering. Their leaders have read and shared ideas from management guru books: *Good to Great,*[9] *Managing for the Future,*[10] *Jack Welch and the GE Way,*[11] *The Fifth Discipline,*[12] and more. Still other initiatives have been drawn from some excellent books tailored specifically for higher education: *Managing Higher Education as a Business,*[13] *On Q,*[14] *Once Upon a Campus,*[15] and *Total Quality Management in Higher Education,*[16] to name a few. Many improvement initiatives seeking to change institutions fundamentally have failed, however, for one or more reasons:

- The failure to make a clear and compelling case regarding the need for change
- Offering solutions without a clear understanding of the underlying problems
- Lack of continued and significant support from the institutions' leaders
- Neglecting to address internal institutional conflicts that overshadowed the change agenda
- Extremely volatile external environments that distracted the institutions from their change agenda
- Inadequate resources to ensure successful implementation of the changes needed[17]

Universities need a comprehensive and integrated approach to intentional institution-wide change based on proven effectiveness. This approach should serve as a model for universities to introduce intentional change that can ensure success in a new and significantly different era for higher education.

1.3 Lean Principles and Practices: An Approach to Organization-Wide Change and Improvement

Lean principles and practices have the potential to provide the needed philosophical framework and tools that can dramatically improve the effectiveness of higher education. Over the past decade, organizations throughout the world embraced the "Lean" approach as a carefully designed and highly successful system for organizational change and improvement that incorporates organizational culture, guiding principles, and a practical set of methods and tools. The Lean system, developed and championed by the Toyota Motor Company, evolved over 50 years with data to support that its balanced "top-down" and "bottom-up" approach can lead to immediate, significant, and long-lasting improvements. Originally developed for the manufacturing operations at Toyota, all areas of the organization (e.g., product development, order management, supply chain management, customer service, parts distribution) now benefit from the "Toyota Way." Toyota openly shares its system and principles with competitors and other organizations throughout the manufacturing sector. The International Motor Vehicle Program at MIT, which was researching emerging changes in manufacturing pioneered by the Toyota Motor Company, named this approach "Lean Production."[18]

Since its gradual introduction and implementation in the United States beginning in the 1980s, Lean principles and practices have been widely embraced as an effective approach to organization-wide change and improvement. Japanese organizations transplanted to the United States using U.S. employees, as well as applications in existing North American-based manufacturing companies, have demonstrated its effectiveness. Lean principles and practices, originally developed in manufacturing plants, have been extended to a wide variety of non-manufacturing settings including hospitals and health care, retail operations, government, and, most recently, higher education.[19] The robustness of the effectiveness of Lean principles and practices across cultures, industries, and professions suggests it may be well-suited for application in higher education settings.

Chapter 2 discusses Lean principles more generally, and subsequent chapters extend these principles to the field of higher education. For the present purpose, Lean principles[20]

- Define the value of the process from the perspective of the beneficiaries of the process

- Identify the flow of the process, from both the beneficiary and provider perspectives, to determine whether and how each step in the process adds value
- Eliminate the many types of waste that add no value to the process
- Make the process flow smoothly, with its delivery "pulled" as needed by the beneficiary rather than "pushed" by the provider
- Pursue perfection through a combination of continuous improvement and radical transformation of the process

1.4 Lean Higher Education: The Application of Lean Principles and Practices in Higher Education

The goal of this book is to extend Lean principles and practices to universities to achieve academic and operational excellence in an intentional and disciplined approach toward organizational change and improvement. Lean Higher Education (LHE), the translation of Lean principles and practices for application in higher education, incorporates both radical organizational transformation and a relentless pursuit of continuous improvement. LHE can help higher education strengthen its contributions to society in the current (and future) environment of limited resources, higher enrollment, and increased accountability. Using an integrated approach that both leverages the abilities of employees and the commitment of leadership, LHE can help universities reduce or eliminate waste that adds no value to their services and operations. The principles and practices contained in this book can help institutions of higher education, regardless of size and mission, become leaders in the global competitive market of higher education through high-quality, low-cost, and timely processes that their beneficiaries value and expect.

LHE adapts Lean principles and practices using nomenclature more easily understood and accepted by those in higher education. Japanese terms common to Lean applications (e.g., kaizen, genchi genbutsu, andon, jidoka) are used sparingly to make the book more readable to a broader audience in higher education. However, several Japanese words and phrases (e.g., "muda," or waste for which the beneficiary is unwilling to pay) commonly used by Lean practitioners are occasionally referenced. Typical situations found on many university campuses provide the scenarios and examples used throughout this book. In addition, this book includes the small but growing number of existing applications of LHE that demonstrate the range of possibilities for improving higher education. Finally, this book is written for a wide audience of individuals who are stakeholders in higher education and, importantly, must understand and advocate for LHE: college and university administrators and employees, faculty, trustees, students in higher education administration and leadership programs, business and community leaders, politicians, and alumni. Overall, the tone and style attempt to create broad interest and support for Lean principles and practices in higher education.

In contrast to the mixed success of other interventions used in higher education, LHE can provide results that are notably different based on well-established Lean principles and practices (Table 1.1).

LHE is a comprehensive approach to institutional change and improvement. Many interventions focus on a single limited area of change: total quality management, statistical process control, team building, process re-engineering, responsibility centered budgeting, management by objectives, goal setting, and so on. Attempts to improve one aspect of an institution leave other ingrained and potentially antagonistic or incompatible practices in place, reducing the likelihood that the intervention will succeed over time. In contrast, LHE is a system-wide intervention that introduces an integrated system of changes that affects many aspects of a university simultaneously, increasing the likelihood of lasting attitudinal and behavioral changes among faculty, staff, and administration.

LHE respects and balances the needs of the institution with those of its employees. LHE recognizes that institutions become successful by

Table 1.1   Advantages of LHE over Traditional Higher Education Change Initiatives

LHE is a **comprehensive** approach to institutional change and improvement
LHE strikes a **balance** between the long-term needs of the institution and its employees
LHE provides **practical** tools for implementing institutional change and improvement
There is considerable **evidence** supporting the extension of Lean principles and practices to higher education

developing exceptional employees and work teams that are committed to the philosophy of LHE and the success of the university, and then listen to and incorporate their ideas. The goal of LHE is to eliminate unnecessary steps and activities that overburden employees and contribute no value to a process designed to benefit students, faculty, etc. Improving the flow of the process relieves employees of unnecessary and nonproductive tasks, thereby allowing them to reinvest this time in new ways that add value to an existing university process. This enriches their jobs, and enhances their own satisfaction and performance. In this way, both the employee and the university benefit, creating a climate of trust and mutual support.

LHE offers practical tools for implementing change and improvement. Over the years, Lean practitioners have accumulated a large number of techniques that may be readily applicable for use in higher education settings. As an example, LHE includes an accepted set of steps for assessing the effectiveness of any university process. The application of available techniques for mapping and evaluating each step in a process (including selecting metrics for measuring performance) and other Lean tools provides comprehensive support for the introduction of LHE interventions throughout an institution. The availability of standardized tools and materials makes it easier to implement LHE with confidence.

There is considerable evidence supporting the extension of Lean principles and practices to higher education. Over 50 years of practice, review, and improvement across different organizations and business sectors provide strong support for the effectiveness of Lean. For the Canadian Postal Commission, implementing Lean principles and practices resulted in a 28% reduction in travel time for mail, a 37% reduction in the length of time mail is waiting to be processed, and a 27% reduction in needed space at its Hamilton, Ontario, mail sorting facility.[21] Pratt & Whitney, the jet engine manufacturer, more than tripled its pretax earnings on virtually the identical revenues through the application of Lean principles and practices.[22] The British grocery chain Tesco applied Lean principles and practices to its stock reordering process and increased the percentage of supplier shipments that arrived just in time and in just the right amount from 92% to 98%.[23,24] Chapter 3 provides examples of the successful application of LHE in a number of university settings. These and many other successful applications of Lean lend strong support to the effectiveness of LHE.

1.5 The Potential of Lean Higher Education

LHE holds significant promise for improvements in higher education. "Lean Thinking" can help universities improve their processes in ways that provide the beneficiaries with what they expect: a process that respects their time, is free from errors or mistakes, and is available exactly when needed by the beneficiary. In an era of declining resources, growing demands for account-ability and cost effectiveness, and the importance of higher education to economic development and quality of life, higher education must reinvent itself to retain its reputation as a preeminent institution that is valued and supported. LHE principles and practices can contribute to creating the new "LHE university" on a number of levels.

An institution's processes have an indirect but important impact on success. A number of core processes provided by different functional areas of the university support student enrollment, faculty reputation, aca-demic program quality, student learning, advancement, and community engagement. For example, the application of LHE to processes in the univer-sity's career placement center can benefit graduating students and prospec-tive employers, improving student placement and the business community's regard for the university. At the same time, the LHE initiatives can help the center use its resources more effectively, serve more students, enhance exist-ing services, or introduce new services without increasing staffing levels. The application of LHE has the potential to improve significantly the institu-tion's overall performance and reputation.

Students, faculty, and staff benefit from improvements introduced through LHE initiatives. Student learning, persistence, success, and sat-isfaction are influenced by students' experiences with the critical processes at the university: recruitment and admissions, orientation, housing and food service, financial aid and bursar, course and program development, advising, course registration, and academic and nonacademic support services (e.g., writing lab, technology support, health center). Faculty success and morale are affected by university processes that support teaching (e.g., proposing a new course or program, obtaining permission to include copyrighted work in course materials); scholarship (e.g., institutional grant approval process, obtaining laboratory or studio space); and service (e.g., reporting and docu-menting community engagement activities, establishing exchange relation-ships with non-U.S. colleges and universities). Members of the support staff are both internal recipients and providers of processes, and their ability to provide valued, timely, and quality processes hinges on the effectiveness of these processes in the areas and offices with whom they interact. The impact of LHE efforts can benefit all members of the university community.

LHE is scalable to improve university processes at any level. The application of LHE can range from a simple process that takes place within a single office or function at the university to a complex process that cuts across many offices and vice presidential areas. Using LHE to improve the process of preparing summer teaching contracts provides a micro-level application that can benefit the staff members who are involved in contract preparation as well as a significant number of faculty members who teach during the summer. However, macro-level processes at a university will also benefit from LHE initiatives. As an example, LHE can be used to examine the freshman-year experience, with all of its various activities and experiences, as a single process. Examining the "flow" of new students as they move through all the academic and nonacademic first-year experiences can provide significant insight into inefficient and unnecessary experiences that are inconsistent with LHE principles (e.g., duplicative efforts that waste university resources, unmet student expectations that impact student retention), and Lean tools can provide specific recommendations for improving this macro process. Taking this one (very large) step further, LHE provides a framework for understanding and improving the entire 4-year degree process. Depending on the university's needs and interests, LHE is scalable to whichever level of focus is most important.

LHE engages and empowers faculty and staff to use their untapped knowledge and ideas to improve the processes in which they are involved. LHE Project Team members receive training on Lean tools used to understand a process and implement changes. Team members are given the authority to recommend and implement changes, allowing those employees who perform the steps and activities of the process to change them to meet the expectations of the individuals or offices that are its chief beneficiaries. Jobs become more fulfilling as employees focus on work that adds value and makes the institution more effective.

Overall, the application of LHE can serve as a unifying framework for introducing and creating change in higher education. With the support and commitment of the institution's leadership, LHE provides a powerful tool for implementing change within the university that meets the expectations of the individuals served, frees up resources for reinvestment, and helps transform the university into a true learning organization.

Endnotes

1. See Eckel, P., Hill, B., and Green, M. 1998. *On change: En route to transformation*. Washington, DC: American Council on Education. p. 1.
2. To make the writing less cumbersome throughout this book, the term "process" refers to both general university processes as well as specific university services.
3. More accurately, it is the individuals who make up the university who commit it to improvement.
4. While drafting the manuscript for this book, financial support for public higher education became even worse as the recession taking hold in the Fall of 2008 reduced state budgets and shrank endowments.
5. See Vedder, R. 2004. *Going broke by degree: Why college costs too much*. Washington, DC: American Enterprise Institute for Public Policy Research.
6. See Schmidt, P. 2004. A public vision for public colleges. *The Chronicle of Higher Education,* June 11, pp. A16-A18.
7. See Eckel, P., Hill, B., and Green, M. 1998. *On change: En route to transformation*. Washington, DC: American Council on Education.
8. By definition, the American Council on Education's Project on Leadership and Institutional Transformation defined transformational change as any change that "… (1) alters the culture of the institution by changing select underlying assumptions and institutional behaviors, processes, and products; (2) is deep and pervasive, affecting the whole institution; (3) is intentional; and (4) occurs over time." (From Eckel et al., 1998, p. 3.)
9. See Collins, J. 2001. *Good to great*. New York: HarperCollins Publishers.
10. See Drucker, P. 1992. *Managing for the future*. New York: Dutton.
11. See Slater, R. 1999. *Jack Welch and the GE way: Management insights and leadership secrets of the legendary CEO*. New York: McGraw-Hill.
12. See Senge, P. 1990. *The fifth discipline: The art and practice of the learning organization*. New York: Doubleday.
13. See Lenington, R.L. 1996. *Managing higher education as a business*. Phoenix, AZ: American Council on Education and The Oryx Press.
14. See Seymour, D. 1993. *On Q: Causing quality in higher education*. Phoenix, AZ: Oryx Press and the American Council on Education.
15. See Seymour, D. 1995. *Once upon a campus: Lessons for improving quality and productivity in higher education*. Phoenix, AZ: American Council on Education and The Oryx Press.
16. See Sims, S.J., and Sims, R.R., eds. 1995. *Total quality management in higher education: Is it working? Why or why not?* Westport, CT: Praeger.
17. See Eckel, P., Hill, B., and Green, M. 1998. *On change: En route to transformation*. Washington, DC: American Council on Education.
18. See Womack, J.P., Jones, D.T., and Roos, D. 1991. *The machine that changed the world: The story of lean production*. New York: Harper Perennials.

19. For example, the National Association of College and University Business Officer's 2004 webcast titled *Quality Initiatives: The Lean University in Action* (http://www.nacubo.org/x3725.xml, August 25, 2005); and The University of Central Oklahoma's PowerPoint presentation titled *Performance Contracts and Lean University: Two Routes to Quality Improvement* (http://www.ncci-cu.org/online/docs/Kreidlerpres_files/frame.htm, February 15, 2005). Chapter 3 presents a number of examples of the application of Lean in higher education settings. Note that both these examples focus on nonacademic processes or operations.

20. The Toyota Motor Company did not develop a list of Lean principles. Different authors have abstracted their own list of principles that differ in number but are inclusive of the general themes put forth by the Toyota Motor Company.

21. See Liker, J.K. 2004. *The Toyota way: 14 management principles from the world's greatest manufacturer.* New York: McGraw-Hill, pp. 272–275.

22. See Womack, J.P., and Jones, D.T. 2003. *Lean thinking: Banish waste and create wealth in your corporation.* New York: Free Press, pp. 305–309.

23. See Womack, J.P., and Jones, D.T. 2003. *Lean thinking: Banish waste and create wealth in your corporation.* New York: Free Press, pp. 44–47.

24. See Slater, R. 1999. *Jack Welch and the GE way: Management insights and leadership secrets of the legendary CEO.* New York: McGraw-Hill. In contrast, it is difficult to determine which of Jack Welch's management insights and leadership secrets were responsible for GE's increases in market value and profits during his leadership. This makes it difficult for university leaders to know exactly which of Welch's traits or behaviors to emulate in an effort to create a world-class institution. LHE is a structured and proven approach to organizational change and improvement.

Chapter 2

Lean Higher Education in Practice
An Overview and Case Study

In the United States, more than 4,000 non-profit colleges and universities serve the needs of many important constituencies: prospective and current students and their families, faculty and staff, employers and local businesses, federal and state agencies, and oversight boards. Two-year schools play a major role in job preparation and supplying local businesses and organizations with well-trained technical and nontechnical employees. Programs and faculty at metropolitan universities provide focused outreach to support and enhance the urban centers in which they are located and extend the application of their work to other urban areas. State-supported colleges and universities provide expanded access and opportunity to their communities and citizens of the state through subsidized tuition and campuses strategically located to meet the needs of underserved areas. Carnegie-classified, research-extensive universities invest in a strong research infrastructure to support externally funded basic and applied research. This broad variety of options is a great strength of the U.S. higher education system because different constituencies may have different preferences or values (e.g., low cost versus academic selectivity). In addition, individuals may have different preferences or values at different points in time (e.g., a residential experience while pursuing an undergraduate degree and an online option while pursing professional development coursework for career enhancement).

Nevertheless, it is not enough for a college or university to commit itself to a mission designed to meet the needs of one or more of its constituencies. Suppose an institution has a registration system that makes students wait in line (or the digital online equivalent)—a line to register as a student, a line to see an advisor, a line to register for courses, a line to pay for courses, a line to purchase course books, a line to get an ID card, a line to get a parking permit—and all at times designed to be convenient for the school rather than the student. Regardless of institutional mission, this registration process may lead prospective and current students to pursue other options (including not enrolling anywhere). If the metropolitan university's only option for full-time workers seeking academic credentials for career advancement is a bachelor's degree requiring several years of part-time study and mandatory general education classes, prospective students will look for alternative programs that meet their professional needs (e.g., a narrowly focused professional certificate program designed specifically for individuals working full-time). State-supported institutions that require students to complete a certain number of courses "in residence" (i.e., taken on the main campus) rather than delivering entire programs online or at convenient off-campus locations will lose these students to other schools that better accommodate their needs. If the research-extensive institution restricts proposal writing assistance or budget consultation to times that staff prefer rather than the work schedules of the faculty, the university will lose grants and perhaps have its best faculty recruited away by institutions that are more responsive to the needs of research faculty. Finally, any institution that makes it difficult for individuals from the external community to park and visit campus, recruit student interns, address their company needs with faculty expertise, find a campus service, or attend an event or performance has squandered opportunities to strengthen community support.[1]

2.1 Higher Education: Falling Short of the Mark

Unfortunately, universities fall short of providing for the needs of the beneficiaries of higher education, and in some cases very short, despite their best intentions. Each university is an amalgam of processes created and supported to fulfill the overall institutional mission. Examples of these typical university processes include

- ■ Admitting students.
- ■ Hiring faculty.
- ■ Moving students into residence halls.
- ■ Purchasing supplies or services.
- ■ Adding or dropping a course.
- ■ Establishing a partnership with an international institution to support education abroad.
- ■ Remodeling laboratory space for faculty research.
- ■ Reserving a classroom.
- ■ Providing medical or mental health services.
- ■ Offering a new course or major.
- ■ Approving a grant submission.
- ■ Advising students.
- ■ Preparing mandated reports to state or federal agencies.
- ■ Reimbursing professional travel.
- ■ Communicating with donors.
- ■ Scheduling instructors for summer courses.

These individually important processes can also be clustered to address the needs of distinct beneficiaries of higher education: processes that define the freshman-year experience, processes that impact students' ability to graduate within four years, processes that support a new faculty member's growth into a nationally recognized scholar, or processes that extend the university's expertise into the community to support the region's economic growth. The responsibility and accountability for different aspects of these processes typically are distributed across university offices in the belief that this functional decentralization makes the institution more efficient and effective. Unfortunately, the suboptimal integration of the different parts of the process frequently results in a poor experience by the beneficiaries of higher education served by this process (e.g., students, parents, faculty members, alumni, employers, legislators).

What the beneficiaries of higher education expect, and how universities actually deliver on these expectations, can be far apart. Students, faculty, parents, alumni, legislators, employers, and so on expect value from each university process in which they are involved. This value or expectation may differ by beneficiary. For example, parents may expect that one call to the university should completely solve their problem. Faculty members may expect that the university does not waste their time with needless waiting, completing forms, and so on. Donors may place great value on courteous and personal treatment. Legislators may expect that the university fulfill their request exactly as requested and in a timely manner. If the university does not provide what is valued or expected, the beneficiary will be disappointed. The beneficiary may look elsewhere in the diverse and competitive marketplace of higher education or impose sanctions to obtain what he or she expects or values:

■ Students can enroll in or transfer to another university.
■ Faculty members will be recruited away by other universities, taking their reputation and grant money with them.
■ Companies can recruit elsewhere.
■ Donors can find other causes to support.
■ Legislators can mandate measures of accountability and lend their support to other universities.

At the same time, university employees are increasingly frustrated by less-than-pleasant interactions with these different beneficiaries who are not receiving what they value and expect. And many of these employees know that processes can and should be improved *and* have ideas on how this could be done.

2.2 Lean Higher Education (LHE)

Lean Higher Education (LHE) follows a set of guiding principles that provides a conceptual framework for improving any university process. Table 2.1 presents the five principles of LHE.[2] LHE begins with developing a clear understanding of what the beneficiary wants from the process.[3] The voice of the beneficiary must be the principal guide for any change to the process. While improvements to the process may also benefit employees and offices involved in the process, the primary focus is meeting—and if possible exceeding—what the beneficiary values or expects from the process. The second principle is direct observation of all steps and activities in the entire process to completely understand the current process and assess whether these steps and activities contribute value to the process as viewed through the eyes of the beneficiary. Each step or activity in the process taken by those providing or benefiting from it is identified, and all steps and activities are carefully reviewed to see whether they add value from the perspective of the beneficiary. The third principle seeks to remove all waste

Table 2.1 Principles of Lean Higher Education

Define the value of the process from the perspective of the beneficiaries of the process.
Identify the flow of the process, from both the beneficiary and provider perspectives, to determine whether and how each step and activity in the process adds value.
Eliminate the many types of waste that add no value to the process.
Make the process flow smoothly, with activities or services "pulled" as needed by the beneficiary rather than "pushed" by the provider.
Pursue perfection through a combination of continuous improvement and radical transformation of the process.

from the process because, by definition, waste adds no value to the process for either the university or the beneficiary. The fourth principle focuses on creating a smooth flow across the remaining (i.e., value-added) steps of the process for both the university provider and the beneficiary. Finally, the fifth principle acknowledges that LHE is an ongoing pursuit of perfection. Employees are empowered to propose additional solutions for removing waste and improving flow, with each change making the process closer to what the beneficiary values or expects. These well-established principles of Lean thinking, treated in a more detailed fashion in subsequent chapters, have developed over the past fifty years and provide a powerful conceptual framework that focuses on the person served by the process.[4]

Implicit in the LHE principles is inviting all employees who are part of a process to learn and apply LHE practices (methods and tools) to arrive at solutions that improve the process. Although there is no single, best way to combine LHE principles, methods, and tools, the application of LHE typically includes the following general steps:[5]

1. Establish an LHE project team and confirm a supportive climate for applying LHE principles and practices.
2. Identify what the beneficiary of the process values or expects.

3. Develop performance metrics to show the extent to which the process provides value and meets expectations.
4. Identify all steps in the current process required by both beneficiaries and providers.
5. Use LHE methods and tools to propose solutions that eliminate waste and improve flow in a "future" improved process.
6. Pursue perfection by monitoring performance metrics on an ongoing basis and introducing additional improvements to the process.

Overall, LHE is a structured approach to help universities meet the needs of those they serve by adapting the successful application of Lean principles and practices in manufacturing and service organizations to higher education. LHE is expected to result in university processes and services that deliver the value expected, use resources more effectively, and provide university employees with more meaningful work.[5]

2.3 An Example of the Application of LHE: The Freshman Move-In Process

How would LHE work in a university setting? The following subsection describes the application of LHE to improve the residence hall move-in process for new freshman. These critical first experiences for new students and parents shape early first impressions of the university's commitment to student service and support. This fictitious example, based on freshman move-in processes at several universities,[6] provides a useful demonstration of the application of LHE to understand and improve processes in higher education.

2.3.1 Freshman Move-In Day

One highlight of the beginning of the fall semester is freshman move-in day. In a roughly 14-hour period, several thousand new students (with their families) arrive at the university to begin their on-campus residential experience. The students and parents are unprepared for what to expect despite some passing familiarity with the campus from previous visits, including a brief summer orientation and registration experience. The university staff feels prepared, having survived freshman move-in day many times. They have modified traffic patterns on campus to help ease congestion, assigned paid staff and volunteers to each freshman residence hall to check in students and assist them with their belongings, and scheduled custodial and maintenance staff to keep the buildings clean and respond to problems.

Even with preparation, it is always a difficult day. Students and parents begin arriving early, finding their way to the four-story, horseshoe-shaped Meredith Hall. Students are welcomed and processed in a first-come, first-served manner, queuing in car lines as they make their way toward Meredith Hall. Upon arriving at the nearest unloading zone, the new freshman is directed to the lobby desk where she receives her room key and essential information. The student can then sign out a "rolling tub" to help transport her belongings to her new room. Parents and volunteer helpers begin to unload the vehicle once the student returns, fitting as much as they can into the single tub to minimize the number of round trips. Students and parents make their way toward the line for the single elevator at the nearest residence hall entrance, navigating the rolling tub through a throng of incoming students and families. There they wait patiently in line for their turn to use the elevator. Two tubs can fit on the elevator simultaneously, and the students and their helpers finally get their turn to ride the elevator to the appropriate floor and wheel their belongings to their new rooms.

Loft beds, the most typical configuration chosen by students, are the default option for rooms with two students. Changing to a bunk bed arrangement requires a little muscle and a hammer, with the biggest challenge being how to reconfigure the beds while the room is filling up with boxes, electronic equipment, and clothes. After two or three trips up and down the elevator, the student has everything in her room. It is common that a piece of furniture from home does not quite fit in the room, so the parents re-tub it and bring it back to their vehicle.

As the day goes on, the line continues to move slowly and never gets much longer. Parking spaces near Meredith Hall and rolling tubs are in short supply as parents help their students unpack. The elevator queue is also quite steady, but the elevator is expected to make it through the day without breaking down. After a long day, the students settle in and families drive home. This year, volunteers delivered cold bottles of water to vehicle passengers as they waited patiently for a space in the unloading zone, which helped keep tempers in check. Next year, the university is considering closing additional streets to divert traffic away from the freshman residence halls during move-in, thus reducing the number of blocked intersections that require the presence of campus safety officers. Overall, another successful freshman move-in day for the university is completed.

The scenario above would please most universities. Dealing with several thousand students and families in a period of 14 hours is a seemingly overwhelming task. The university works hard to accommodate infrastructure limitations: There are only so many roadways around the residence hall, parking spaces in the vicinity, check-in stations for completing paperwork and picking up keys, and entrances and elevators in the residence halls. Staff deal immediately with problems, and recommend changes to expedite the process the following year. It would be impractical for the university to install more elevators just for move-in day, not to mention more roads or parking spaces for something that occurs one day a year. What more can be expected?

When viewed from the perspective of the freshmen and their families, several expectations of the freshman move-in process were unmet:

- *Making the entire process flow smoothly and predictably from start to finish is expected and valued.* Getting their daughter's belongings up three flights of stairs is just part of the problem for the parents. Getting to the right place on campus, bringing no more than will fit in the room, and knowing which side of the double room is their daughter's side interrupt the flow of what students and families can do during the move-in process. Although volunteers offered help with moving the student's belongings into her room, without a room key and moving tub it came at the wrong time.

- *Students and families do not want their time wasted.* Waiting in traffic, waiting for an open parking space, waiting for the room key, waiting for a moving tub, waiting for an elevator, and so on contribute no value to the freshman move-in process.

- *Students and families value solutions that are brought to them rather than having to find solutions for themselves.* After parking, the student had to leave to go to the commons area to pick up her key. Then she proceeded to another line inside the common area to wait for the next available moving tub. A nonworking electrical outlet in their daughter's residence hall room forced the family to search the building for a maintenance person. Many families interrupted their move-in activities to find an off-campus store that sold fans, because no one told students that a box fan would make their un-air conditioned rooms more comfortable during the last weeks of summer.

- *Students and families want decisions that add stress and hold up the move-in process eliminated.* There were lots of parking options on the way to the residence hall, but families were unclear whether they should park at the first available spot outside the building or wait in line with other cars and hope closer parking would be available. They also wanted to wait until the daughter's roommate arrived in case she had any preferences about loft beds versus bunk beds, where the refrigerator would go, the sharing of storage areas, etc.

■ *Students and families want solutions tailored to their specific needs.* A "one-size-fits-all" moving tub was unable to accommodate a refrigerator, computer, packing boxes, and loose clothing on hangers. Their temporary parking space, while close to the building, was far away from the building entrance most convenient for their residence hall room. The student and parents had hoped to meet briefly with an advisor to discuss the daughter's completion of two summer courses at their local community college. However, only representatives from financial aid and the bursar's office were available.

University administrators who oversee the freshman move-in process certainly care about new students and parents. They see the lines of cars, the elevator backlogs, and the controlled chaos during peak periods of arrivals. They work hard to address complaints and problems quickly and effectively. But their focus has been on managing the move-in process from the university's perspective (e.g., dealing with the inherent shortages of parking spaces and the number of elevators; balancing budget constraints with the need to pay overtime for staff deemed essential to the move-in process; raising the morale of staff and volunteers, who are the first to hear complaints and have little authority to resolve them) rather than delivering what freshman students and parents expect from the process. LHE provides a unique opportunity to understand and improve the freshman move-in process to deliver the value expected, use resources more effectively, and engage and develop employees. In the following subsection, we demonstrate the application of LHE principles and practices to this fictional example of the freshman move-in process.

2.3.2 Applying LHE to the Freshman Move-In Process

Establish a LHE project team and confirm a supportive climate for implementing LHE principles and practices. During the university president's bi-weekly cabinet meeting, the president and senior leaders concur that freshman move-in is an important university process that could be improved using LHE principles and practices. The president requests Vice

President Richard Smith, Office of LHE Initiatives, to serve as project sponsor. VP Smith drafts a project proposal with input from university employees who are involved with the move-in process and see opportunity for improvement. He consults with other vice presidents to appoint the LHE Freshman Move-In Project Team (or "Project Team"), composed of six to eight members representing a cross-section of employees and volunteers who work closely with students and families during the move-in process, to lead the initiative. One of the team members, Katy Lockhart, from the Office of Student Housing, is appointed team leader, recognizing her many contributions on a previous LHE team as well as her excellent listening and organizational skills. Matt Liam, one of the university's "LHE Champions," agreed to serve as consultant to the Project Team. Liam is a mid-level supervisor in plant operations with considerable background in LHE (i.e., training and extensive hands-on experience as team member and leader on earlier LHE project teams).

VP Smith confirms a positive climate for the Project Team, especially important because this project crosses VP areas of responsibility. The vice presidents and other cabinet members have been vocal supporters of previous LHE initiatives across campus. In addition, they have released employees from their formal job responsibilities in order to participate on LHE teams, and they provided wide latitude in identifying and implementing LHE solutions proposed by previous LHE teams. Overall, VP Smith identified no barriers that require a more extensive climate assessment or issues to address before the Project Team begins its work.

All members of the Project Team receive copies of the university's "Guide for LHE Team Projects." The guide provides information on LHE principles, methods, and tools as well as a detailed outline of major steps with accompanying support materials. Team members commit to a 5-day "Rapid Improvement Workshop" that will culminate in a set of recommendations for improving the freshman move-in process. The workshop, which overlapped with the next freshman move-in day at the university, began with 1.5 days of training on LHE principles and practices and Lean methods and tools used to eliminate waste and improve flow.

Identify what the beneficiary of the process values or expects. The Project Team reviews survey data collected from a sample of freshmen and families who took part in the most recent freshman move-in process. The Team also has access to survey data from admitted freshmen and their families who would be participating in the upcoming freshman move-in process. Survey items were simple and direct, with probes for eliciting detailed information. In addition, other evaluative comments about the freshman move-in process (e.g., complaints or compliments received, responses to previous student or parent surveys) were located and combined with the survey data. Project Team members reviewed these data and met as a group to reach consensus on what the beneficiaries of the freshman move-in process value or expect; that is,

- Students and families expect to know exactly what is needed of them (e.g., what they should or should not bring, where they should go when they arrive on campus, what help they can expect during move-in).
- Students and families value their time. They do not want to wait at any step in the move-in process, and they want to complete the move-in as quickly as possible in the fewest number of round trips from their vehicle.
- Students and families expect that everything in the residence hall room will be arranged according to their preferences. Everything should also be in working order.
- Students and families expect to meet with individuals from other areas of campus (e.g., advising, student disability services) and have their concerns completely addressed on move-in day.

The Project Team decided to develop performance metrics around the first three values or expectations to measure improvement in the freshman move-in process as defined by students and their families. They felt that the last expectation was outside the team's charge, and forwarded it to VP Smith for discussion with the senior leadership team.

Develop performance metrics to show the extent to which the process provides value and meets expectations. The Project Team established metrics to evaluate performance during the upcoming freshman move-in process as well as to monitor performance following changes recommended by the Project Team. These measures of performance include

- *Total time*: the total amount of time from arrival on campus until the move-in process is completed.
- *Percent value added time:* the percentage of total time spent on move-in that actually added value to the move-in process (i.e., transporting the students' belongings to the room adds value; waiting for an elevator is "wasted" time).

- *Number of "round trips" to unload vehicle:* average number of trips it takes to completely unload the car (using available campus moving resources such as rolling tubs and volunteer moving help).
- *On-time delivery of move-in services*: the percentage of room move-ins that were completed within the established cycle time (i.e., the amount of time an actual move-in should take as established by the Project Team).
- *Room quality:* the percentage of student rooms with one or more errors or malfunctioning services (e.g., nonworking electrical outlet, incorrect bed frame setup).
- *Parent/freshman feedback:* freshman and parent assessments of the move-in process.

Identify all steps in the current process required by both beneficiaries and providers. All Project Team members serve as observers during freshman move-in day at the university. Project Team members walk through the complete process from beginning to end, identifying what actually occurs based on their own direct observations. They follow new students and their families (i.e., the beneficiaries of the process) through the process, identifying every step as well as any time spent waiting between steps. Similarly, Project Team members physically travel the path of the steps performed by university staff and volunteers (i.e., providers of the process) during the move-in process, asking questions along the way to understand the purpose of the step or activity, the flow of information during the process, and so on. The Project Team documents the amount of time needed to complete each step or activity and the length of time that both students and families and university staff and volunteers spend waiting between steps. Interviews with parents and students and key employees supplement the Project Team's understanding of the move-in process. Finally, the Project Team gathers the data needed for calculating the performance metrics for the move-in process.

Based on their direct experiences with the process and information gathered during freshman move-in, the Project Team draws a map of the current move-in process, highlighting the steps that they agree contribute value (from the perspective of students and families) to the move-in process, and calculate the performance metrics chosen to evaluate the process (see Figure 2.1). The Project Team gains a number of insights by following this LHE method of "learning by seeing" the entire move-in process from the perspectives of beneficiaries and providers.

The Project Team discovered that only 29% of the time spent by students and families during move-in actually contributed value to getting a student moved in. Of the average 260 minutes that it takes students and families to complete the university's current move-in process, only 76 minutes were identified as contributing value to move in students. For example, waiting in traffic for temporary parking to open up to begin the move-in process is not contributing any value to the move-in process, but rather is a waste of student and family time. Similarly, "wayfinding" to the student's residence hall also wastes time because students and families value knowing clear campus directions ahead of time (which campus entrance to use and roadways to follow). The team uncovered many other examples of how the time of students and their families is wasted:

- Waiting in line to obtain a room key.
- Waiting in line to sign out and return a moving tub.
- Requiring families to re-park their cars in secondary parking lots.
- Wheeling moving tubs an excessive distance to the entrance of the residence hall.
- Waiting for elevators.
- Reconfiguring furniture.
- Reporting and waiting for room repairs.
- Sending home personal belongings that would not fit in the room.

In addition, this mapping of the current move-in process identified examples of poor flow. For example, the limited number of parking spaces and elevators created significant chokepoints in the move-in process that constrained the flow of the entire move-in experience.

The Project Team discovered that only 17% of the time spent by university volunteers and staff during move-in actually contributed value to getting a student moved in. Of the average 83 minutes that university staff and volunteers spent helping each freshman move in to the residence hall, only 14 minutes contributed value from the perspective of the student and his or her family. This estimate excludes any time wasted reconfiguring room furniture (which students want to be correctly configured on arrival) or repairing room problems (which students want to be resolved before arrival). Some examples of waste in the move-in process from the provider's perspective were identical to those of the beneficiaries (e.g., staff and volunteers who wait for elevators along with the student they are assisting). Other examples of waste in the current steps of the move-in process completed by the university are the

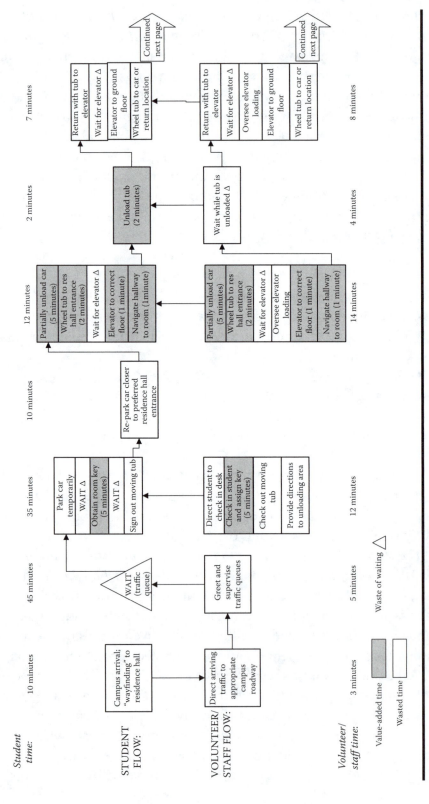

Figure 2.1a Visual map of the current freshman move-in process.

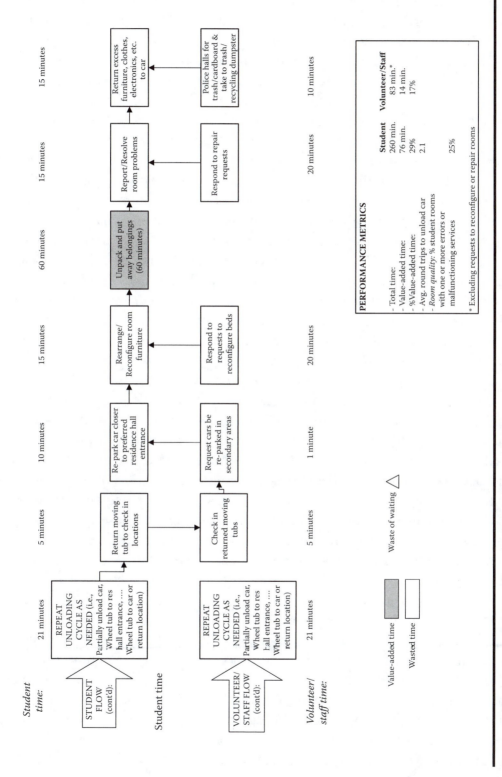

Figure 2.1b (continued) Visual map of the current freshman move-in process.

causes of waste for students and their families (e.g., staffing time required to sign out and sign in rolling tubs used by students). Finally, the Project Team identified some examples of waste unique to steps performed by university staff and volunteers (e.g., staff members in the first-floor lobby who monitor elevator loading and unloading). When the amount of staff and volunteer time wasted per student is multiplied by the number of new freshmen who move in this day, it serves as a powerful impetus for change.

The additional performance metrics also provided useful insights for the Project Team. For example, students averaged just over two round trips from their cars to move all their belongings to their rooms. This repetition of the unloading cycle requires families to spend more time waiting, longer queues waiting to use the elevator, and delays in re-parking cars so that other families can begin unloading. In addition, the Project Team documented that one in four rooms (25%) required a reconfiguration or repair (e.g., electrical outlets, cable TV, and Internet connections that do not work). This "quality control" challenge required the presence of many maintenance staff (many of whom receive overtime pay), and required students and families to wait in their rooms for staff help to arrive and fix the problem.

The Project Team recognized that waste and poor flow in the move-in process negatively influenced the perceptions and attitudes of those involved in the process. Parent and incoming freshman feedback underscores shortcomings in the current move-in process. Starting college provides an emotional and stressful backdrop for students and their families, and they may arrive tired from packing their car and driving to campus. In this context, students and parents are more sensitized to shortcomings in the move-in process, with some attributing the delays and problems to an uncaring large bureaucracy (an unfair portrayal of a university pursuing LHE). These frustrations influence parent and student interactions with volunteers and staff, who get to hear all the complaints in their roles as representatives of the university during the move-in process. The Project Team also notes that staff and volunteers feel their time could be used more productively, but they do not believe they can do anything about it.

Overall, the Project Team has developed a comprehensive understanding of the move-in process. Their documentation of the amount of time wasted by each student and his or her family, multiplied by the number of freshmen participating in the process, underscores the decision to focus on meeting students' needs and expectations through the application of LHE. Similarly, poor flow and waste suggest that future improvements to the move-in process can have benefits for university volunteers and staff (e.g., greater ownership and engagement) and the university (reducing their commitment of resources while simultaneously providing better service).

Use LHE methods and tools to propose solutions that eliminate waste and improve flow in a "future" improved process. The Project Team followed the overarching principles of LHE to propose solutions that will enhance the value freshmen and their families expect from the university's move-in process. After separating into two LHE Specialist Teams (i.e., a team focusing on removing waste and improving flow from the beneficiary perspective, and a team focusing on removing waste and improving flow from the provider perspective), they developed tailored recommendations for reducing waste and improving flow using LHE methods and tools. Together the two Specialist Teams quickly proposed a number of solutions to eliminate or improve steps and activities during the move-in process that add no value or disrupt its flow.

Allow freshman students to confirm in advance how they want their rooms configured (bunk beds or loft beds). Freshman students would receive a scale floor plan of their rooms with movable icons of university-provided furniture. They would return this form to the university prior to move-in day so that the room can be prepared to meet their expectations. The floor plan with room dimensions will also help students determine which personal furniture and appliances will physically fit in the limited space available. The university should consider providing (or renting) a combination microwave/refrigerator that is perfectly sized for the space and can be comfortably shared by students.

Purchase new moving tubs that better accommodate student belongings and maximize elevator space usage. The new moving tubs should accommodate more items of different shapes and sizes, and transport hanging clothes. Resized tubs will provide more capacity for student belongings and allow four tubs to fit in an elevator at the same time. Moving tubs should have an erasable surface to identify the room number for the belongings currently loaded in the tub. Tips for packing (e.g., preferred sizes of boxes or containers, recommendation that the students delay bringing winter clothes until later in the semester) will help freshman students facilitate the move-in process.

Schedule freshman students' move-in times to smooth out the peaks and valleys of activity throughout the day. Equally distributing the number of freshman arrivals throughout the day minimizes congestion in and around the residence hall and uses university staff and volunteers more efficiently. Freshman students would select their preferred window of time for move-in, and the university can develop incentives (e.g., free family meal) to shift some students to less-popular time windows.

Send detailed on-campus directions to freshman students prior to move-in. Campus directions should be clear (e.g., a color-coded graphical map that corresponds to campus features and temporary color-coded signage created specifically for move-in). Directions should guide students and their families to the precise residence hall parking location where they can begin the move-in process immediately upon arrival. The location of students' rooms in the building or their need for an elevator will determine their parking assignment outside the residence hall.[7]

Bring registration and room keys to the student rather than having the student go to a centralized registration area. University staff will bring the hall registration and room key assignment "carside." Knowledge of arrival time window and parking assignment will support this effort.

Confirm room quality prior to student arrival. Residence hall staff should inspect rooms prior to student arrival and "sign off" that the room is properly configured and all services (electrical outlets, light fixtures, cable TV, phone, Internet) are in working order. Each room should have contact information for students requiring assistance with furniture, electrical, phone, and so on during move-in.

Assign moving tubs to small "moving teams" of university volunteers. Team size and the number of tubs per team should be determined to accomplish student move-in in a single trip.

Assign moving teams to residence hall entrances based on average "cycle time" (i.e., the average time for a complete move-in). Each moving team should complete a certain number of complete move-ins every hour based on average cycle time. A whiteboard posted in a visible location will present up-to-date information on whether the moving teams at a particular location are falling behind schedule. Other moving teams that are ahead of schedule, or one or two floating movers, can use this information to provide assistance and get things back on schedule.

Transport moving tubs in elevators without members of the moving team. Moving teams can use the nearby stairs to meet up with their tub at the correct floor. Moving tubs will be placed in the elevator so that the tubs closest to the elevator door are the first off the elevator. A volunteer assigned to each floor will remove full tubs from the elevator at their correct floor and load empty tubs on the elevator for their trip down. Moving team members (and the student and family) can use the stairwells to transport fragile, odd-shaped, or extra items to the student's room. The moving team member who returns the emptied tub to the elevator should place any discarded cardboard and packing material in the tub for deposit in recycling and refuse containers outside the residence hall, keeping the narrow hallway clear of trash, which makes it difficult to navigate.

Move unloaded cars immediately to nearby parking so that moving teams can assist the next freshman student. The moving team completely unloads each freshman student car. The car can be driven to nearby parking (perhaps converting non-parking space into a temporary parking lot for use on move-in day) as the team transports belongings into the residence hall.

Provide all staff and volunteers with an overview of the entire move-in process and cross-training on assignments. Staff and volunteers involved in the move-in process must understand the importance of completing their roles and responsibilities as expected to the success of the freshman student move-in process. Standardized steps ensure that work is coordinated with the work of others, and training staff and volunteers for multiple assignments provides flexibility in responding to unanticipated needs.

The Project Team draws a new map of the proposed or "future state" move-in process following the implementation of the LHE solutions noted above (see Figure 2.2). They highlight steps in the improved process that they agree contributed value (from the perspective of students and families) to the move-in process, and project revised performance metrics for evaluating the process.

By applying LHE methods and tools to remove waste and improve flow during the move-in process to meet the expectations of new students and families, the impact of the Project Team's recommendations on the established performance metrics are striking:

- The amount of time freshman students and their families spend on the move-in process could be reduced from over 4 hours to less than 1.5 hours, a 69% decrease. Of the 81 minutes needed for move-in, 96% of that time (compared to 29% of their time during the current move-in process) contributes value to the move-in process.
- The university also gains similar savings in time and effort. By eliminating steps that add no value to the move-in process and by using LHE tools to improve the flow of the process, the amount of time required for a typical freshman would drop from 83 minutes to a projected 36 minutes (a 57% decrease). Of the estimated 36 minutes needed to move in a new student, 47% of the time directly contributes value to

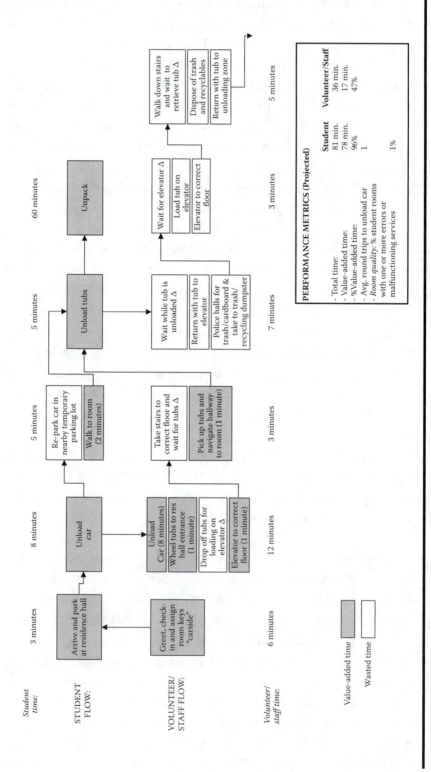

Figure 2.2   Proposed future state visual map of the freshman move-in process.

the process—a significant improvement over the 17% value-added time observed in the current move-in process.

■ The paid staff and volunteers who represent the university in the move-in process should have a more positive experience: greater engagement in the process, fewer complaints from frustrated students and parents, fewer reported room problems, more efficient use of their time, and less stress.

■ Implementing these LHE solutions reduces the level of resources required for freshman move-in while at the same time providing greater service to the new students and their families. The reduction in staff resources needed for freshman move-in may result in actual cost savings for the university, and the reduction in volunteer resources can be redirected toward other services that new freshman and their families value (e.g., having academic advisors available on move-in day).

Overall, the Project Team is confident that the proposed LHE solutions to improve the move-in process will result in a more positive experience for freshman students and their families, use university resources more efficiently, and provide a more engaging and rewarding experience for university staff and volunteers. The 5-day rapid improvement workshop culminates with a formal presentation of proposed solutions by the Project Team to VP Smith and the Office of LHE Initiatives.

VP Smith invites the LHE Project Team leader, Katy Lockhart, to present the team's recommendations at the next cabinet meeting. (The presentation of LHE project results to the university's senior leadership group underscores the president's commitment to LHE as an important institutional priority.) At the cabinet meeting, Lockhart visually contrasts the proposed future state map of the freshman move-in process with the map depicting the current process; the visible reduction in the number of steps and activities immediately impresses the cabinet. She also presents a table of projected changes on the key performance metrics established by the Project Team to document improvements to the freshman move-in process (see Table 2.2). Consistent with previous LHE projects at the university, Lockhart explained to the cabinet that implementing the proposed LHE solutions would result in immediate savings of university resources while providing a move-in experience more consistent with what new freshmen and their families expect. These savings more than offset the proposed costs of purchasing new moving tubs and a small number of large whiteboards.

The president and cabinet strongly endorse the LHE solutions proposed by the Project Team. The recommendations are approved "as is," in clear

Table 2.2 Current and Projected Levels of Performance on Key Metrics Established for the Freshman Move-In Process

Key Performance Metrics	Current Levels of Performance before LHE Rapid Improvement Workshop	Projected Levels of Performance after LHE Rapid Improvement Workshop
Total Time:		
Student/family	4 hours, 20 minutes	1 hour, 21 minutes
University staff/ volunteers	1 hour, 23 minutes	36 minutes
Value Added Time:		
Student/family	76 minutes (29% of Total Time)	78 minutes (96% of Total Time)
University staff/ volunteers	14 minutes (17% of Total Time)	17 minutes (47% of Total Time)
Number of Round Trips to Unload Cars	2.3	1
On-Time Delivery of Move-In Services	Not known or measured	95%
Room Quality	25% errors	1% errors
Parent/Freshman Feedback	Anecdotal comments suggest mixed to negative reaction to move-in process	≥90% satisfaction as measured by formal survey instruments completed by students and families

deference to the Project Team's detailed and comprehensive understanding of the freshman move-in process from the perspectives of beneficiary (the students and their families) and provider (university staff and volunteers). The university allocates funds to purchase whiteboards for use outside all residence halls on move-in day. Budget constraints require spreading the purchase of new moving tubs across two fiscal years.

Lockhart and VP Smith share the positive results of their meeting with the LHE Move-In Project Team. The project's endorsement and positive comments by the university's senior leadership team validates the hard work and contributions of the Project Team. Consistent with LHE practice, the Project Team quickly establishes an LHE Implementation Team from its membership and a timetable for implementing their recommendations. The Implementation Team invites other key participants in the freshman move-in process to join them as they finalize changes. With support from the Office for LHE Initiatives, the Project Team documents the new freshman move-in process and develops a training program for all individuals and offices that will participate in the next freshman move-in.

Pursue perfection by monitoring performance metrics on an ongoing basis and introducing additional improvements to the process. University administrators who oversee the freshman move-in process and the LHE Project Team monitor the next occurrence of the new freshman move-in process using the established performance metrics (Table 2.2). All faculty and staff participants in the move-in process are urged to propose additional recommendations as part of ongoing continuous improvement efforts for this and other university processes using a standardized and simple, one-page format. The Project Team will forward all meritorious recommendations to the Advisory Council of the Office of LHE Initiatives for its endorsement prior to implementation. The recurring cycles of recommendations for improvement reflect the ongoing continuous improvement process (analyze the situation, implement a solution, study and measure the effectiveness of the solution, and adjust the solution as necessary) that is central to LHE. Project Team members report feeling positively about their professional growth during the workshop experience, gaining new knowledge and tools to improve how they do their work and provide better service to freshman students and their families. Employees who are directly involved in the move-in process appreciate their expanded responsibility for continually adding more value to the move-in process from the perspective of freshman students and their families, the primary beneficiaries of this critical university process.

VP Smith has noted which team members are showing promise as LHE leaders for future LHE rapid improvement workshops. He enters on his calendar when the next freshman move-in process will occur, and will make sure that the LHE Move-In Team is invited to observe the improved process and identify new LHE solutions to the move-in process for the next year.

2.4 Summary

LHE offers a practical framework for understanding and improving processes in higher education. Teams of employees follow a simple set of steps that helps them understand and diagnose an existing process, starting with the value that process is expected to deliver to its beneficiaries. The team then uses LHE methods and tools to create a better process that flows smoothly and minimizes waste, increasing value to the beneficiary of the process, reducing the amount of limited university resources needed to support the process, and making employees' jobs more engaging and fulfilling. Tailored specifically for higher education, LHE presents an opportunity for universities desiring to shift the institutional mindset from "business as usual" to a learning organization that supports the university-wide application of LHE principles and practices.

Endnotes

1. These challenges are no different in other organizations with very different missions and processes. Different types of restaurants exist to meet different types of needs that people may have: food that is fast, predictable, and cheap; a relaxing atmosphere to unwind and be waited on; an opportunity to experience meals that are beyond one's cooking skills; a place to meet new people and have fun (with food as an afterthought). Different types of food stores exist if you prefer to cook your own meals: a corner store that is expensive but where you can find that one missing ingredient at the last possible moment; a full-service grocery store where you might do your weekly shopping based on its wide variety of goods and its reasonable prices; a discount warehouse where you visit every 6 to 8 weeks to purchase prepackaged, nonperishable items at a discount. Different consumers may have different values (low cost versus high convenience), and the same consumer may have different values at different times (lunch on the run at a fast-food drive-thru and a relaxing dinner at an elegant restaurant). But simply establishing an organization or a business to solve a problem is not enough. If the fast-food restaurant has long lines—lines for ordering food, lines for paying for food, lines for picking up food—it will soon find itself with very short lines as consumers who are looking to save time go elsewhere. If the corner grocery store decides to have limited evening and weekend hours, it loses much of its appeal (and business) to working adults who expect the convenience when they need it. Consumers have very clear expectations about their definition of value and how they choose among organizations and businesses to meet their needs.
2 These five principles are commonly acknowledged in the Lean literature, and were originally attributed to one of the most influential books on Lean by Womack, J.P., Jones, D.T., and Roos, D. 1991. *The machine that changed the world: The story of lean production,* New York: Harper Perennials.

3 "Beneficiary" is defined as the end user or recipient of the outcome of the process. Depending on the university process, the beneficiary could be students, parents, faculty, employers, legislators, or others. While it is recognized that there will likely be some differences in needs and expectations within and between the different classes of beneficiaries, all will expect processes that minimize waste and improve flow.

4. Adapted from Womack, J.P., Jones, D.T., and Roos, D. 1991. *The machine that changed the world: The story of lean production.* New York: Harper Perennials. Chapters 1 through 5.

5. The conceptual framework of LHE draws heavily from the pioneering work by Womack, J.P., Jones, D.T., and Roos, D. 1991. *The machine that changed the world: The story of lean production.* New York: Harper Perennials; Womack, J.P., and Jones, D.T. 2003. *Lean thinking: Banish waste and create wealth in your corporation.* New York: Free Press; and Womack, J.P., and Jones, D.T. 2005. *Lean solutions: How companies and customers can create value and wealth together.* New York: Free Press.

6. This "hypothetical" case study is based on a combination of personal experiences over the years at my home institution and second-hand anecdotes about move-in day at other institutions. Subsequent examination of the freshman move-in process at my home institution provided confirmation for the actual time estimates presented in this scenario.

7. The LHE Move-In Team did consider the possibility of parking and unloading vehicles in parking lots on the periphery of the campus, using buses and trams to deliver students and their belongings to the appropriate residence halls. However, the scope and expense of this potential initiative was considered impractical—at this time.

Chapter 3

"Proof of Concept"
Examples of the Successful Application of LHE

Many industry sectors—manufacturing, service, healthcare, government—have used Lean principles and practices with great success. Its ongoing extension to other domains—law, architecture, construction, and, now, higher education—attests to its broad applicability in virtually all work settings. Skeptical audiences within higher education, however, may prefer or even demand direct evidence that Lean Higher Education (LHE) principles and practices can be successfully applied at colleges and universities before pursuing and embracing their implementation:

- Senior administrators may question whether it delivers on its promises, given the significant opportunity costs (time and energy) required to introduce this institution-wide intervention.
- Faculty members may question Lean's applicability to higher education, given their perceptions of the unique qualities of the work done by colleges and universities.
- Administrators and staff may be concerned with how LHE will impact their job responsibilities or employment security.
- All university employees may question whether this proposed program will follow the life cycle of other "flavor-of-the-month" improvement initiatives (i.e., introduced with great fanfare only to wither away over time), squandering limited university resources with no significant benefits for those served.

This chapter provides that evidence. It features several universities that have applied Lean principles and practices, and demonstrates both the breadth of opportunity within higher education as well as the benefits of LHE to the university and its stakeholders. These exemplars of LHE in practice will depict differences across and within institutions in how and why Lean principles and practices were introduced, the breadth of the intervention (i.e., university-wide versus localized in one division or unit), how Lean events were sponsored and conducted, and the documentation of success of LHE initiatives. However, all the examples adhered to the core tenets of LHE:

- Define the value of the process from the perspective of the person who receives or benefits from it.
- Identify the flow of the process, both from the beneficiary and provider perspectives, to determine whether and how each of its steps or activities contributes value.
- Eliminate the many types of wasted steps and activities that add nothing to the value of the process.
- Make the process flow smoothly (more *pulled* by the beneficiary rather than *pushed* by the provider).
- Achieve perfection through continuous improvement and radical transformation of the process.

3.1 University of Central Oklahoma[1]

The University of Central Oklahoma (UCO; http://www.ucok.edu/) is a state-supported, metropolitan university located in Edmond, Oklahoma, a suburb of Oklahoma City. One of the regional universities in the state system of higher education, UCO serves approximately 16,000 undergraduate and graduate students across five academic colleges. Stagnant and even shrinking budgets (e.g., a budget cut of 15% in 2002), the concomitant shifting of the tuition burden to students and their families, and burdensome and inefficient administrative processes all contributed to low morale and declining productivity. Previous efforts to change university processes at best provided inadequate solutions to critical university processes, exacerbating problems with customer satisfaction and employee morale. Focus groups with a range of campus constituents confirmed that a significant number of administrative processes prevented the university from functioning efficiently.

The Executive Vice President of Administration concluded that implementing a Lean program at UCO held great promise for the university, recognizing that many of the complaints registered centered on non-value-added activities (i.e., waste) in key business processes. Consultation with experts in Lean manufacturing at local organizations and retaining the services of a Lean consulting firm led to the development of the Lean University™ process improvement initiative at UCO.

All administrative staff members attended an informational meeting that provided an overview of Lean and stressed the importance of all employees getting involved in Lean University™ initiatives. Each administrative staff member also participated in a one-day Lean training program, tailored to higher education and built around four key steps:

Step 1: Identify the Opportunities. Complete an organization-wide diagnostic search for issues, problems, and opportunities.

Step 2: Solution Design. Create a blueprint for success that involves all employees: training, mapping, and planning.

Step 3: Implementation. Use rapid improvement workshop (i.e., kaizen) events, core teams, and metrics to implement and illustrate change.

Step 4: Continuous Improvement. Monitor performance after projects are completed.

A campus-wide survey and subsequent focus groups provided data to help prioritize projects that could have the greatest impact on customer service. The university selected the work order process in facilities management as the initial project based on acknowledged delays in the completion of work orders, the impact of this process on all campus constituencies, and expressed interest by facilities management staff in improving their service.

The facilities management staff, along with other UCO administrative staff members, participated in a Lean training class focusing on administrative, service, and support processes. The class incorporated a combination of lectures and simulations to demonstrate Lean concepts. This training was followed by a 2-day workshop on "value stream mapping" that taught the skills of developing a visual map of a current "as-is" university process as well as developing a visual map for how the process might be done in the future (i.e., after introducing changes to remove waste and improve flow). The workshop documented the actual current state maps for UCO processes and served as the foundation for a number of Lean implementation projects (also known as "kaizen events"), including the work order process.[2]

An external Lean consultant and a UCO Lean Management Coordinator facilitated a 5-day kaizen event for a core team of five members who were assigned responsibility for improving the facilities management work order process. After fine-tuning the current state map to ensure that it accurately represented the existing work order process, the project team developed an action plan that (1) prioritized Lean solutions to improve the process and (2) identified Lean metrics that measure the effectiveness of the process. The team gathered Lean metrics to prepare a performance scorecard for the current state process, with the initial benchmark levels of performance prominently posted in the team's meeting room. Following from the action plan, team members took responsibility for communicating and implementing Lean solutions to the work order process, and were given the authority to make minor adjustments to ensure an overall workable solution that leads to positive change. The project team assigned any task not completed at the end of the 5-day kaizen event to a core team member with a specific deadline for completion. The project team shared results of the weeklong effort with the management and staff of Facilities Management and the Executive Vice President of Administration. In the six months following the workshop, employees in facilities management proposed additional solutions as part of Lean's continuous improvement efforts to meet customer expectations.

Table 3.1 provides a performance scoreboard, using key performance metrics identified by the Lean team, for the work order process at UCO. Column 2 provides performance information for the "current state" of the work order process prior to Lean intervention. Columns 3 and 4 show significant improvements in performance following implementation of the "future state" of the work order process immediately following the 5-day kaizen event after the workshop and six months following the workshop. The Lean implementation project for the facilities management work order process led to substantial and documented improvement, as shown in the rightmost column of Table 3.1.

The clear success of the Lean initiative is captured in the UCO's technical report, *Becoming a Lean University*™:

> *For 100% of all work orders the customer is contacted within two days of submittal. Over 90% of the work orders are completed within three days and over 80% are completed on the day of request. A process that once had over 3,000 backlogged work orders now has less than 300 at any given time. … Even though the emphasis of this effort is on improving customer service across campus, there*

Table 3.1 Performance Scorecard for Lean Improvements in Work Order Process

Metric	Before Workshop	Immediately after Workshop	Six Months after Workshop	Percent Improvement
Number of pieces of paper generated per work order	19	2.2		88.4
Annual paper cost	$15,597.46	$1,262.39		91.9
Travel path of work order	1265 ft.	253 ft.		80.0
Average number of touches	28	5		82.1
Average number of days waiting until work order is assigned	24.1 days		2.6 days	89.2
Percent of work orders submitted by e-mail	26.8%		91.1%	240.0

have been multiple instances of cost savings through project work. The first Facilities Management project was able to save more than $14,000.00 in annual paper cost with only one week's worth of work. … The overall morale and work ethic of employees in areas where changes have been made has improved significantly. … Students have already begun to see the positive impact on services offered … Faculty members whose responsibilities include the role of building monitor have once again become engaged in the process.[3]

Following the initial Lean project, Lean Core Teams were formed to apply Lean principles and practices to a number of additional processes from all divisions of the university, including:

- Bursar and Financial Aid Coordination Process.
- Graduate Program and International Students Office Student Application Process.
- Purchase Order Process.
- Physical Plant Payroll Process.

- Architecture and Engineering Services Construction Contraction Process.
- Access Control Key Distribution Process.
- Academic Affairs Adjunct Hiring Process.
- Academic Affairs Budget Request for Increase Process.
- Prospective Students Services and Admissions Coordination Process.
- Bursar Check Distribution Process.
- Change Order Process.
- Access Control Key Approval Process.
- Access Control Housing Key Distribution Process.

Overall, UCO's Lean University™ program has significantly improved customer satisfaction by eliminating waste and improving flow in critical administrative, service, and support processes. In addition, university employees who participate in Lean initiatives are reported to feel more empowered (i.e., they have the responsibility to improve their work processes) and accountable (i.e., they can see the impact of their efforts on customer satisfaction and the financial position of the university). Participation in a Lean project provided a professional development experience that improved employee outcomes (e.g., higher job satisfaction, reduced frustration) as well as university performance (e.g., increased productivity, cost savings).

3.2 University of Iowa[4]

The University of Iowa (UI; http://www.uiowa.edu/), located in Iowa City, is a research-extensive state university enrolling more than 30,000 undergraduate and graduate students across 100+ academic areas of study. With an annual budget exceeding $2.4 billion, UI employs over 2,000 faculty and approximately 13,000 professional and general staff. Like many public universities and colleges, UI faced an environment of decreasing state appropriations and increased competition for external grants. In response to these challenges, UI began an aggressive plan in 2005, with the active support and involvement of the president, provost, and vice president for finance and operations, to examine all administrative functions in an effort to better serve students, faculty, staff, and the public with improved and timely services at a reduced cost to the university.[5]

UI's Human Resources created an internal Organizational Effectiveness (OE) unit to provide workplace consultation and work redesign programs to the university community. Recognizing that Lean principles and practices would complement existing consultation services, UI began a partnership with Rockwell Collins, a world leader in communication and aviation electronics with corporate headquarters in nearby Cedar Rapids. Years earlier, Rockwell Collins had adopted Lean methodology and techniques throughout its global operations with great success. Rockwell Collins generously agreed to assist UI in establishing a "Lean in Academia" model tailored to address improvements in administrative and back-office processes that are important to students, faculty, and staff. The company provided extensive "train the trainer" experiences for an internal consultant from OE to develop the university's internal capabilities for implementing Lean across campus. Rockwell Collins also provided a Lean expert who helped lead three Lean events at UI. The Lean expert served as a mentor to the OE consultant, who gained the expertise and experience needed to lead future Lean events at the university independently. The Rockwell Collins partnership continued to support the university's Lean efforts through ongoing consultation and advice.

UI selected Lean events strategically to maximize impact on goals of the university's centralized strategic plan.[6] One administrative process approved for improvement through a Lean event was the UI hiring process. The Office of Equal Opportunity and Diversity (EOD), in support of UI's strategic goal for increased diversity, oversees the hiring process, beginning with the approval of the position description and ending with the approval to extend an offer. The multi-step process affects hiring across campus, and concerns about the time consumed by the process and the level of reworking required by the EOD and departmental units due to inaccurate or incomplete forms made it a critical process to review and improve. Leaders from the EOD met with the internal Organizational Effectiveness consultant to develop a "case for change." This helped the EOD set objectives, project scope and boundaries (e.g., state or federal regulations), the project manager or champion of the Lean event, and event participants (including employees from other departmental/collegiate areas involved in the hiring process, customers of the hiring process, and an IT staff member to help with immediate technological solutions). Table 3.2 lists the key outcomes from these preparatory meetings prior to the hiring process Lean event. Information and data were also gathered to depict the preliminary "current state" of the process (e.g., process and information flow, value and non-value-added activities, performance metrics) targeted for improvement. Figure 3.1 shows the current state hiring process.

Table 3.2 Outcomes of Preparatory Meetings for Hiring Process Lean Event

Case for Change
Desire to streamline the electronic processing of search forms and implement a more proactive and intuitive search and selection process
Desire to meet UI's strategic goal for diversity of faculty, staff, and students
Project Scope
Electronic submission and approval of position requisition/recruitment plans, pre-interview reports, and search and selection documents
Process for waiver of search not included in this Lean event
Boundaries
Regulatory and high quality standards must be met
Existing signature authority (minimum of three signatures) must be met
Maintain integrity of data
Objectives
Educate departments about EEO/AA and recruitment/retention best practices
Minimize risk to UI through appropriate controls
Ensure uniform search and selection procedures and implementation of EEO/AA principles
Complete the search and selection process in a more efficient and timely manner, with recommendations based on complete and accurate information
Modify documents and process to reach OED target goal of 24–48 hour turnaround
Meet employee training needs
Lean Event Members
Sponsor and project leader from OED
13+ participants from OED, academic units, human resources, and information management
Facilitators from Organizational Effectiveness unit

As shown in Figure 3.1, the current hiring process at UI includes 30 steps, with the time needed for all of the steps requiring almost 95 hours of work by UI employees. (*Note:* The process maps developed by the Lean project teams and leaders do not include the time between steps—transport of forms between offices, forms requiring action that languish in in-baskets, and so on—which is acknowledged as significant and adds to the time to completion of the hiring process). While mapping the current hiring process, data revealed that missing or incorrect information led to wasteful rework to correct problems at the final three steps of the process (i.e., for every 100 hires, an average of 26 hours of employee time is spent correcting errors, adding no value to the hiring process).

The hiring process Lean event (kaizen) project team convened for three consecutive days of focused effort under the co-leadership of the team leader and OE consultant. The event began with an overview of Lean principles and practices, followed by a restatement/refinement of the Lean event objectives (developed earlier by OED, "owners" of the hiring process). The project team then worked collaboratively to confirm the accuracy of the current state map of the UI hiring process, carefully documenting areas of waste in the process and identifying disruption to work flow. Table 3.3 presents a partial list of problems identified by the Lean event team as well as initial ideas for eliminating waste and improving flow.

The Lean event team used these observations to propose an improved hiring process for the future, as shown in Figure 3.2. The "future state" process map for the UI hiring process reflected a 17% reduction in the number of steps (i.e., from 30 to 25 steps) and a 54% reduction in the work time invested in the hiring process (i.e., from 94.8 hours to 43.7 hours). Although not documented, the Lean event team reduced the time between the steps in the process (the waste of transport and waiting), decreasing the length of time needed to complete the hiring process. For example, the team reduced the time from initiation of the hiring request to job posting from 45 to 30 days, a 33% improvement. The Lean event team then shifted its efforts to establishing metrics for documenting improvement in the hiring process. These performance measures focused on improvement from the perspective of the customer of the hiring process, confirming the expected reduction in waste and improvement in flow in the 12 to 18 months following implementation of the Lean solutions incorporated in the "future state" hiring process. These performance metrics included:

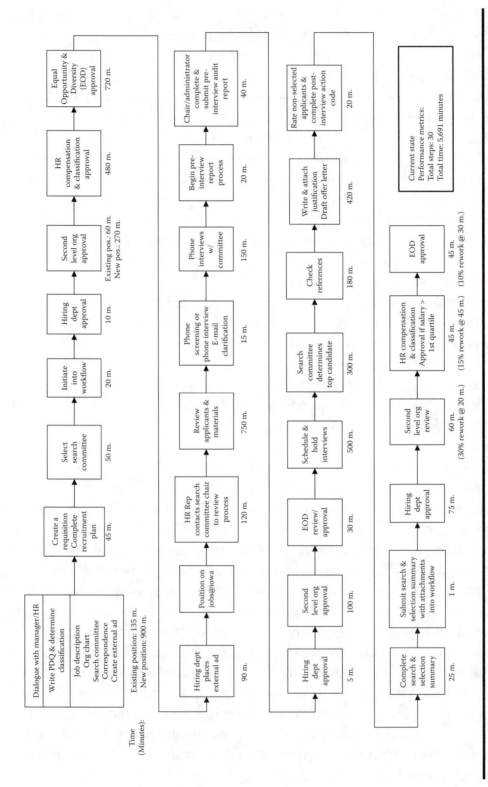

Figure 3.1 Current state process map: University of Iowa hiring process. (Adapted from UI EOD Lean Event: Post-Event Summary.)

Table 3.3   Partial Listing of Conformed Problems and Possible Solutions to UI's Current Hiring Process

Confirmed Problems: Unnecessary Waste and Disruptions to Work Flow	Possible Solutions: Eliminating Waste and Improving Work Flow
Advertising language inconsistent	Encourage centralization of advertising to save dollars and effort
Inconsistent communication with applicants throughout hiring process	Create "smart form" that ensures targeted advertising for job titles that underrepresent women/minorities
Phone interview option/process needs to be clarified	
Conflicting interpretations of "total" vs. "relevant" years of experience	Redesign pre-interview and reference check forms
Search committee and EOD unclear on evaluation of position qualification	Define "years of total" and "years of relevant" job experience
Pre-interview form provides no rationale for required ratings	Automate entry of mid-point salary range data
Capability to edit online forms lacking	Provide instructions on what is expected in the justification of the selected candidate

- Average number of days to complete hiring process.
- Percentage of rework by category of error and by department/organization unit.
- Average total time to hire.
- Percentage of UI employees who have completed training on hiring process.
- Survey of HR representatives in department/organization units on satisfaction with the improved hiring process.

The final formal responsibility of team members at the end of the 3-day Lean event was to present their findings and recommendations to senior university leaders for their endorsement and approval.

Shortly following the Lean event, the project team reconvened to complete a "Gap Analysis," which enumerated the specific actions necessary to transition from the current UI employee hiring process to the recommended future hiring process as endorsed by the university president. A written "Action Implementation Plan" was developed, including deadlines for key milestones and individual accountability for critical tasks (e.g., within 2 to 4 weeks, require electronic submission of applicant resume), to ensure that the recommended Lean solutions were completed. The university formed

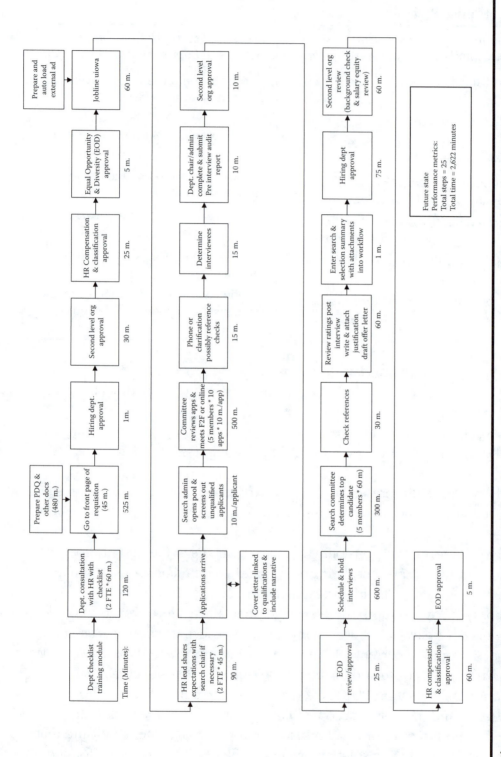

Figure 3.2   Future state process map: University of Iowa hiring process. (Adapted from UI EOD Lean Event: Post-Event Summary.)

"Action Item Teams," including UI employees who had not participated on the Lean event team, to address each key area in the implementation plan. Regularly scheduled follow-up reviews and required reports to management helped monitor progress on the Action Implementation Plan. The established performance metrics were (and are) continually monitored to confirm that the process improvement gains achieved through the Lean intervention are sustained, as well as to identify ongoing opportunities for continuous improvement to the hiring process at UI. In fact, the Lean event team had also envisioned a more distant "future state" process for hiring employees that required technological solutions (i.e., an electronically shared "smart form") not practical at the time of their work. The potential implementation of this yet-unachievable process would reduce the number of process steps to 16 and dramatically reduce waste due to waiting, transport, and errors.

Outcomes from the hiring process Lean event have had a positive impact on the university community, as shown in the first row of Table 3.4. Improvements to the hiring process have also improved the experiences of job applicants, who benefit from a simpler, more informative, and quicker hiring process. UI has completed approximately 20 Lean events since implementing Lean in 2006. Table 3.4 briefly summarizes several of these Lean events.

In its first year, Lean events were estimated to save the university $500,000 (i.e., through actual cost reduction or cost avoidance), and annual savings are expected to increase and compound dramatically as UI implements additional high-priority Lean events in subsequent years. In addition to the savings and improved services that benefit students and faculty, the campus community embraced "Lean in Academia" as a practical tool for improving business processes. A number of Lean events were being planned at the time of this writing (e.g., course add/drop process, human subject review board application process, conflict management process), all with the strong backing of the UI's president, provost, and vice president for finance and operations.[7] Overall, employees across campus see "Lean in Academia" as a great success:

> *The concept, interest, and results of corporate partnerships have been overwhelmingly positive. It has been well received on campus by faculty and administrators due to the improved efficiency, decreased costs, improved relationships, improved change management, and ongoing evaluation.*
>
> *The benefits of collaboration are recognized well beyond the confines of the university. Students benefit by gaining a better*

Table 3.4   Summary of Lean Projects and Outcomes at the University of Iowa

Lean Project	Project Outcomes
Human resource transactions: simplify the employee hiring process	• Decreased time from initiation to job posting from 45 to 30 days (33% improvement) • Decreased number of process steps from 30 to 25 (17% improvement) • Reduced number of attachments to HR forms by 75% • Decreased reworking submissions by 50% • Decreased number of applicant files to review by 50%
Research administration contracts: simplify process for faculty and improve accuracy	• Reduced number of steps in the process from 45 to 17 (62% improvement) • Decreased number of process loopbacks from 21 to 10 (52% improvement) • Decreased the number of total days in process contract waits for action from 42 to 15 (65% improvement) • Reduced review time for complex contracts from 38 to 32 weeks (16% improvement); simple contracts reviewed in <48 hours
Research administration grants: simplify process for faculty and improve accuracy	• Reduced time to inform grants accounting of award notice from 10 to 5 days (50% improvement) • Projected reduction of 25% in rework and post-grant submission corrections • Established research liaison role to improve understanding of process within the decentralized university structure • Improved information gathering: decreased number of unnecessary phone calls and e-mails to Office of Sponsored Research
Large bid (>$1M) contracting process: reduce the time from bid opening to contractor begins project	• Eliminated 20 days between the time bids are opened and the time contractors begin work

Table 3.4 (continued) Summary of Lean Projects and Outcomes at the University of Iowa

Lean Project	Project Outcomes
University billing office: improve efficiency of process and increase student satisfaction	• Reduced annual mailing expenses by $100,000 • Projected reduction in bank transaction costs through expanded use of e-payments by students
Americans with Disabilities Act request process: simplify process for faculty, staff, and students	• Reduced number of required forms from 4 to 1 (75% improvement)
Departmental scholarship process: improve scvholarship application and approval process	• Automation of process eliminated data entry for 4,000 scholarship applications annually ($7,000 annual labor savings)

education at a lower cost and exposure to Lean practices while at the university – highly sought skills in new college graduates. Consequently, industry benefits through hiring students who have gained knowledge, skill and ability in Lean business improvement methodologies during their university experience.[8]

3.3 University of New Orleans[9]

The University of New Orleans (UNO; http://www.uno.edu) is a public comprehensive institution enrolling approximately 11,000 undergraduate and graduate students. In addition to its main campus located 15 minutes from the French Quarter district, UNO has several academic centers in nearby cities as part of its role as a metropolitan university. Several senior faculty members with federally funded grants to teach Lean Six Sigma to the U.S. Navy asked UNO's chancellor to consider using Lean Six Sigma as a way of improving university processes. The chancellor offered his strong support for establishing a Lean Six Sigma Initiative pilot program at UNO. He shared his personal and institutional commitment to this effort through an e-mail to the entire campus community, and worked closely with his direct reports to ensure their commitment and support as well. One of the three Lean Six Sigma initiatives chartered by the chancellor was the personnel payment process required when there was a change in source of funding for a position.[10] This process, referred to as Personnel Action Form 101, was perceived as a great source of frustration by department heads and deans because of both the large number of steps involved and the high likelihood of errors that delayed the process while forms were returned to an office for correction. At least one instance where a graduate student left the university because he had not received a paycheck after 3 months exemplified that the process did not meet the needs of the individuals served.

UNO formed a Lean Six Sigma project team to study and improve Personnel Action Form 101. The team included the process "owner" (a higher-level administrator who was responsible for the overall process), a Lean Six Sigma champion (faculty members with Lean Six Sigma credentials and experiences), a vice chancellor (representing the chancellor's office commitment to the project), a team leader (with experience in facilitating Lean Six Sigma events), and other university employees and students. Several team members were invited to participate in Northrop Grumman Ship Systems' Lean Six Sigma "green belt" employee training program, where they were introduced to key concepts and practices that would be used by their UNO project team. The project team met regularly and was required to complete its work within 4 months.

The team focused on two key performance metrics for the Personnel Action Form 101 process: the number of submittals that required reprocessing because of errors and the cycle time from initiation of a payment request to entry into the payroll system. Information reviewed by the team estimated an error rate of 9% for payment requests, and a minimum cycle time of 20 days (i.e., assuming no errors in the payment request). The team established new performance targets for Personnel Action Form 101: a 1% error rate and a maximum cycle time of 14 days. The project team then applied both Lean tools (e.g., current state value stream mapping) and Six Sigma tools (e.g., Design-Measure-Analyze-Improve-Control cycle) to describe and diagnose the Personnel Action Form 101 process. The current state value stream map for the payment process identified more than 33 discrete steps; preliminary discussions of the steps helped the team realize immediately that several steps thought to be required by the Louisiana State University system were in fact not required, indicating some obvious opportunities for improvement.

After confirming that the current state process map was accurate, the project team held a "rapid improvement workshop" focused on redesigning the Personnel Action Form 101 process. The project team proposed several key recommendations for the "future state" value stream:

- Steps that added no value to the Personnel Action Form 101 process were marked for elimination. This resulted in reducing the process from 33 or more steps to just five steps.
- Because many errors were due to inadequate training in how to complete Form 101, the project team recommended that an electronic template replace the current paper form. The template would have drop-down menu options to help complete the form, and the template would reject any form that did not have required information fields completed or included information that was obviously wrong.
- Because much of the cycle time for Personnel Action Form 101 was due to the wasted time transporting the form from person to person and office to office, an electronic signature and routing system was proposed.

The Lean Six Sigma team presented its recommendations to the chancellor and his cabinet, who embraced the recommendations enthusiastically. UNO implemented the new Personnel Action Form 101 process as recommended. Evaluation of this new process indicated that errors were reduced markedly, reaching the performance target of 1% or fewer errors that required returning the request for rework. Most impressive was that the cycle time for completing a Personnel Action Form 101 decreased from 20 days to 45 minutes, a 98% reduction in the time from initiation of request to entry into the payroll system.

With the success of this and the other two chartered Lean Six Sigma initiatives, UNO was poised to implement an expanded Lean Six Sigma program across the university. Unfortunately, Hurricane Katrina inflicted massive damage to the campus, resulting in a downturn in enrollment and declaration of financial exigency by the university. UNO placed the expanded Lean Six Sigma program on hold because of this campus disaster. Despite the very unfortunate turn of events for UNO, from which it is slowly recovering, the Lean Six Sigma resulted in remarkable improvements for the university and those it serves.

3.4 Bowling Green State University

Bowling Green State University (BGSU; http://www.bgsu.edu) is a state-assisted, research-intensive institution with approximately 18,000 undergraduate and graduate students enrolled on its main campus in northwestern Ohio. BGSU is committed to undergraduate success inside and outside the classroom, with a wide number of first-year programs to help ensure a smooth transition to college. In response to reduced state funding (and concomitant expectations from the state that the university use their support more efficiently) and BGSU's commitment to improve services to students, the president and several vice-presidents supported a pilot program to implement Lean principles and practices (referred to as Lean Higher Education or LHE). As part of its ongoing efforts to improve efficiency and service quality, the Division of Student Affairs had formed an advisory committee to plan for a new facility that co-located three student support offices (Counseling Center, Student Health Services, and Office of Disability Services) in a comprehensive "Health Center." It was felt that physically bringing these offices together would be convenient for students (e.g., students could receive health and wellness services and advice in a single location) and leverage naturally occurring efficiencies (e.g., sharing a common record-keeping system). The Office of Student Affairs leadership team embraced the introduction of LHE to study critical processes in an effort to eliminate waste and improve flow in existing processes that could inform space needs and floor plans in the program statement for the new health center.

The LHE Steering Committee (three faculty members familiar with Lean and a doctoral student) provided general oversight and facilitation for two LHE Project Teams: Counseling Center and Student Health Services.[11] The teams worked independently and met approximately every other week, with individual and group assignments completed between meetings.[12]

Counseling Center. The Counseling Center Project Team included five center staff members, with the Director of the Counseling Center serving as team leader; additional center staff members joined the team over time as their expertise was needed. Two members of the LHE Steering Committee served as project team facilitators.

Early impressions of project team members were that students (and parents) desired speedier access to assessment and therapy services provided by the center. Emergency counseling services were available for crisis situations, and regularly scheduled group sessions provided "drop-in" opportunities for students dealing with stress and other common college adjustment issues. Nevertheless, students requesting personal appointments for nonemergency problems would typically wait several weeks from their initial contact with the Counseling Center to their first counseling appointment (a common challenge many university counseling centers face given increased demands for services and limited resources to meet them).[13] In response to this delay, there was the sense that some students would escalate the seriousness of their request in order to receive immediate services normally reserved for real emergencies, which then contributed to the waiting for services by other students. Therefore, the project team focused on improvements to the general "Assessment and Therapy Services" process, which was composed of two key internal subprocesses: the "Consultation and Assessment" subprocess and the "Client Assignment" subprocess. The Consultation and Assessment subprocess provided initial screening/intake to determine whether ongoing counseling services were needed beyond this first session and, if so, the most appropriate type of service. The Client Assignment subprocess paired new clients with center counselors based on counselor availability, counselors' areas of expertise, students' preference for the gender of counselor, etc.[14]

Project Team members shared their initial perceptions of the Assessment and Therapy Services process from both the perspectives of service provider (center staff) and service beneficiary (the students). This task identified several potential areas of focus:

■ Perceptions of unmet student/client expectations (e.g., students want immediate service, too much paperwork).
■ Waste that could be targeted for elimination (e.g., students waiting for appointment, staff waiting for files to be completed, waiting for meetings to assign student clients for individual counseling).
■ Factors that impeded the flow of services (e.g., handling paperwork multiple times for entry into the electronic database, nonstandardized steps for completing and forwarding paperwork).

Team members then walked through all of the individual steps of both the students and center staff to create a map of the current Assessment and Therapy Services process. This "current state" map provided an accurate description of the individual steps in the process as well as detailed review of the forms used, flow of people and information through the processes, and key performance metrics (e.g., average time from initial contact to Counseling and Assessment meeting; number of student "no-shows" for scheduled Counseling and Assessment appointments, number of emergency service sessions). Figure 3.3 presents the "current state" map for the Assessment and Therapy Services process.

As shown by the triangles between the steps of the flow for students in Figure 3.3, this process is rife with waiting by students. Students wait, on

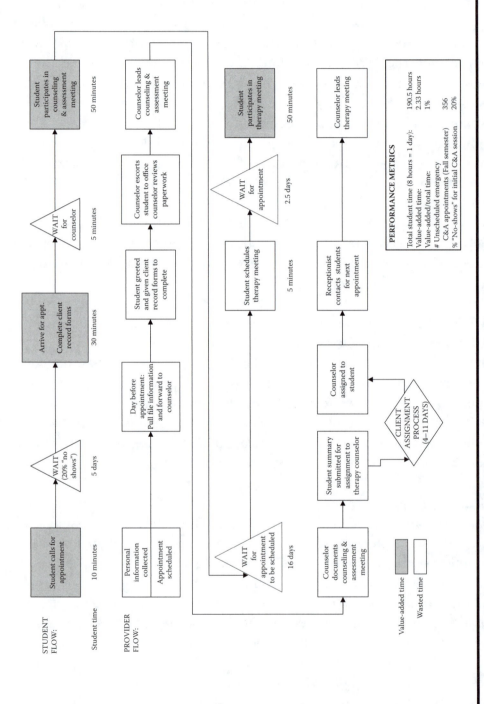

Figure 3.3 Current state process map: BGSU counseling center assessment and therapy services.

average, 5 days from their initial contact with the counseling center to their first consultation and assessment meeting, 16 days until they are assigned a counselor with whom they can schedule their first therapy session, and 2.5 days for the first therapy session to occur. The client assignment process (an embedded subprocess depicted by the diamond shape contained in the provider flow) contributes significantly to student waiting. If the intake counselor does not submit the required paperwork for assigning the student to a therapy counselor, the discussion of this student at this weekly meeting may be held over to a subsequent week. The shaded boxes underscore that only a small fraction of time (2.33 hours) in this lengthy process spanning more than three weeks contributes real value to students. The large number of unscheduled emergency appointments (356 in the fall semester alone) and the significant percentage of students who fail to show for their initial counseling and assessment meeting (20%) interrupt the planned schedule of services to students and contribute to the poor flow of the Assessment and Therapy Services process.

The LHE Project Team applied Lean tools designed to remove waste and improve the flow of this process. The team made more than 70 recommendations across the two subprocesses that made up the Assessment and Therapy Services process. One radical change proposed for the Counseling and Assessment subprocess was implementing same-day "walk-in" appointments. This would eliminate one identified point of significant waiting, allowing students to access assessment and counseling services more quickly. Walk-in appointments would also drastically reduce the number of "no-shows" for appointments. A second, equally significant recommendation was to eliminate the Client Assignment process. From the Lean perspective of eliminating waste and improving flow, it became strikingly clear to the team that this process took approximately 2 weeks to complete and required a significant amount of staff time but added little value from the perspective of a student client. A number of other recommendations identified by the Lean project team were also implemented (e.g., reducing duplication in record keeping, revising client information forms to provide greater focus during assessment, standardizing work flow by counselors, providing signals to counselors to minimize the number of counseling sessions that ran overtime). The Project Team recruited other members of the counseling center staff to join an LHE Implementation Team to put these recommendations into practice and monitor their impact.

Figure 3.4 shows the future process map for Assessment and Therapy Services that the LHE Implementation Team put into action at the BGSU

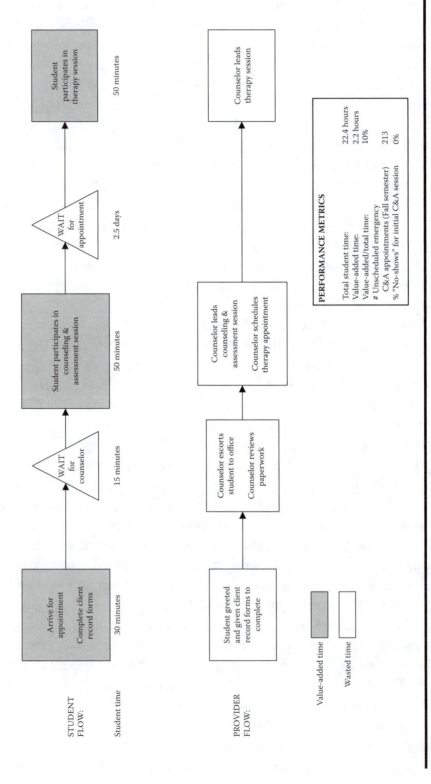

Figure 3.4 Future state process map: assessment and therapy services.

counseling center. The revised process reduced the total number of steps, providing a more simplified flow of services for students and counseling center staff. Walk-in counseling and assessment services dramatically reduced waiting time for students. With walk-in service, the disruption to the work flow of the counseling center caused by students who fail to show up for their scheduled counseling and assessment meeting is eliminated. Demand for unscheduled emergency appointments has dropped, and the counseling center redirected counselor time historically reserved for unpredictable emergencies appointments toward other pressing student needs.

Table 3.5 summarizes the gains achieved in the Assessment and Therapy Services process following LHE intervention. Overall, the delivery of services has improved dramatically. With the implementation of walk-in services and immediate assignment to a counselor for any continuing therapy,[15] students are now able to schedule their first therapy appointment that same day (the amount of waiting until the initial therapy appointment depending on available times that are mutually convenient for the student and counselor). Appointment no-shows dropped dramatically (as would be expected with walk-in service), which minimized the inefficient redirection of counselors' time when students failed to show for appointments. The number of self-identified emergencies decreased 41% with the availability of walk-in service for all students. Most impressively, the reduction in no-show appointments and emergency services visits and the elimination of the Client Assignment process freed up considerable staff time to support the improved Assessment and Therapy Services process, avoiding the need to hire additional staff. All of these improvements took place at the same time the number of student requests for service *increased* approximately 25%. As might be expected, student satisfaction with this new service delivery model was extremely high, as measured by surveys completed after experiencing the new process. Although not formally assessed, the Counseling Center received positive reactions from campus offices that commonly refer students to the Counseling Center. The center's leadership team continues to look for continuous improvement opportunities to enhance further the Assessment and Therapy Services process. Overall, the application of Lean principles and practices to identify and remove waste and improve flow allowed the counseling center to offer assessment and therapy services to more student clients when they wanted them with no increase in staffing.

Student Health Services. Student Health Services (SHS) formed an 11-person LHE Project Team to improve the process of delivering medical services to students. The team identified a number of unmet expectations

Table 3.5 Counseling Center Performance Metrics Before and After LHE Improvements

Performance Metrics	Before LHE Intervention	After LHE Intervention	Percent Change
Student waiting time until initial appointment (days)	5	<1 (same day)	Decreased ≈500%
Student waiting time from initial appointment to assignment to individual counselor (days)	16	<1 (same day)	Decreased ≈1600%
Number of unscheduled emergency assessment/ counseling services interviews[1]	356	213	Decreased ≈41%
Percentage of no shows for consultation and assessment interviews	20%	<1%	Decreased ≈2000%
Percent student satisfaction with "walk-in" counseling appointment process[2]	n/a	100%	
Total number of students requesting counseling services[1]	761	950	Increased ≈25%

[1] Fall semester data.
[2] "Strongly Agreed" or "Agreed" that "walk-in services were easy to use."

of students who used student health services: long waits when phoning the SHS, inability to get timely appointments, long waits for obtaining lab results, and an inefficient and complicated system to access (and provide) care.

Team members began with a physical "walk-through" of the most frequently used process, the primary care visit (i.e., a scheduled appointment for diagnosis and treatment). The walk-through provided a common understanding of each step of the process from a student's perspective. It immediately surfaced examples of waste and poor flow (e.g., health professionals would escort students from examination rooms to the lab because of concerns that students would get lost due to poor signage; the same staff conducted student check-in and check-out, creating a poor flow of students through the process as well as numerous staff interruptions). These initial observations led the LHE Project Team to break into four LHE Specialist Teams, each focused on a distinct component of the process thought to be critical to the student primary care experience: (1) Patient/Information Flow, (2) Front Desk (Reception/Check Out), (3) Exam Room/Provider Flow, and (4) Laboratory/Pharmacy Services. The LHE Project Team invited additional SHS staff members to participate voluntarily on one of the four LHE Specialist Teams.

Teams met regularly over an 8-week period. For each of their areas, teams drew up a "current state" process map, which provided a visual flow-chart for all steps and activities in the process by staff or students as they naturally occur, highlighting problem areas that can be targeted for improvement in the future. In addition, process observation worksheets were completed that provided detailed information for every step or activity identified in the current state process map (e.g., average time for each step, average time waiting between steps, distance traveled between steps). To document visually the physical flow of students, staff, and information in the physical workplace, the team created "spaghetti diagrams" (i.e., drawing the paths that people and information travel). The teams presented their findings at a combined meeting of the Office of Student Affairs and SHS leadership teams. Team members noted examples of waste and poor flow throughout the entire medical services process, and proposed specific recommendations based on common Lean solutions. The SHS leadership formed several LHE Implementation Teams (e.g., building signage, electronic health records), including both Project Team members and other SHS staff volunteers, and charged them with implementing the endorsed Lean solutions. For example, the LHE Implementation Teams standardized the equipment and supplies in all examination rooms and initiated a formal process for restocking supplies. This greatly minimized the need for healthcare providers to search for medical supplies or educational materials, allowing them to provide uninterrupted service to students while using their time more efficiently. Table 3.6 includes the list of the Lean solutions implemented according to the four focal areas examined by the LHE Implementation Teams.

Preliminary results indicate that the LHE intervention led to improvements in a number of the key performance metrics identified by the LHE Project Team, as shown in Table 3.7. While the reported saving of time may seem modest, reducing the average waiting time for each student by 2.3 minutes across the almost 37,000 SHS visits each year results in a savings of more than 1,400 hours of waiting by BGSU students. It is also worth noting that SHS accomplished this reduction in wait time (i.e., faster service delivery

Table 3.6 Examples of Problems of Waste/Flow and Lean Solutions: SHS Processes

SHS Process	Problems of Waste and Flow	Lean Solutions
Patient/ Information Flow	• Lost patients due to inadequate signage; escorting patients wastes time • Locating and moving single set of paper charts/records for each primary care patient • Patient education pamphlets must be located by caregiver; posted materials out of date • Students arrive on schedule and then required to wait for appointment	• Enhanced signage and clearly designated waiting areas • Expanded use of readily shared electronic charts/ records among caregiver team • Accountability assigned for updating and stocking educational materials • Educational materials located on a shared drive system so care providers could print out up-to-date pamphlets as needed • Staff schedules revised to align staffing levels with varying levels of student demand for services
Front Desk (Reception/ Check-Out)	• Single registration queue for all patients/visitors • Incoming phone calls disrupt front desk staff interactions with patients • Repetitive steps for chart handling	• Electronic "self check-in" by students • Separate queues focusing on different services needed • Incoming phone calls assigned to staff member not involved in front desk services • Standardized system/schedule for transporting charts/ records
Exam Room/ Provider Flow	• Care provider leaving exam room to retrieve missing supplies/equipment • Wasted movement retrieving refrigerated allergy/vaccine serum • Duplicate charting of patient information	• Standardized list of items and stocking schedule/ system for exam rooms • Centralized relocation of allergy/vaccine serum refrigerator • Designation of responsibilities for charting information • Student work-ups conducted by staff were standardized and streamlined

Table 3.6   (continued) Examples of Problems of Waste/Flow and Lean Solutions: SHS Processes

SHS Process	Problems of Waste and Flow	Lean Solutions
Laboratory/ Pharmacy Services	• Wasted movement filling prescriptions and conducting lab tests • Students wait in narrow hallways for lab results or filled prescriptions • Employees leaving lab to hand-deliver results to care providers	• Reconfigure shelving and work areas; replace stationary islands with moveable task carts • Comfortable common waiting area with student paging system • Networked computers to send lab results to care provider

Table 3.7   Student Health Service Performance Metrics: Before and After LHE Improvements

Type of Student Waiting	Average Waiting Time before Lean (minutes)	Average Waiting Time after Lean (minutes)	Student Time Saved Waiting for Services (% Time Saved)
Primary care appointment	20.1	18.1	2.0 min (10.0%)
Flex care (walk-in) appointment	21.5	18.3	3.2 min (14.7%)
Pharmacy visit	3.5	2.5	1.0 min (30%)
Laboratory visit	7.6	8.1	0.5 min *increase*
Overall average	20.4	18.1	2.3 min (11.4%)

Note: Data reflect averages from a full week of student health service appointments, using comparable weeks (i.e., the second week of April) from 2 school years.

to students) with minimal cost and no increase in staffing. Over 90% of SHS staff members were involved in the LHE initiative as participants in the project, specialist, or implementation teams. This broad level of participation provided staff member with insights into the "student care process" from the perspective of students and a better understanding of the roles of each department in the delivery of services. A survey of SHS staff found that over 80% felt that the LHE project resulted in improvements in medical services and that their own experience with LHE was positive.

BGSU completed a number of other LHE projects outside the student affairs area. For example, a LHE Project Team reviewed the university's international wire transfer process that sends funds to education abroad programs overseas, which used Lean solutions to reduce the time to transfer funds from 21 days to 3 days. Lean solutions improved the process for contracting instructors for non-credit courses, resulting in faster and more accurate completion of contracts while saving the contract coordinator more than 44 hours of non-value-added effort each year. Overall, the pilot LHE initiatives at BGSU demonstrated the transportability of Lean principles and practices to business processes in higher education.

3.5 University of Scranton[16]

The University of Scranton (http://www.scranton.edu) is a private Jesuit university located in northeastern Pennsylvania enrolling 5,000 undergraduate and graduate students. The Lean example described here, improving processes in the university's admissions office, was conducted to provide a hands-on learning experience for students as part of a university course on Lean thinking.

A faculty-supervised student team conducted two projects with the full support and cooperation of the admissions office. The first project sought to understand and improve the process of responding to external inquiries regarding the University of Scranton, as over 90% of these inquiries came from prospective new students. A Lean team composed of students and admissions staff identified that the expectations of the individuals served by the "faculty calling process" (i.e., faculty were responsible for initial callbacks to the inquiries) included a quick response, helpful information, and the timely forwarding of contact information to the appropriate admissions office staff member for prompt follow-up with potential new students. The mapping of the current state value stream (Figure 3.5) for this process identified 13 steps from the initial call for information to when the admissions officer had the necessary information to call back prospective students. Several areas of waste and poor flow were identified, as shown in the first column of Table 3.8. The entire process took an average of 2 to 3 weeks.

The team applied a number of Lean concepts to eliminate steps that added no value to the process and wasted time and university resources. The result reduced the 13-step calling process to three steps. The second column of Table 3.8 describes the Lean solutions implemented. With only

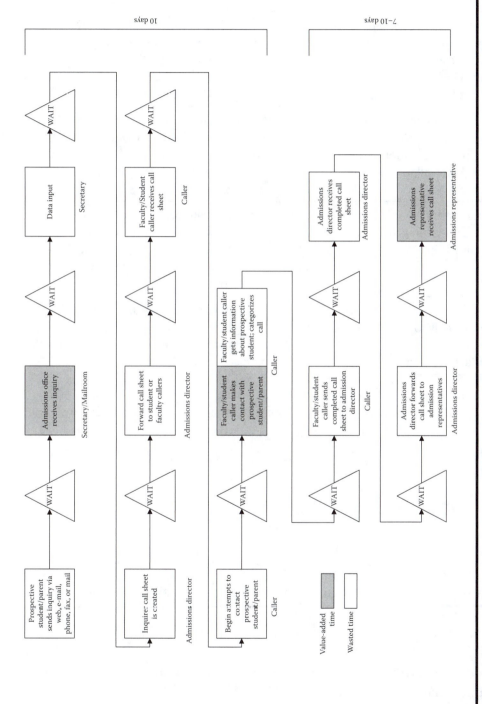

Figure 3.5 Current state process map: Admissions prospect calling process—University of Scranton. (Adapted from Tischler, L. 2006. Bringing Lean to the office. *Quality Progress* 39(7): 32–38.

Table 3.8 Examples of Problems of Waste/Flow and Lean Solutions: Faculty Calling Process

Problems of Waste and Flow	Lean Solutions
Admissions director reviewed inquiries weekly to assign faculty members to make initial call to prospective students; paper form sent to faculty members via campus mail.	Using admission director's criteria, electronic forms were created to be completed for online and phone inquiries. Completed forms were sent electronically via e-mail.
Faculty members were more likely to try and reach prospective students during the day when the students were in school and unavailable, requiring multiple calls.	Professional callers were hired to respond to an inquiry the same day the inquiry was received. Professional callers were available day and night to respond to inquiries.
Faculty members would fill out paper version "completed call" form and send to admissions director via campus mail.	Electronic call forms were completed by professional callers and routed to admissions representative. Immediate e-mail "thank-you" messages were also sent to prospective students.
Admissions director reviewed completed call forms weekly to assign prospective students to an admissions office representative.	This step was eliminated. Automated management report generated as needed to track progress of inquiries and times of contact.

modest costs for the university's ITS to set up the automated system, and the cost of training and paying the professional callers at a local call center, the future state value stream process (Figure 3.6) was established with immediate benefits:

- The time from the beginning of the process to the end was reduced from 2 to 3 weeks to less than 1 day, with many students or parents receiving a personal phone call within hours or minutes of their enrollment inquiry.
- Faculty involvement was reduced, allowing them to refocus their energies on teaching and research (improving the quality of education and the reputation of the university).
- The admissions director could reinvest his freed-up time in other activities that add value to the admissions process.
- An annual savings of $500 in paper costs and a reduced burden on the campus mail system.

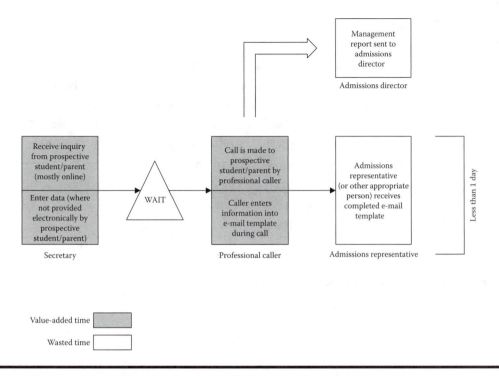

Figure 3.6 Future state process map: Admissions Prospect Calling Process—University of Scranton. (Adapted from Tischler, L. 2006. Bringing Lean to the office. *Quality Progress* **39(7): 32–38.**

The second project focused on the application process for student admission. In this process, prospective students submitted an application that the admissions staff reviewed; at the end of this process, the staff informed students of the admissions decision. The Lean team identified eight overlapping steps in the current state value stream occurring in no prescribed order by many different individuals. Working with the admissions staff to focus on the value-creating purpose of the process—that is, to process applications so that qualified prospective students learn of their admission acceptance as quickly as possible—the Lean team created a simplified future state process map. With the development of an operations manual, employees involved in the application process for student admission had a clear understanding of their role and the roles of others in the process. In addition, the Lean team created a system to allow everyone in the value stream to track an applicant's progress. ITS created a visual tracking system that clearly indicated when all admissions information has been received for an applicant, moving the application forward for review to accept or reject. The university developed a webpage to allow applicants to check on the progress of their admissions application (and know what information is still missing from their application). The university also built a software interface to allow information sharing among admissions, financial aid, and the registrar, reducing the number of times data are entered into the system, the number of data entry errors made, and wasted time in sharing information. While write-up of this project does not report the decrease in time necessary to complete the application process for student admission, it does document less overall work, shorter wait times, and improved information sharing on the status of every application. On the basis of these successes, the faculty sponsor of these Lean initiatives received multiple requests to lead additional Lean initiatives from administrative areas across campus.

3.6 Rensselaer Polytechnic Institute

Rensselaer Polytechnic Institute (RPI; http://www.rpi.edu) is a research-extensive university enrolling approximately 7,300 undergraduate and graduate students on its main campus in Troy, New York, and its smaller campus for working professionals in Hartford, Connecticut. The Hartford campus offers graduate degrees and certificates in several disciplines, including an MBA degree and an M.Sc. Management degree through the Lally School of Management and Technology (http://www.ewp.rpi.edu/hartford/academic/lsmt/index.html). RPI offers these part-time, face-to-face programs to working professionals in the area, who typically return for an advanced degree with ten to fifteen years of work experience and holding supervisory, mid-level management, or executive positions in local organizations.

The part-time working professionals in these executive master's programs face challenges, including professional demands such as business travel and work-related responsibilities and deadlines, and personal commitments such as family responsibilities and civic involvement. Many executive, evening, and weekend programs have modified their full-time graduate programs in an effort to accommodate these students, but these changes fall short of being fully responsive to the expectations of their beneficiaries (i.e., students and their sponsoring organizations). For example, changes in course format and delivery (e.g., extended class sessions on weekends and evenings) are helpful to many working professionals. However, other, more meaningful changes in (e.g., course objectives and pedagogy) are less likely to be considered if the student/employer has not had an opportunity to share his or her expectations for a single course or the complete program with an educational provider intent on listening and responding to these expectations.

A faculty member in the Executive Master's Program (EMP) in Management with an extensive background in applying Lean principles and practices in business organizations conducted two projects. The first Lean project was an individual initiative by the faculty member to improve his course on the topic of leadership.[17] The second project was a "bottom-up" effort supported by the senior administration that expanded the scope to include all ten courses that comprised the M.Sc. Management program.[18] These demonstrations of how Lean principles and practices can be used to transform the educational process represent both an informal and independent effort by a course instructor and an institutionally supported Lean project completed using formal Lean teams. They are also the only Lean projects found that directly focus on the student learning process, the core activity of higher education.

Leadership course project. As a first step in applying Lean principles to course redesign, it was important to identify student/employer expectations for the course. The professor of this course used several sources of information to specify course expectations:

- *Student data:* Published writings about the needs of working professional students as well as feedback from students enrolled in the program.
- *Alumni data:* Published data from MBA alumni identified a number of topics and skills that are perceived as valuable, including dealing with organizational politics, managing value conflicts, and integrating social responsibility throughout the curriculum.
- *Employer data:* Published data from employers of MBA students identified a number of topics and skills that are perceived as valuable, including stronger writing, speaking, and team building skills; applying the scientific method to business and management problems; and the integration of business concepts (finance, marketing, strategy, etc.) within a single course.
- *Accreditation standards:* Recent accreditation standards proposed by the Association to Advance Collegiate Schools of Business identified a number of topics and skills perceived as valuable, including a focus on basic management skills, differentiation designed for relevance to the market niche it serves, and diversity of participants and instructors.

Together these sources provide an indication of the value that students and employers desire from their graduate courses and degree program, and should be considered along with reflective thinking by the faculty member (as opposed to simply repeating the course as previously taught) of the value he or she hopes to create in students who successfully complete the course.

Following Lean principles (e.g., create value for end-use client, eliminate waste, respect for people, continuous improvement), the "current state" of the conventional course design and delivery system was constructed for the graduate course in leadership. For example, course assignments play an important role, both in reinforcing course learning outcomes and assessing student mastery of key concepts and skills. But in a traditionally designed course, the professor rarely communicates to students either the objective of each course assignment or how it relates to previous course material. As a second example, faculty members assign a smaller number of lengthier assignments, maybe due every few weeks. But this can lead to a "satisficing" response (e.g., focusing more on page length than on an unspecified learning outcome) to these tasks by students balancing competing work and family responsibilities. Furthermore, feedback in the form of a grade (and hopefully developmental written comments) is returned after some delay because of the time it takes the instructor to read and evaluate lengthy assignments.

In contrast, the professor can use traditional Lean tools to propose changes in the role course assignments should play in the "future state" design of the course, creating an improved course that meets the educational expectations of the working professional students and their sponsoring employers:

- Shorter and more frequent assignments (i.e., load smoothing).
- Simplify assignments to focus students on desired learning outcome (i.e., standard work).
- Specify learning outcome, standard format, and grading criteria for all assignments (i.e., respect for people; standard work).
- Return graded assignments in time for discussion in next class (i.e., just-in-time).

Table 3.9 summarizes how the professor applied Lean principles and practices to seven key elements in his graduate course in leadership. For each course element identified in the first column of the table, potential limitations in conventional (or "current state") course design and delivery are noted in the second column. Following the application of traditional Lean tools (e.g., just-in-time, load smoothing, standardized work, error proofing,

Table 3.9 The Application of Lean Principles and Practices to Key Elements in the Design and Delivery of a Graduate Course on Leadership

Course Element	Potential Limitations in Conventional Course ("Current State" Design and Delivery)	Recommended Modifications for Improved Course ("Future State" Design and Delivery)
Course philosophy/ principles	• Course philosophy/ principles are not explicit nor fully explicated through course materials	• Course philosophy/ principles are explicitly stated (e.g., world business community should play an important role in improving economic and social conditions)[19]
Syllabus: content and organization	• Syllabus is long (5+ pages) and not always followed • Syllabus does not include clear expectations for students • Syllabus does not identify typical errors that result in poor grades	• Syllabus is limited to critical information (3–4 pages) and closely followed and referenced throughout the course • Syllabus clearly and simply defines student expectations • Syllabus includes information on how to avoid typical errors that result in poor grades
Required readings	• Required readings, out of tradition, are extensive and lack clear learning objective • Required readings emphasize case studies whose solutions lack transferability to other settings	• Required readings are focused and thematically consistent and achieve planned learning outcome • Required readings emphasize root cause analysis and scientific method

—continued

Table 3.9 (continued) The Application of Lean Principles and Practices to Key Elements in the Design and Delivery of a Graduate Course on Leadership

Course Element	Potential Limitations in Conventional Course ("Current State" Design and Delivery)	Recommended Modifications for Improved Course ("Future State" Design and Delivery)
Assignments	• Assignments are infrequent and lengthy • Assignments do not include clear learning objectives and grading rubric	• Assignments are shorter and assigned weekly • Assignments follow a clear grading rubric that supports well-defined learning objectives
Examinations	• Limited number of examinations (midterm + final)	• Shorter bimonthly or weekly graded assignments
Student feedback	• At end of course with no or little impact on current or future course design and delivery	• At mid-term and end of course with response to students on whether and how their suggestions will be used
Impact on degree program and career	• Course notes, graded assignments, and readings may be collated and stored away	• One-page narrative/graphic summary of course content and learning outcomes • Simplified list of common errors made by senior managers in this course content area

visual management systems), changes in course design and delivery are recommended (see third column in Table 3.9) to create an improved (or "future state") graduate course in leadership.

The professor implemented the proposed "future state" for course design and delivery, and feedback from students and experiences of the professor were used to refine the course over five semesters (i.e., continuous improvement). Student course evaluations, using a nationally benchmarked assessment instrument, showed a steady and positive trend in student reactions to the "Overall Excellence of the Course" and "Overall Excellence of the Teacher." Over this same period of time, student evaluations of other courses at RPI were approximately 10% lower than this Lean-improved course. Written comments on the course evaluation survey (e.g., clear learning objectives, consistent and timely feedback, professor "walks the talk," like the one-page course summary) show that the innovations introduced are recognized and appreciated by students who have completed this course.

Executive Management Program Project. Based on the success of the initial Lean project to improve a single course, the faculty member received enthusiastic support from senior administration, faculty, and staff to conduct similar rapid improvement workshops for all ten courses in the graduate program. Student surveys identified four major classroom components of the educational process targeted for improvement:

- *Purpose and learning objectives:* a clear rationale for the topics, readings, assignments, and so on included in the course.
- *Course content:* the relevancy of topics, the level of technical/analytical rigor, the inclusion of global comparative analyses of companies, the applicability of course skills to their workplace, and the appropriateness of technological solutions.
- *Organization and sequence:* a logical flow and organization of course materials.
- *Classroom experience:* an interactive and engaging experience (i.e., limited lectures and slide shows).

Lean teams of five or six members (including the course instructor, other faculty members, a senior manager or staff member, a program alumni, and a trained facilitator) were recruited for each course. Prior to participating in a 2-day workshop, team members received a packet of information about the course (e.g., syllabus, key instructional materials) and written guidelines on expectations, member roles and responsibilities, and an agenda of activities. The length of the Lean workshops for each course ranged from 1 to 2 days, and the project team presented its improvement results to senior managers, faculty, and staff at the conclusion of each workshop. Table 3.10 summarizes the course-level improvements implemented following the ten Lean rapid improvement workshops. The team also recommended several program-level improvements:

- Eliminate ambiguity in grading criteria and assignments across courses.
- Standardize syllabi format (e.g., course description, course objectives) across courses.

Table 3.10 Summary of Improvements to Critical Classroom Components Implemented Following Lean Rapid Improvement Workshops

Classroom Component Targeted for Improvement	Implemented Improvements (Examples)
Purpose and learning objectives	• Written statement of purpose or learning objective for each class session and class assignment • Oral review of purpose or learning objective by instructor
Course content	• Updated course materials, with current articles incorporated into class discussions • Incorporate root cause analysis methods (e.g., "5 Whys") into courses, where appropriate • Include non-U.S. case studies, class readings, and current articles • Demonstrate (orally, written, visually) how class concepts are applied in real business settings • Incorporate explicitly the role/impact of technology on course subject matter
Organization and sequence	• Re-order course-level and class-level sequence of topics to improve flow and make best use of time
Classroom experience	• Increase diversity of "adult learning methods" that enhance student participation and match student learning styles

- Eliminate duplicate teaching materials (e.g., case studies, assigned readings) across courses.
- Ensure adequate opportunities for students to demonstrate learning and mastery of course materials (e.g., 4–12 graded assignments versus final exam only).
- Identify thematic "leadership and strategic thinking" connections among the ten program courses.

Self-reports by participants in a debriefing session following the work-shops supported the expected goals of the Lean workshops (e.g., the changes resulted in courses better aligned with student expectations, pro-fessors were energized to look for additional continuous improvements beyond those identified in the workshop). In addition, subjective ratings also indicated positive perceptions of workshop outcomes by the workshop participants.

Overall, Lean principles and practices to course and program design and delivery can challenge professors to rethink the value they offer to their stu-dents (and other beneficiaries), providing a framework for eliminating waste and improving flow in this educational experience:

> *The application of Lean principles and practices is an opportunity to better understand value from both the students' and employers' perspectives, and offer more substantive and focused educational challenges. Of course, the voice of the customer—both students and employers—should be incorporated in balance with the knowledge areas that the professor must be presented in the course to achieve the desired learning outcomes, and consistent with accreditation and school requirements.*[20,21]

3.7 Summary

Overall, results from the application of Lean principles and practices in higher education are positive and promising. Each LHE project demonstrated improvements on key performance metrics, providing immediate benefits to the different constituencies served by the process. Students were the clear beneficiaries of a number of the processes improved using LHE. The LHE projects made student admission decisions more quickly, provided prospec-tive students with quick and personalized contact, simplified the process for paying student bills, made scholarship award decisions more quickly, veri-fied financial aid eligibility more quickly, made counseling services more readily available when needed, required less waiting for medical appoint-ments, and more. Faculty, a key constituency at every institution, also ben-efited from the application of LHE principles and practices. In the cases presented, LHE provided a quicker review of grant applications, improved on-time paychecks for supplemental teaching, processed reimbursements for faculty travel more quickly, and streamlined the process for filling open faculty positions. LHE principles and practices brought improvements to processes that served all offices and employees. The institutions completed work orders in a more timely fashion, started (and completed) capital building projects sooner, and posted and filled vacant staff and faculty positions more quickly.

Positive outcomes from these LHE events also extended to college and university employees who served on one of the LHE teams or whose positions were embedded in the business processes targeted for improvement. Consistent with findings reported outside of higher education, anecdotes and testimonials from employees indicate that LHE projects improved their work situations and/or provided useful professional development. Employees who were part of a poor process experienced firsthand the personal stress that comes from customer complaints, work that is physically or psychologically taxing yet adds little value, and the lack of authority to make obvious changes in their own jobs to improve efficiency. These LHE initiatives resulted in changes to how work should be done to better meet the needs of students, faculty, or others who are served, changed employees' work (e.g., unnecessary and wasteful tasks were eliminated, work responsibilities clarified, less time spent correcting errors, fewer client complaints). These changes, in turn, contributed to increases in job performance and job attitudes (e.g., satisfaction, autonomy, involvement).[22] Employees also benefited from the professional development and growth associated with being part of an LHE initiative. Employees reported gaining greater insights into the importance of their roles and the roles of colleagues in critical processes that serve students and other constituencies. This insight helped expand employees' perspectives and empowered them to assume a more active role in improving the success of their college or university.

It is also worth noting that these LHE initiatives were successful across a wide range of situations and circumstances. LHE principles and practices worked across large and small institutions, across private and public institutions, with or without presidential endorsement and support, with or without a formal LHE office to sponsor events, with extensive training and preparation as well as with just-in-time training, in intense multi-day workshops as well as less compressed schedules that accommodate participants' work responsibilities, and addressing nonacademic support areas as well as the core academic process. The success of LHE projects appears to be robust across a wide variety of higher education settings and circumstances in much the same way that Lean has been shown to generalize across different industries and institutions. That said, there are some constraining factors that would influence the approval and scope of LHE initiatives. For example, it would seem unlikely that, without presidential support, an institution would choose to undertake an LHE initiative with cross-functional impact that would fundamentally change the way a university does business in the future. Likewise, a college dean would not choose to establish a college-wide LHE effort when there is limited trust in the college's leadership team or the university's overall climate is at odds with a climate conducive to introducing LHE principles and practices. The next chapter discusses these and other factors that help establish a favorable environment for LHE initiatives.

Endnotes

1. This summary is based on information from the following source: Moore, M., Nash, M., and Henderson, K. 2007. *Becoming a Lean University.* Report available at http://www.sacubo.org/sacubo_resources/best_practices_files/2007_files/UnivofCentralOkla-LeanUniversity.pdf.
2. UCO does not share current or future state process maps with outside organizations, restricting their use to campus Lean events and their executive training program offered to universities interested in starting Lean initiatives.
3. Moore, M., et al. 2007. p. 12.
4. This summary is based on information from the following sources: Reed, L., and Berry, K. 2007, April. Academia going lean. Presented at the *Annual Meeting of the Higher Learning Commission*, Chicago, IL. In addition to the manuscript, slides of the presentation can be found at http://www.ncahlc.org/download/annualmeeting/07Handouts/GMON945a.pdf.
5. The State of Iowa Government began its own Lean efforts (http://lean.iowa.gov) in 2003 with help from the Iowa Coalition for Innovation & Growth. More than 25 Lean events across eight different agencies were completed by Summer 2005. Iowa's then-Governor Vilsack envisioned that Lean would be implemented throughout state government. Lean support is offered through the Iowa Department of Administrative Services, Human Resources, Workforce Planning; http://das.hre.iowa.gov/wp_revising_processes.html.
6. When this program was first introduced under the former president, all vice presidents, deans, and directors annually created a prioritized list of critical business processes requiring improvement based on input from unit employees. Senior leaders considered all recommendations when establishing a university-wide set of priorities, according to an established set of criteria: strategic importance to the university, expected improvement in work flow, expected improvement in employee/student/patient satisfaction, financial impact, and capability of the unit's leadership to implement change. As the

new president and provost become familiar with Lean events at UI, there is the possibility that this original process of strategic review and priority setting could resume.

7. Interestingly, graduate students from UI's Tippie College of Business are also given the opportunity to participate in upcoming corporate partners' Lean events. These students receive hands-on experience in implementing Lean principles in the workplace, adding knowledge and skills that will be of great value in a competitive marketplace where many organizations are considering Lean initiatives to improve their performance and effectiveness.

8. Reed, L. and Berry, K. 2007, April. *Academia going lean.* Presented at the Annual Meeting of the Higher Learning Commission, Chicago, IL. Page 6.

9. See http://www.ncci-cu.org/Visitors/Documents/LeanSixSigma070905AC. pdf and http://www.ncci-cu.org/Visitors/Documents/LeanSixSigma070905AC. pdf for PowerPoint slides of the pilot Lean projects at the University of New Orleans, presented at the 2005 and 2007 annual conferences of the National Consortium for Continuous Improvement in Higher Education.

10. The other Lean Six Sigma initiatives selected by the chancellor were (a) the travel reimbursement process, which was perceived to be inefficient with too much paperwork and lots of processing errors, resulting in delayed reimbursement to faculty and staff for university-related travel; and (b) the financial aid verification process, where missing information and errors delayed the approval of financial aid awards as quickly as needed to strengthen enrollment, and students and parents complaining to the chancellor's office when their phone calls to financial aid are not answered as quickly as they would like.

11. Progress was limited in the Office of Disability Services because both the ongoing workload and small number of staff made it difficult to introduce an LHE initiative under any meeting format. Thus, only LHE initiatives for the Counseling Center and Student Health Services are reported.

12. The decision to schedule rapid improvement workshops using a meeting format that met for several hours across several weeks rather than the more typical intensive multi-day meeting was made for a variety of reasons, including the limited availability of team members who held critical service delivery roles for students.

13. See Farrell, E.F. 2008. Counseling centers lack resources to help troubled students. *Chronicle of Higher Education* LIV(25): A1; A28.

14. Other processes considered by the team included (a) "Emergency Service" process, where on-call counselors are assigned to meet with students who have been identified (self- or otherwise) as needing immediate attention; (b) "Consultation" process, where faculty, staff, or parents call the Counseling Center for help in addressing a student mental health issue; (c) "Individual Counseling" process, where students receive one-on-one counseling (up to a maximum of 30 sessions) from a professional staff member; (d) "Group Counseling" process, where groups of students meet with a professional staff

member; and (e) "Outreach" process, where professional staff members led workshops or made classroom presentations on relevant mental health issues (e.g., body image, coping with stress).

15. The process allows for this counselor to reassign a student to an alternative counselor based on student preference, special area of expertise, etc. This was accomplished through an immediate e-mail or phone call, resulting in only a minimal delay in reassignment.

16. See Tischler, L. 2006. Bringing lean to the office. *Quality Progress* 39(7): 32–38.

17. Emiliani, M.L. 2004. Improving business school courses by applying Lean principles and practices. *Quality Assurance in Education* 12(4): 175–187.

18. Emiliani, M.L. 2005. Using Kaizen to improve graduate business school degree programs. *Quality Assurance in Education* 13(1): 37–52.

19. See Caux Roundtable. 2004. Principles for business. www.cauxroundtable.org/documents/PrinciplesforBusiness.doc.

20. Emiliani, M.L. 2004. Improving business school courses by applying Lean principles and practices. *Quality Assurance in Education* 12(4): 183.

21. For an additional example where Lean principles and practices were used to redesign an MBA course on operations management using Lean, see Shevlin, J., and Van Dongen, L. 2006, October. Learning through Lean: Applying Lean thinking to education. Presented at the Linking Lean Thinking to Education Conference, Worcester Polytechnic Institute, Worcester, MA. Conference information at http://www.wpi.edu/news/conf/leaned/. Copy of presentation can be found at http://lean.mit.edu/index.

22. It should be noted, however, that Lean initiatives may result in negative short- and long-term consequences for employees. For example, stress may increase due to greater responsibility and accountability, employees may worry that changes to their jobs will affect relations with team members or level of authority, and a general anxiety associated with organizational change. All this suggests the importance of collecting better measures of employee attitudes and outcomes as part of the full assessment of the implementation Lean initiatives.

Chapter 4

Getting Started
*The Successful Launch of
Lean Higher Education*

The decision to pursue Lean Higher Education (LHE) is the critical first step, signaling readiness on the part of the university's leadership to improve institutional effectiveness through the application of Lean principles and practices. The success of LHE requires the commitment of key leaders, regardless of whether it is implemented as a comprehensive university-wide change program, a local pilot demonstration project, or somewhere in between these two ends of the LHE project continuum. Equally important to success, however, is the institution's readiness for LHE. Ensuring the successful launch of LHE requires establishing a supportive context for LHE to thrive, identifying the focal area(s) for implementing LHE initiatives, and establishing, training, and supporting LHE Project Teams.

This chapter provides an overview of key issues to consider and practical steps to take that will help prepare a university for the introduction of LHE and the successful completion of one or more LHE initiatives. While no amount of preparation, organization, and planning can guarantee positive outcomes from LHE, the recommendations and suggestions offered can help increase the likelihood of its success.

4.1 LHE: University-Wide versus Local Implementation

LHE is an institutional philosophy and set of operational practices that influence all aspects of the university: mission and goals, strategic planning, leadership, and work roles. Ideally, then, universities will implement LHE principles and practices university-wide because the most important processes of a university that contribute the greatest value to beneficiaries are university-wide. In a university setting, faculty hiring and retention, academic degrees and coursework, student recruitment and success, facilities operations, support for teaching, research and outreach missions, and alumni development and private support all encompass a large number of critical processes that cut across different functional areas (e.g., Academic Affairs, Student Affairs, Finance, Facilities and Operations, Advancement). Introducing LHE at the highest levels of the university can result in greater benefits for the university. It allows the university to focus on critically important university-wide processes whose complete sets of steps have not benefited from a careful examination by LHE principles and practices designed specifically to provide the value expected by the beneficiaries of that process, reduce costs, and improve employee attitudes. Introducing LHE across all divisions and levels at the university would create a true learning organization that understands and provides what its beneficiaries expect, eliminates waste that adds no value, and improves the flow of critically important processes.

Table 4.1 includes other possibilities that vary in the breadth or scope for implementing an LHE initiative.[1] As shown in the table, the scope of LHE initiatives can vary significantly, and the focus selected has implications for the levels of resources and leadership support needed to introduce and implement the initiative. For example, choosing an LHE initiative with a global-level focus will require the highest level of leadership support from the leaders of all institutions that contribute significant components of the identified service or process. At the other end of the continuum, an LHE initiative that focuses on a process embedded within a single office or operation that is under their local control might only need immediate supervisor support to accomplish the initiative. The expectation is that university leaders will support LHE initiatives at a university-wide or cross-functional level. Both provide manageable boundaries for implementing LHE initiatives: They are under the control of mid- to senior-level leaders within the university and hold real promise for making a significant impact on adding value,

Table 4.1   Level of Focus for LHE Initiatives

Level of Focus	Description	Example
Enterprise-wide	Focus on a process that spans beyond the university's boundaries to include other institutions, companies, etc.	The building design and construction process that includes state agencies, outside architects and contractors, and internal university offices
University-wide	Focus on all university processes that support a single external consumer	The comprehensive on-campus orientation process for new freshman students
Cross-functional	Focus on a process that spans several university functional areas	The application and approval process for faculty improvement leaves
Unit level	Focus on a process that is internal to a specific university office or function	The filing and archiving process for written documents within an academic department office

removing waste, and improving the flow of the university's most important processes.

Applying LHE principles and practices to any university-wide or cross-functional process will require presidential and vice presidential support. For example, suppose the director of student employment recognizes that the current process for advertising student employment opportunities and matching students to available positions is overly time consuming and fails to meet the needs of both student employees and the offices that hire them. Implementing change will affect areas well beyond student employment, including the hiring departments/areas, advising, financial aid, human resources, and internal marketing and communication. Without the authority to change the major steps in the student employment process, efforts to reduce waste and improve flow would depend on mutual consent from all of the "owners" of each of the individual process steps and activities. Without senior leadership support, foot dragging or active resistance by just one of the affected owners of a process step outside of student employment would derail the entire LHE initiative.

While institution-wide implementation of LHE offers the greatest gains to a university, LHE can be implemented within select areas of the institution as a set of principles and practices designed to introduce intentional change. Although smaller in scope and impact, a "local" LHE initiative can easily improve local processes under local control (e.g., updating an alumni database, determining faculty teaching assignments, fulfilling transcript requests, scheduling college advisor appointments, assigning graduate teaching and research assistantships, arranging x-ray and lab tests for ill students). For example, a university's continuing education unit can create an LHE team to hold a rapid improvement workshop to improve its process of recruiting and approving instructors for noncredit programs. This will help the unit better meet client expectations (i.e., offer more high-demand programs taught by knowledgeable and proven instructors) and improve university outcomes (i.e., greater enrollment and revenue from enhanced business and industry training while better serving the community in which it resides). To the extent that this targeted process is owned and controlled by the continuing education unit (e.g., the university's office of human resources does not dictate recruitment and hiring practices for this group of temporary employees), the unit can identify and introduce changes that reduce waste and improve flow as suggested by LHE principles and practices. The benefits, while significant for the unit and the clients it serves, will have a more limited impact on the overall effectiveness of the university.

Leaders of universities may choose to implement LHE in select areas of the university as the first step of a planned university-wide phase of LHE or as demonstration projects to introduce and demonstrate the effectiveness of LHE. Several successful "proof-of-concept demonstrations" of LHE may provide the evidence senior leaders need to endorse and support the university-wide expansion of LHE prior to a university-wide rollout. A second reason for pursuing local LHE initiatives may be the lack of "readiness" for implementing any university-wide change (including LHE). As discussed in the following section, LHE initiatives have a greater chance of success in an organizational climate that complements the philosophy of LHE as well as leadership practices that clearly support LHE initiatives. In those situations where the degree of readiness for LHE is limited to a few areas of the university, it may be both prudent and appropriate to implement LHE initiatives locally so that the university can begin to achieve some benefit (albeit on a smaller scale than would be possible institution-wide). Of course, local LHE projects must have the endorsement and support of local university leaders as well as members of the senior leadership team with line authority over the targeted process.

It is worth noting that this recommendation to pursue "local" implementation of LHE within select areas of the institution is contrary to the arguments made by several authors who write that organization-wide support is essential for the long-term success of Lean principles and practices, that is, the evolution of a true learning organization.[2] While their points are valid, it can be both appropriate and beneficial to introduce LHE in select areas within the institution. Chapter 3 presented many such examples that show that the benefits of LHE are not limited to only university-wide implementation of initiatives.[3] Many complex organizations have successfully introduced Lean principles and practices within select areas or plants, demonstrating the effectiveness of implementing LHE in more circumscribed areas. Successful implementation of LHE in select areas within a university can achieve immediate gain, and their success stories can help draw university-wide endorsement and support. For example, in the absence of presidential support, the success of local LHE initiatives can generate grass-roots interest in additional localized LHE projects, providing more support and greater impetus for expanding the implementation of LHE university-wide. In summary, while a motivated and committed champion of LHE can find some corner of the university to introduce LHE principles and practices that better the university, the greatest potential for benefit is derived from broader institutional acceptance and implementation at the highest institutional levels.

4.2 Institutional Readiness for LHE: The Importance of Workplace Climate and Leadership Practices

Launching a major organizational change effort such as LHE is an ambitious undertaking, and institutional leaders should think carefully before implementing any new initiative.[4] Assuming for the moment that the system-wide change intervention has evidence to show its effectiveness, failing to provide the right conditions for introducing the initiative can result in resistance by individuals, groups, and ad hoc coalitions. Analogous to the preparation of the soil to improve the survival and vitality of a newly planted sapling, the goal of institutional readiness is to ensure that the university "soil" is prepared to accept and support the introduction of LHE. Workplace climate[5] and leadership practices are two key factors to consider when assessing institutional readiness for LHE.

4.2.1 Workplace Climate and LHE

Workplace climate refers to employees' shared perceptions and attitudes about their work environment. Climate permeates the workplace, shaping how employees think and feel about their role in the organization. Climate's influence on employee attitudes and motivation, in turn, influences individual and work group performance. Thus, organizational climate can have a significant impact on employees' understanding of what they are supposed to do, their motivation to show up for work and complete their tasks and assignments, and their individual and group contributions to university goals and outcomes.

Consider the following workplace climate examples:

Climate A: University employees are clear on what their job duties are and feel the need to work hard to reach the high standards that are set for their job performance. They know that they are personally responsible for the work they do, but trust and depend on their supervisor and co-workers to provide needed help and support. When they are successful, employees feel that the university recognizes them for their contributions and hard work. Overall, employees feel very engaged and committed to what the university is trying to accomplish.

Climate B: There is some ambiguity among university employees about the full range of their job duties, and their understanding of what is expected is not particularly challenging. They do not feel any personal responsibility for whether they are successful or unsuccessful at work, and no one seems to notice their performance except when there is a problem. The supervisor and co-workers are nice, but everyone would rather avoid confrontation than challenge the status quo. They will not help when needed, however, especially when asked by someone outside their area. Employees feel no great loyalty to either their department or the university, but have no intention of leaving.

In which workplace climate are most employees with the prerequisite knowledge, experience, and equipment likely to be motivated to excel and contribute more to the overall performance of the university? In which climate are employees more likely to support their supervisor and make a commitment to LHE, a significantly different philosophical approach in the way university employees contribute at work? Answers to these questions underscore the important role that organizational climate plays in the workplace.[6] A healthy climate provides a positive context that arouses higher levels of motivation within employees and, through their increased commitment and improved job performance, contributes to the university's success. Conversely, an unhealthy climate provides a dysfunctional workplace setting that never achieves the benefits of psychologically engaged faculty and staff, causing the success of the university to suffer.

Litwin and Stringer have identified six dimensions of climate that can influence workplace attitudes and motivation:

■ *Structure*: the extent to which employees feel that the university is well organized and they understand their roles and responsibilities.
■ *Standards*: the extent to which employees feel pressure to improve their performance and the pride they take in doing a good job.
■ *Responsibility*: the extent to which employees feel they are their own boss and have the autonomy and authority to make job decisions.
■ *Recognition*: the extent to which employees feel the emphasis is placed on reward versus criticism and punishment and that they are recognized for a job well done.
■ *Support*: the extent to which employees feel a sense of trust and mutual support within their work group and can go to others (including their supervisor) for help.
■ *Commitment*: the extent to which employees feel a pride in being part of the organization and are committed to its goals.[7]

Universities (and areas within a university) will differ in their profile on these six different climate dimensions. A short, simple-to-complete climate survey is available to measure these six climate factors for the entire university or in selected areas, and templates exist for providing feedback on how employees perceive the overall climate (or the local area or unit climate).[8] Alternatively, the consensus judgments of key individuals at the university can provide a qualitative assessment of climate if a survey is determined to be impractical.

Of particular interest here is whether there is an optimal workplace climate profile that reflects institutional readiness for LHE. That is, is there a preferred "LHE Climate" profile (i.e., a pattern of low and high levels on some or all six climate dimensions) that provides institutional support for LHE, allowing it to take root and flourish? The writings of Lean authors suggest that three of the six climate dimensions proposed by Litwin and Stringer may be particularly helpful for creating a healthy environment for introducing (as well as providing ongoing support for) LHE:[9]

■ *A climate of standards:* Faculty and staff should feel a sense of pride in their unit or department for doing their jobs as well as possible. They should also feel that their supervisor and workgroup are interested in finding ways to improve performance and that everyone plays a role in making this happen. The climate should motivate faculty and staff to establish and meet high standards of individual and unit/department performance. Overall, the climate should support a workplace that is committed to meeting the needs of the individuals or offices they serve through high standards and continuous improvement.

◼ *A climate of support:* Faculty and staff should feel that they have the support of their university colleagues and supervisors and are part of a well-functioning unit or department. They should feel that they can go to their supervisor or colleagues for assistance at any time, and that they will not be inappropriately blamed or punished when mistakes occur on new and challenging assignments. The climate should motivate faculty and staff to obtain the knowledge needed to do their jobs as well as possible and not make them fearful of making mistakes. Overall, the climate should support professional development and risk taking that expands faculty and staff talents and ideas in an effort to meet the needs of those they serve.

◼ *A climate of commitment:* Faculty and staff should feel proud to be part of their unit or department and care about its success. Each should feel a personal responsibility to help the unit or department accomplish its goals and overall mission. The climate should motivate faculty and staff to maintain a sense of loyalty and commitment as active members of their unit or department. Overall, the climate should stimulate personal enthusiasm and energy to make it as good as it can be in the eyes of individuals inside and outside the university.

An assessment of these three dimensions of climate provides decision makers with insights into the level of institutional readiness prior to introducing LHE. If institutional readiness is determined to be a significant concern, particularly in the areas of standards, support, and commitment, Litwin and Stringer also identify interventions that may improve the climate and increase support for LHE.[10] University leaders can affect three aspects of the workplace to create a more sustainable environment for LHE:

◼ *Leadership practices:* day-to-day behaviors of the leaders in an organization. Evidence from both research and practice identifies the area of leader behavior as the most important determinant of climate.

◼ *Organizational arrangements:* formal aspects of the organization, including job responsibilities, reward system, policies and procedures, and the physical location and layout of the organization.

■ *Strategy:* the understood direction and purpose of the organization, how it sets goals, and how it allocates resources.[11]

Knowing the available levers that can help university leaders create a more LHE-friendly workplace climate (university-wide or within areas of the university) allows senior leaders at the institution to shape their practices, arrangements, and strategy in a purposeful and concerted manner. For example, if a vice president at the university wants to move toward a climate of high standards, he or she can coach and incentivize other leaders (i.e., his or her direct reports) to set challenging performance goals for their employees, provide then with formal feedback on goal success, and model a participatory, problem-solving approach with their subordinates. Organizational arrangements can be altered to build more responsibility and accountability into employees' jobs, tie performance incentives to work quality, and provide a physical workplace that supports employee success on the job. Communication with employees should frequently restate the university's commitment to the highest standards of performance as part of its overall mission, and show how it has invested resources to accomplish this priority. The alignment of leadership practices, organizational arrangements, and strategy to support high standards of performance would help create an overall climate more amenable to the introduction of LHE. The assessment and improvement of institutional readiness for LHE can increase the likelihood of success of LHE initiatives introduced at the university.

The next subsection provides a more expanded discussion of leadership practices, given their signal role in establishing a level of institutional readiness to support the success of LHE initiatives.

4.2.2 Leadership Practices and LHE

By their words and actions, presidents, vice presidents, deans, directors, department chairs, and other formal university leaders contribute significantly to a climate that can support or thwart the implementation and outcomes of any LHE initiative. The practices of other leaders, including the leadership of faculty and staff councils, unionized employee groups, highly influential faculty and staff, and elected student officials, can also influence the workplace climate and level of institutional readiness to introduce and sustain LHE initiatives.

As with many change initiatives, LHE principles and practices will alter the way employees of the university view and perform their jobs: more autonomy from supervision, more responsibility for success, more involvement in proposing changes, and the potential reassignment of duties and responsibilities as processes are redesigned to remove waste and improve flow. These changes can be unsettling as employees speculate how the changes will affect them (i.e., How will my job change, and will I like all the changes? Am I able and willing to adapt to these changes? Do the changes threaten my status and power, and even my job security?). Similar thoughts may also be going through the minds of supervisors because the implementation of LHE affects their jobs as well. Leadership practices that demonstrate support for LHE implicitly, and often explicitly, endorse the coming change and the redirection of resources to implement the change. Consider the following two scenarios:

Leadership Practices A: Department Chair Julia Carey sees how LHE can help the department improve advising services for anthropology majors. Her goals are a redesigned advising experience that is more responsive to student needs, a more effective use of faculty and staff advisor time, and eliminating advising complaints from students, parents, and the associate dean. After receiving approval for her LHE project proposal, she works with the LHE Project Team to design a strong communication plan for helping skeptical faculty and staff members understand the need for the initiative. Carey also shared her decision to make a modest investment of departmental resources to support the project's success. As the departmental chair, she made the LHE initiative one of her own priorities, actively participating when requested by the LHE Project Team and becoming a vocal cheerleader for the project and team members. She also awarded one faculty member a course release, given his significant leadership role on the LHE Project Team. The level of involvement by Department Chair Carey convinced many faculty members to embrace the LHE initiative to improve the advising process, and convinced still another subset of faculty not to pursue any active resistance.

Leadership Practices B: Department Chair Ed Bradley does not really understand what LHE is all about, but is willing to concede that advising for anthropology majors could be improved if only to reduce the number of complaints he receives from students, parents, and the associate dean. In his own mind, there are several other, more pressing departmental priorities, including a shortage of faculty to teach unstaffed course sections next semester (not realizing that removing waste and improving flow in the current advising system might free up faculty resources to reallocate to the teaching mission). Nevertheless, he does not want to say no to colleagues who appear very committed to LHE. When the university approves the LHE project proposal submitted by his faculty colleagues, Bradley assigns these colleagues the responsibility of leading the project as part of their service contributions to the department. While offering lukewarm public support for the LHE project, Bradley does allow LHE Project Team members to update the faculty and staff members when requested (assuming there is time available on the faculty meeting agenda). The faculty and staff quickly sense their chair's ambivalence toward the LHE initiative and, in turn, limit their own involvement in and support for the project.

The differences in leadership practices by the two department chairs in the scenarios above show their influence on faculty and staff members' perceptions of LHE, their level of engagement in pursuing an LHE initiative, and the likelihood of success of the initiative should it be approved. All else being equal, LHE is more likely to be successful with the leadership support provided by Department Chair Carey, whereas the indifferent public support and interest by Department Chair Bradley undermines the probability of a successful LHE project (and wastes precious faculty time and effort). Taking a neutral stance may be as damning as outright refusal; the absence of supportive leadership practices may compromise any change effort, including LHE, resulting in the same effect as would actively lobbying against it. Overall, the extent to which leadership practices are supportive of LHE can influence its success.

Factors that may influence the need for leadership practices that support LHE initiatives. In the absence of a commonly accepted or data-verified set of factors that influence the *need* for leadership practices that support LHE initiatives, the following factors may serve as a reasonable set when considering how much leadership support may be needed for the successful introduction and implementation of LHE:

- *Significance of the process to the university community.* LHE initiatives that may lead to changes in processes central to the functioning of the university will require higher levels of leadership support than LHE interventions in processes more limited in scope and significance. For example, changing the faculty hiring process or the student admission process will have a broader and more visible impact on the university than will revising the process for requesting instructional media support and, thus, will require more leadership support.
- *Number of individuals within the institution who are affected.* LHE initiatives that affect a large number of individuals or offices within the university will require higher levels of leadership support than LHE initiatives that affect fewer individuals and offices. Changing the advising process within the anthropology department, thereby affecting only faculty and staff members who are involved in advising in that

single unit, would require less leadership support than an LHE initiative that would change the advising process for all university students.

■ *A climate that is neutral or hostile to organizational change.* Universities whose climates are ambivalent or resistant to any type of organizational change will require higher levels of leadership support practices than universities whose climates are predisposed to embrace and support change. At universities where institutional memory includes vivid examples of change initiatives that faltered and failed, or negative consequences for employees as a result of successful or unsuccessful change, considerable leadership support may be required to avoid a dismissive attitude toward LHE initiatives. In contrast, less leadership support would be needed at universities where continuous improvement, customer service, best practice, and commitment to excellence are part of the ingrained beliefs or values of employees, and successful projects have resulted in fair outcomes for faculty and staff affected by the change.

■ *Number of individuals outside the institution who are affected.* LHE initiatives that affect individuals outside the university will need more active leadership support than LHE initiatives that affect university community members only. Changing the process by which students from a variety of community colleges transfer into the university will require more leadership support than an LHE initiative focused on the process by which students change their academic majors among departments in a single college.

■ *External mandates for change initiatives.* LHE initiatives that may be mandated by individuals or agencies perceived as external to the university community (e.g., boards of trustees, state boards of regents, legislators, federal agencies) will require greater leadership support practices by university leaders than LHE initiatives that are developed within the institution. Regardless of whether the external mandate (e.g., developing shared purchasing processes or record-keeping systems across all state-assisted universities within a single state) is ultimately in the best interest of the university, more extensive leadership support practices will help diffuse internal resistance and assure members of the faculty and staff that the LHE initiative is appropriate and will be supported.

Factors that may influence the availability of leadership practices that support LHE initiatives. Given the need for leadership practices to support the introduction and implementation of LHE initiatives, will they be available? Similar to above, a commonly accepted or data-verified set of factors that influences the availability of leadership support practices is absent. Thus, the following set of factors may influence the expected availability of leadership practices to support the introduction and implementation of LHE.

■ *Power of the leader.* Leaders with higher levels of institutional or personal power may have more influence on leadership practices to support LHE initiatives than will leaders with lower levels of power. A popular and respected university president would have considerable power inside and outside the university to support the introduction and implementation of LHE than would a new department chair. Influential individuals, with or without formal positional authority (e.g., faculty recognized as exceptional teachers or scholars, well-respected coaches), may also wield significant power to support LHE initiatives. For example, a former president of the faculty senate recognized for her effective handling of important issues may use her power to marshal support for LHE initiatives.

■ *Personal and sustained commitment of the leader.* Leaders with higher levels of personal and sustained commitment to the success of LHE may have more influence on leadership practices to support LHE initiatives than will leaders who are not personally invested in its success. Committed leaders "walk the talk" and can demonstrate their support of LHE (e.g., commitment of resources, public acknowledgment of the LHE initiative, encouragement of LHE Project Team members). Conversely, the influence of leaders with no personal investment in LHE is limited (e.g., lukewarm statements of support, limited follow-through on promises made, interests shifting to other issues and interests over time).

■ *Competition for the leader's available resources.* Leaders faced with less competition for their available resources can invest more of their leadership practices in support of LHE initiatives than can those with multiple or shifting priorities. One vice president with an unwavering priority of commitment to student retention may choose to focus his leadership practices on an LHE initiative for a key university process. Another vice president may divide her support among multiple priorities that continue to shift with changes in the environment, with the consequence of never investing enough to launch and sustain an LHE initiative through completion.

■ *Leadership stability.* Leaders who continue in their positions have more opportunities to offer consistent leadership support for LHE initiatives over an extended period than leaders who are new to their positions and may feel less commitment to their predecessor's priorities. New leaders often will feel a need to take their area in some new directions, reallocating their leadership support toward change initiatives they implemented rather than continuing what their predecessors had started (and not completed). The promotion of an existing dean to a vice presidency, in part due to recognized progress on LHE initiatives she consistently supported through her ongoing leadership activities, may result in the passive withering or proactive dismantling of the college's LHE accomplishments as the new incoming dean seeks to make his mark on the college.

A key consideration before embarking on LHE should be an evaluation (formal or informal) of the correspondence between the leadership practices needed versus their available level to support the introduction and implementation of LHE. Given the role leadership plays in communicating the need for LHE, committing adequate resources, overcoming resistance to change, and providing ongoing encouragement and support, it is essential to the success of any LHE initiative. Sponsors of the LHE initiatives should determine whether the level of leadership support expected to be available is sufficient, based on the extent to which leadership support is needed given key characteristics of the proposed project. The conclusion from this qualitative assessment may result in a formal request for a greater commitment of leader support commensurate with the scope and impact of the project. Alternatively, the conclusion may result in scaling back the proposed LHE initiative (e.g., shrinking the scope of the LHE initiative from university-wide to an effort within a single division of the university) to align the level of support needed from leadership with the level of support expected to be available. Postponing the LHE initiative until a time when the required level of leadership support is available could also be the preferred alternative. Rather than chance a failure by moving ahead with inadequate support from leadership at the university, sponsors may decide to defer the LHE initiative pending the future availability of leadership commitment from current leaders or a change in university leadership. Overall, moving forward with LHE without an appropriate level of commitment of leadership support could seriously undermine the effective introduction, implementation, and sustainability of LHE. Leadership support is a necessary, but not by itself sufficient, condition for the success of LHE.

LHE Leadership Practices			
		Consistently Low Support	Variable Support	Consistently High Support
LHE Workplace Climate	Consistently Non-Supportive	ABANDON	DEFER	FIX: CHANGE CLIMATE, THEN REASSESS
	Variable Support	DEFER	READI-NESS FOR LOCAL LHE INITIATIVE	READI-NESS FOR LOCAL LHE INITIATIVE
	Consistently Supportive	FIX: CHANGE LEADERS, THEN REASSESS	READI-NESS FOR LOCAL LHE INITIATIVE	READI-NESS FOR UNIVERSITY-WIDE LHE INITIATIVE

Figure 4.1   Readiness for LHE: leadership practices and workplace climate as critical factors for the success of LHE.

4.2.3 Institutional Readiness for LHE: The Joint Consideration of Workplace Climate and Leadership Practices

The assessment of institutional readiness to pursue LHE, and the chosen scope of the LHE initiative, should include consideration of both workplace climate and leadership practices. Figure 4.1 depicts how three levels of climate, and three levels of leadership practices, each representing a different level of support for LHE, interact to create nine discrete conditions of institutional readiness for introducing LHE. As shown in the darker shaded section of Figure 4.1, conditions to pursue university-wide implementation of LHE may be optimal, given both consistently high levels of leadership practices that support LHE and a workplace climate supportive of LHE. In this situation, employees are inclined to engage in LHE initiatives and accept their new roles and responsibilities in a university committed to LHE because they recognize that this initiative has strong backing from university leaders and their belief that the university will support and recognize their efforts with their involvement in the LHE initiative.

Figure 4.1 also suggests explicitly that if the level of institutional readiness is not supportive of university-wide implementation, then LHE can be introduced in a more circumscribed way (within a division, college, department, etc.) where conditions are more likely to support its successful implementation. The decision to pursue a "local" LHE project in a unit whose leadership practices and local climate support LHE may be preferred where university-wide leadership practices may offer less consistent support for LHE (e.g., limited public commitment by the most senior university leaders) and the institution's workplace climate is only modestly aligned with LHE principles and practices (e.g., employees as a whole feel limited responsibility for the university's goals). For example, if the director of the university bookstore is a strong advocate for using LHE to improve customer satisfaction and increase net revenue, and bookstore employees feel that they have an important role in improving bookstore operations and a commitment to meeting the needs of their customers, this would provide a favorable setting to pursue an LHE initiative focusing on processes within and under the control of the bookstore. Local workplace climate will have a strong influence on the motivation and performance of faculty and staff, perhaps even to a greater extent than would the university-wide climate (e.g., how their colleagues in biological science feel may have more influence on the attitudes and behaviors of biology faculty members than would how university faculty members outside the department feel). The local workplace climate may also be more malleable by the local leaders within a division or unit, and LHE could be implemented locally without the precondition of university-wide improvement in the workplace climate.

Figure 4.1 suggests that LHE may not be worth pursuing, either at this time or in the near future, at every university. In situations where leadership practices provide consistently low support for LHE, coupled with a workplace climate that is uniformly nonsupportive of any type of planned change, it may be wise to reconsider any proposal to introduce LHE. The probability of success is likely to be low, and its failure will make university leaders and employees less sanguine about the success of future programs proposing planned change. Figure 4.1 also suggests that there may be situations where the sponsor of LHE may wish to defer to a later time the decision to pursue an initiative where the level of support is consistently low on either workplace climate or leadership practices. In situations where the level of support is consistently high on one of the factors but consistently low on the other, the LHE project sponsor may first wish to consider a planned intervention to improve conditions on the low factor and then reassess whether the level of institutional readiness is adequate to support the introduction and implementation of LHE.

4.3 Creating Structure to Support LHE

The decision to pursue LHE requires that the university establish some level of organizational structure to provide leadership, oversight, and support for LHE initiatives. The extent and formalization of this organizational structure will vary considerably across institutions, depending on a number of factors, including:

- *Commitment to LHE.* Universities committed to the introduction of LHE as part of a long-term philosophy or strategy will require more structure than universities that introduce LHE as one of many endorsed practices over time.
- *Institutional impact of LHE initiatives.* Universities planning university-wide initiatives will require more structure than universities focusing their LHE initiatives at the unit level.
- *Number of LHE initiatives.* Universities that anticipate supporting a large number of LHE initiatives, many of which may be underway simultaneously, will require more structure than universities where initiatives are infrequent.

Consideration of these and other factors (e.g., availability of resources, presence of existing structures that have oversight responsibility for process or quality improvement) can inform the choice of structure that might be most appropriate for organizing LHE efforts in an efficient and effective manner. The structures created in universities that have applied Lean principles and practices (see Chapter 3) have varied widely, from very formalized and centralized to more localized, ad hoc efforts. With the hope that many universities will choose to implement LHE university-wide, in accord with an overall institutional philosophy that adopts Lean principles and practices, an example of a centralized and formalized structure to support this effort is presented.

4.3.1 The Office of LHE

The charter for an Office of LHE must complement the existing structures already in place at the university to organize and coordinate its efforts. Senior leaders in academic affairs, student affairs, finance, planning, and so forth provide top-down oversight for issues that affect the institution's academic mission, student experience, financial health, and long-term direction, respectively. In contrast to this typical vertical organization by functional area, the university's horizontally delivered processes cut across these functional areas to provide the valued services that students, parents, faculty, staff, and other beneficiaries of higher education expect. For example, the registration process for freshmen crosses many of the university's functional areas (e.g., which academic courses are offered for incoming freshmen, available housing and dining options, co-curricular opportunities to support academic and personal growth, determining tuition and fee charges and providing payment options). No single leader or office is directly responsible for—nor has the formal authority to ensure—a smooth, efficient, and satisfying process from the critical perspective of new freshmen and their families. The introduction of LHE will focus the institution's attention and effort on understanding and improving critical cross-functional processes.

In light of existing university structure and the planned efforts of LHE, a university president could create an Office of LHE to provide a formal, centralized structure responsible for overseeing LHE efforts university-wide, led by a "Senior Process Officer" (SPO) who is given the responsibility and authority to oversee and improve critical value-creating processes at the university.[12] Optimally, the Office of LHE and the SPO would report directly to the president, and the organizational chart and SPO position title would reflect equal status with current senior leaders of the university. The SPO would establish an LHE Advisory Board that includes both members of the university community and individuals from outside the university (e.g., business leaders and employees, alumni) possessing knowledge and experience with Lean principles and practices.[13] This advisory board would assist the Office of LHE in drafting a strategic business plan to advance the university's adoption of and transition to a LHE philosophy. Board members would each serve as liaison to a distinct "family" of processes (e.g., student processes, faculty processes, staff processes, external constituent processes). Board members would also serve as consultants on key LHE initiatives (i.e., early initiatives where the skills and experiences of university members are limited, prominent initiatives whose scope affect extremely visible and critical university processes).

The Office of LHE would also establish an internal LHE Steering Committee, consisting of university colleagues possessing a wide range of competencies (e.g., information technology, team-based leadership, statistical analysis, project facilitation) to assist with the successful implementation of LHE. Members of the steering committee would serve as liaisons between the Office of LHE and each LHE Project Team (discussed below). After receiving LHE training and serving on several LHE project teams, steering committee members may serve in the role of LHE project team facilitator/ mentor, offering practical advice and support to a team chosen to address a specific LHE initiative. The LHE Steering Committee can also serve as strong advocates for LHE efforts to the university leadership, providing energy and guidance in strengthening the university's commitment to LHE principles and practices that improve and sustain the university. The steering committee would advise the SPO on promoting and encouraging LHE projects across campus, prioritizing and selecting LHE initiatives, and reviewing and endorsing recommendations to improve processes. Members of the LHE Steering Committee would receive release time from their current responsibilities to provide the necessary time and energy required by their temporary, part-time assignment with the Office of LHE. An appointment to the steering committee would be an excellent professional development "rotation" for rising university leaders, broadening the university's LHE talent pool and creating more advocates who can strengthen the university's climate for LHE and lead the implementation of LHE initiatives throughout the university.

4.3.2 Summary

Regardless of the scope and scale of LHE efforts, the university's leadership should ensure that an appropriate structure is in place for their support. For LHE efforts focused on unit-level processes and sponsored by unit-level leaders, no formal structure is needed. A decision by university leaders to implement LHE at the cross-functional level may require some degree of new structure to coordinate (and negotiate) LHE initiatives that impact processes that span two or more functional areas of the university. For a university-wide commitment to building an LHE philosophy that is expected to introduce a large number of LHE initiatives that impact the most critical processes, university leaders should consider making a reasonable investment in a new or existing office that can lead and advocate for LHE at the institution. While one model of an Office of

LHE is presented above, it is by no means the only alternative. There are no "best-practice" guidelines for designing offices of LHE, and recommendations from for-profit organizations may not be compatible with the unique characteristics of institutions of higher education (e.g., faculty governance).[14]

4.4 Selecting an LHE Initiative

A university is an amalgamation of an almost unlimited number of processes that, in theory, are designed to fulfill its mission and goals in an efficient and effective manner. Many processes fall short of these expectations; in fact, students and their families, faculty and staff, business leaders and legislators, and alumni and friends can probably suggest one or more processes that could be improved. University leaders and LHE project sponsors (e.g., individual campus leaders, an Office of LHE Steering Committee) can identify potential LHE initiatives from:

■ Walks around campus (e.g., observing students waiting in line, watching office support staff "walking" a form across campus for appropriate signatures).

■ Surveys of students, faculty, and staff (e.g., simplifying the travel reimbursement process, waiting for appointments with a financial aid counselor).

■ Personal involvement in a university process (e.g., waiting for laboratory space renovations to occur, navigating the process for obtaining approval that an existing course can be designated as satisfying an "international perspectives" requirement).

■ Reviews of complaints (e.g., a student's difficulty in scheduling a mandatory advising appointment prior to open registration, losing a top faculty candidate due to a slow and cumbersome hiring process).

■ Requests for advice from those outside the university (e.g., difficulties adult learners face when transferring course credit from community colleges, employers' concerns that recent graduates are ill-prepared for graduate school or the global workplace).

For any institution looking for opportunities to remove waste and improve the flow of processes that are important to the beneficiaries they serve, there will be no shortage of potential LHE initiatives. With all these possibilities, how might university leaders and LHE project sponsors select a process as the target of an LHE initiative?

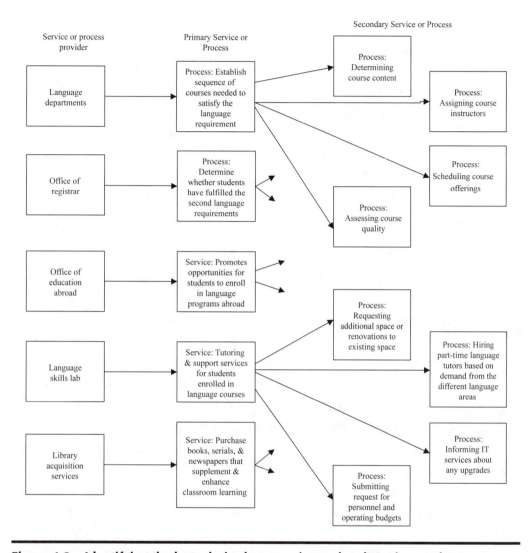

Figure 4.2 Identifying the boundaries between interrelated services and processes: university language requirement.

4.4.1 Factors to Consider When Selecting an LHE Initiative

Determine the clear boundaries for the process being considered for an LHE initiative. University processes are often highly interrelated and interdependent, with no clear or natural boundaries. To keep the scope of the LHE initiative manageable, it is important to establish boundaries that define the process and therefore the offices and individuals involved in the process. As an example, the provost might be interested in improving the processes that support the university's expectation that all students fulfill a language requirement. Figure 4.2 shows several departments and offices that provide a process that supports the second language requirement, including the language departments, registrar, education abroad, language skills lab, and library. Each of these areas has a number of primary and secondary processes that are relevant to the university's language requirement. For example, the language departments have their own processes wherein faculty members are involved in establishing the sequence of courses needed to satisfy a language requirement. In addition, each language department also has distinct processes for determining what content material will be included in each language course, assigning course instructors, scheduling course offerings, and assessing course quality. The provost, with the help of LHE sponsors, needs to establish clear boundaries that define the process(es) to be included in the LHE initiative. At the highest level, this initiative could include a comprehensive examination of the many processes provided by the set of five departments and offices. This would be an ambitious initiative that encompasses the majority of processes that together contribute to students' experiences with a second language requirement. In contrast, the provost could choose to focus on the processes in one area that have been identified by students as most frustrating (e.g., the current scheduling of language courses does not allow students to make adequate progress on their second language requirement, which results in students taking coursework over the summer or delaying student graduation). Determining the boundaries for the LHE initiative will keep the scope of the project clear and defined, and allow the LHE sponsor to consider the level of leader support needed to introduce and implement the project.

Select a process that is in crisis. Crisis conditions, real or otherwise, create a context for change and receptiveness to new ways of doing business, for example:

■ A dramatic decrease in student satisfaction with academic advising.
■ A significant increase in students who need to be placed on internships without a concomitant increase in operating budget to support the placement process.
■ An online university entering the university's market and offering greater flexibility in the dates that courses begin and end.
■ A marked increase in the number of transfer students from community colleges.

Crises present opportunities for implementing LHE to understand and solve process problems. For example, suppose the state's higher education agency implements a new policy that requires all state universities to provide freshman applicants with earlier feedback about their admission and financial aid status. The office of admission must now reduce by half the time for processing applications without receiving additional resources from the state or university. The criticality of the admission process to the success of the university will make the response to this mandate one of the highest priorities of the university. In other circumstances, the university's leadership might create a "manufactured" crisis to introduce a new initiative (with or without an influx of new resources) that will substantially change the way the university operates. For example, a commitment by the president to expand and improve student services to increase student enrollment and retention, during a period of budget cutbacks and declining enrollments, necessitates a new approach to improvement that goes beyond the well-worn admonitions to "work smarter, not harder" and "do more with less" without a clear way to do this. The implementation of one or more LHE initiative offers a planned response to a significant challenge identified by the university's leadership.

Select a process where necessary leadership support for LHE will be available. Many processes extend across the functional responsibility areas of a single leader. The LHE Project Team must have the necessary authority to ensure cooperation of those who are involved in and oversee the process. In addition, implementing radical changes to the process will require significant leadership support. Choosing a "unit-level" process may guarantee the local leadership support needed to implement LHE. Although deans, directors, department chairs, and other supervisors and managers may not have the organizational authority to commit the entire university to an LHE initiative, their span of control and sphere of influence are enough to provide the needed leadership commitment and support within their area. For example, the director of the university bookstore would possess both the authority and leadership to endorse LHE principles and practices within bookstore operations. One potential drawback, however, is that the impact of the benefits of a unit-level LHE initiative may be local and limited as well, in contrast to the potential effects of cross-functional or institution-wide LHE initiatives. A corollary recommendation is to select an LHE initiative that focuses on a process "internal" to the university, that is, a process by employees or volunteers under the complete control of the university. Choosing a process that depends on the services or products of individuals or organizations outside the university may be missing the control needed to introduce an LHE initiative and implement any subsequent LHE solutions.

Select an important and visible service or process where the LHE initiative can demonstrate clear benefits. Achieving significant improvements in a university process following an LHE initiative will help LHE gain wider support and commitment from the university community.[15] An LHE initiative to improve the bursar billing process can be expected to have a larger payoff for the university (higher parent and student satisfaction, reduced billing errors, faster billing and collections, reduced staffing needs) than would one that focuses on providing inter-university library card borrowing privileges. Selecting a process that is particularly important to leaders at the university will draw their attention and show the effectiveness of LHE in an area of personal interest. For example, if the university's president is known to have a strong interest in internationalizing the campus through greater diversification of the faculty, an LHE initiative could examine the faculty hiring process with special attention to the additional steps necessary when hiring non-U.S. citizens. Alternatively, the process chosen could be one that is a chronic frustration to key university constituencies (e.g., temporary parking privileges for a campus visitor, opening a university computer account, the lack of centralized ticket purchasing for university events, long bookstore lines during the first week of classes) who would recognize and appreciate improvements that followed from the LHE initiative. Given the reported gains obtained from the application of Lean principles and practices outside of higher education[16] as well as those reported from LHE applications (see Chapter 3), significant improvements can be achieved. LHE initiatives that yield large financial savings can provide a powerful success story for LHE sponsors and university leaders. The effect of LHE initiatives on outcomes (i.e., faster, higher quality, and less costly processes) that are important to the university community will raise the visibility and credibility of LHE on- and off-campus.

4.4.2 Summary

Any university process can be a candidate for improvement using LHE. The selection of the first LHE initiative,[17] and the prioritization of subsequent LHE initiatives, should consider the significance of the service or process to the university, recognizing that various factors (e.g., available leader support) will remove some potential LHE initiatives from consideration for the immediate future. Nevertheless, prioritization of LHE initiatives should focus, when possible, on processes most critical to the institution, as defined in a number of different ways:[18]

- *It is the (or one of the) most important process(es) to the institution.* For an automotive company, it might be designing or building vehicles. For a hospital, it might be in-patient services or scheduling of operating rooms. Within higher education, critical processes include course or program development, faculty hiring, student admissions, and course scheduling.
- *Data suggests significant problems that need to be addressed quickly.* For a law firm, it might be a delay in getting invoices out to clients. For a home construction company, it might be an increase in the number of repairs appearing on the "punch list" during final walk-through inspections. Within higher education, these may include a spike in the number of freshman complaints about the availability of advising appointments or faculty resignations due to the inability to provide timely counteroffers.
- *The process is a strategically important new direction or focus for the university.* A retail pharmacy chain may choose to focus on supply chain issues associated with its strategic decision to develop regional distribution centers. A local computer company may work on scheduling home visits as it strategically expands in-home upgrade and repair services. Within higher education, these may include attention to the international student recruiting process as competition increases for highly qualified doctoral students in the physical sciences, or improving the process to identify and summarize faculty outreach projects in response to the state governor's explicit emphasis on institutional community engagement.
- *The process is extremely salient and important to a key internal or external constituency.* For a company supplying plastic molded parts, it might be a key customer's request to reduce plant-based buffers of not-yet-needed parts. For a school system, it might be a school board member's concerns about the length of time some students spend on the bus due to bus route configurations. Within higher education, it might include prospective students' complaints about outdated university Web pages or a legislator's concern about her daughter's difficulties in transferring credits among the three state-supported institutions she attended.

Overall, a considerable investment of leadership support, employee time, and institutional energy will be required for each LHE initiative. Thus, the prioritization of processes as candidates for LHE initiatives should be determined strategically and rationally (e.g., significant savings from an initial initiative will free up resources to invest in later initiatives). The selection of a "quick-and-dirty" project for demonstration purposes might be a reasonable decision to introduce and establish buy-in for a broader rollout of LHE, but the institutional payoff and commitment to LHE is more likely when the process is fundamentally important to the success of the university.

4.5 Organizing LHE Project Teams

At any point in time, faculty and staff are suggesting or introducing changes at work to deal with ineffective policies and practices, accommodate to new systems and technology, resolve complaints, and respond to externally imposed rules and regulations. At universities adopting LHE, these efforts would continue to occur, with many faculty and staff using LHE principles and practices to add value to a process by reducing waste and improving flow in an ongoing cycle of continuous improvement. LHE Project Teams will be chartered where the Office of LHE (or some similar coordinating system) determines that a particular process is a high priority for the university. For example, The Office of LHE may decide to form an LHE Project Team when the process cuts across functional areas of the university, is technically complex, or has a broad impact on the university's core services.[19] It might also charter an LHE Project Team to develop a new process for the university (e.g., design a university-wide alert system for campus emergencies), improve an existing process (e.g., streamline the personnel budget proposal process for academic units), or respond to a significant challenge or problem (e.g., reduce the time required to process financial aid awards due to an unplanned increase in applicants).[20]

4.5.1 Forming an LHE Project Team: Membership and Roles

An LHE Project Team will typically include 7 ± 2 members, each of whom brings some degree of process knowledge and personal motivation to make a significant contribution to the LHE initiative. The Office of LHE can help assign LHE team members to one of three roles: team facilitator/mentor, team leader, or team members.

Team facilitator/mentor. The team facilitator/mentor should be a member (or designee) of the LHE Steering Committee. His or her responsibilities include facilitating the efforts of the LHE Project Team and serving as a mentor to the team leader. Including a member of the LHE Steering Committee on the LHE Project Team signifies the importance of the LHE team to the university's leadership. This "LHE champion" should be very knowledgeable of LHE principles and practices, and have personal hands-on experiences with implementing Lean initiatives in (preferably) higher education or the public/private sector. While the presence of the team facilitator/mentor is not required at all team meetings, he or she would be readily available to the team leader to offer advice, advocate for the needs of the team, and provide constructive criticism and feedback to ensure the team's faithful adherence to LHE principles and practices.

Team leader. The team leader is a member of the university community who has a personal stake in the process identified in the team's charter. Team leaders should have the respect of team members, be knowledgeable and comfortable with guiding the team in the application of LHE principles and practices to improve the selected process or service, and have facilitation skills to maximize the contributions of team members. The team leader has a number of responsibilities during and between LHE team meetings:[21]

- Provide support for LHE team members throughout the LHE initiative.
- Coordinate team meetings and prepare meeting agenda.
- Use LHE practices and tools (e.g., developing a visual map or flowchart of the process under investigation; engaging team members to provide ongoing recommendations for continuous improvement after implementing initial changes to the process or service) to maximize the contributions and participation of LHE Project Team members.
- Provide updates and forward concerns to the Office of LHE and the team facilitator/mentor.
- Understand team dynamics, monitor the team for signs of resistance and apathy that could impede progress on the LHE initiative, and address team process and performance issues in a constructive fashion.
- Invite individuals with specialized expertise to attend team meetings on an as-needed basis to share their knowledge with members of the LHE Project Team.

Following the implementation of LHE solutions, a team leader with ongoing involvement in the improved process can then provide continued oversight, helping to ensure that all LHE solutions introduced remain in place after the LHE team has disbanded and that a climate for employee-driven continuous process improvement develops.

Team members. The success of LHE Project Teams depends heavily on members whose personal knowledge and hands-on experience provide the critical insight needed for improving the process through the application of LHE. Team members who are involved in the process targeted for improvement will have significant insights, when guided by LHE principles and practices, on identifying waste, improving flow, and adding value to the process expected by its beneficiaries (e.g., students and their families, faculty, employers, legislators, alumni). Team membership should represent the functional areas involved in the LHE initiative. Because the team is limited in size, team membership may not include all areas or offices that contribute to the process; therefore, it is important that team members actively communicate with colleagues from unrepresented areas to ensure that the team benefits from their insights into the process and recommendations for improvement. In some instances, the team might include an "outsider" unfamiliar with the particular process targeted for improvement. This member has no preconceived expectations of how things are done and can ask naïve but insightful questions (e.g., Why is that signature required? Why are extra copies of the report produced if they are never distributed?). In addition, external suppliers or customers who have some role in the university process may bring excellent insights as team members and, in turn, bring LHE principles and practices back to their own organizations.[22] For example, high school counselors who help students navigate the admissions process, donors who experience the stewardship process by the university's office of development, and employers with expectations of the competencies of recent graduates of a professional program can all offer unique insights from their vantage points in the process.

How might the Office of LHE select team members, given that the number of possible team members will exceed the number of openings? One suggested strategy is to use a two-stage screening process.[23] The Office of LHE would first identify potential members based on their knowledge and experience with the LHE process, their technical expertise, and their general knowledge of the university and the area they represent. After this initial review based on ability and experience, the Office of LHE would then factor in personal characteristics and personality styles thought to bolster or amplify the ability/experience contributions of potential team members to a collaborative team effort and solution. Those individuals with a strong interest in participating in the LHE initiative, a reputation as a respected peer or leader, and a willingness to support implementation recommendations would be included on a prioritized list of finalists for the LHE Project Team.[24] All things being equal, the deciding factors to consider for the final selection of team members may be their knowledge and experience with LHE (e.g., knowledge of just-in-time delivery, experience in preparing visual maps of processes) or political influence (i.e., including a university opinion leader or prominent faculty member or administrator can help generate support for the LHE project).[25]

Summary. Overall, a large proportion of the LHE Project Team members should be involved in the process identified for the LHE initiative. Their personal knowledge and experience with the process, combined with training on the application of LHE principles and practices, will help identify and implement improvements to the targeted process. The broad involvement of university employees on LHE Project Teams is central to the employee-centered philosophy of LHE. Greater employee involvement in improving processes that are part of their job can increase job satisfaction, reduce stress, and raise job performance. The voluntary participation and enthusiasm by the LHE Project Team members create a sense of ownership for recommendations to improve the process, which supports the implementation of LHE solutions and a commitment to continuous improvement of the process over time.

4.5.2 LHE Project Team Formation and Training

LHE team formation. The Office of LHE takes responsibility for drafting an LHE Project Team "charter," which is shared with the LHE Project Team at an initial kickoff meeting led by the LHE project team facilitator/mentor and team leader. The charter includes:

- The scope of the LHE initiative (e.g., the process by which employees request and receive travel reimbursement).
- Why this process was chosen (e.g., employees are upset that they incur interest charges on their personal credit card while waiting for business expense reimbursements that are regularly questioned and slow to be reimbursed).

- What results are expected (e.g., reduce the number of travel reimbursement requests that have to be returned for additional information by 80%, reduce errors by 90%, and reduce time from submission to reimbursement by 50%).
- A timetable for completing their task (e.g., recommendations due within a week).

As liaison to the Office of LHE and a representative of the institution's commitment to LHE, the team facilitator/mentor can use this meeting to identify the resources available to LHE Project Team members for their work on this LHE initiative. In addition, the meeting provides a forum for the newly formed LHE Project Team to raise questions or concerns they have to enhance their performance as a team.

The LHE Project Team should clarify ground rules that will support team effectiveness.[26] For example, the team should understand the role and responsibilities of the team leader. Team members may be assigned responsibilities to help support team functioning (e.g., timekeeper role to keep team process on track; recorder role to capture the team's mapping of the process or document their recommendations to improve the process). In addition, the team should establish its own norms and expectations for members (e.g., the level of participation expected, the importance of listening to and respecting the opinions and recommendations of all team members, how the team will deal with conflict and disagreement, how best to keep team members on task).

LHE team training. LHE emphasizes "learning by doing." Thus, hands-on, just-in-time training on LHE principles and practices should occur in the workplace close to the process being reviewed.[27] One rule of thumb is that at the early stages of an LHE initiative, 80% of the time should be spent doing LHE and 20% on training. In addition, for training to be most effective, the opportunity to implement what has been learned should immediately follow training (or very focused training topics should follow immediately after hands-on experiences with the steps of LHE).[28]

Abbreviated training modules should be available to LHE Project Team members tailored to their familiarity with LHE. These may include:[29]

- Overview of LHE principles and tools.
- Understanding value and waste.
- Creating visual process maps.

■ Metrics for measuring the effectiveness of university processes and services.

■ Communicating and implementing LHE recommendations.

   Overall, training should be practical and delivered during the LHE initiative when it can be applied immediately. Individuals with considerable LHE experience will need little training, whereas those new to LHE may benefit from short and tailored training experiences that coincide with their needs to know the information (e.g., learning about value and waste immediately prior to investigating the university process targeted for improvement). Those interested in learning more about LHE or broadening their understanding of LHE can avail themselves of additional training resources and reference materials as desired.

Endnotes

1. Adapted from Keyte, B., and Locher, D. 2004. *The complete lean enterprise: Value stream mapping for administrative and office processes.* New York: Productivity Press. Chapter 2.
2. Liker, J.K. 2004. *The Toyota Way: 14 management principles from the world's greatest manufacturer.* New York: McGraw-Hill. Chapter 22.
3. Lean did not begin as an organization-wide change initiative. Toyota evolved the "Toyota Production System" over many decades, starting with local initiatives on the level of the shop floor or assembly line, and developing and revising the principles and tools that would later become known as Lean. Over time, as Lean practices matured, Toyota leadership recognized the potential of an expanded application of these principles and tools throughout the company and beyond (i.e., to include suppliers, parts distributors, etc.). They recognized that a company-wide system, supported by an organizational culture and commitment by senior leaders, would offer more value to their customers and create a self-sustaining learning organization committed to continuous improvement. Organizations that subsequently embraced Lean chose to implement the "evolved and matured" company-wide Lean system that required commitment by senior leadership and efforts to reshape organizational culture. In addition, most Lean proponents underscore the critical importance of leadership commitment and a supportive organizational culture as essential to the effective implementation of Lean.

4. Jeffrey Pfeffer and Robert Sutton's book, *Hard facts, dangerous half-truths and total nonsense: Profiting from evidence-based management*, Boston: Harvard Business School Press, 2006, offers an extraordinarily practical list of eight questions that should be asked—and answered honestly—before introducing a major organizational change.

5. The more typical term used in the professional literature is "organizational climate." While a university is clearly an organization, the term "workplace climate" was thought to be more understandable when describing university settings.

6. Lean authors and advocates recognized early the role that context, referred to as *organizational culture*, is believed to play in the successful transformation to a Lean organization. See, for example, Liker, J.K. 2004. *The Toyota Way: 14 Management principles from the world's greatest manufacturer.* New York: McGraw-Hill. Chapter 2; Womack, J.P., Jones, D.T., and Roos, D. 1991. *The machine that changed the world: The story of lean production.* New York: Harper Perennials. Chapter 4; Shinkle, G., Gooding, R., and Smith, M. 2004. *Transforming strategy into success: How to implement a Lean management system.* New York: Productivity Press. Chapter 5; Holbeche, L. 1998. *Motivating people in Lean organizations.* Oxford: Butterworth-Heinemann. Chapter 3. This chapter reaffirms the importance of context, but instead focuses on a context that is more readily discernable and changeable: *organizational climate.* My choice of climate rather than culture is pragmatic, not semantic. Culture reflects the shared basic assumptions that *underlie* the visible aspects of an organization. These implicit assumptions can include the traits, activities, or behaviors that the organization values, unstated beliefs of how the organization works, legends or stories about the organization and its leaders, traditions that perpetuate cultural values, and norms for workplace attire, work hours, and interpersonal interactions. Culture provides a broadly defined and difficult-to-measure concept that, while theoretically important, is limited in its practical usefulness for many organizations (and areas or units within the organization). The time and expertise needed to uncover a university's true culture would be significant, and the clinically oriented approach (used because structured surveys would be limiting in the assessment and interpretation of culture) can lead to disagreements in interpretations. In contrast, climate is seen as the collection and pattern of *observable and measurable* factors in the employees' environment that influence their motivation at work. Climate has been defined more narrowly and clearly than culture, and good standardized measures of climate exist. Many believe that there is considerable overlap and mutual reciprocal influence between organizational culture and organizational climate.

7 Stringer, R. 2002. *Leadership and organizational climate.* Upper Saddle River, NJ: Prentice Hall. pp. 10–11.

8. See Schneider, B. 1975. Organizational climates: An essay. *Personnel Psychology* 28(4): 447–479.

9. Liker (2004) wrote in his book, *The Toyota Way,* (2004, New York: McGraw-Hill) that there are three underlying beliefs or values that make it possible to become a learning organization that follows Lean principles: top executives are committed to a long-term vision of adding value to consumers, top executives are committed to developing Lean thinking and skills in all employees and partners, and the commitment to Lean will not waver with a change in leadership. Spear and Bowen's 1999 *Harvard Business Review* article on "Decoding the DNA of the Toyota Production System" (http://twi-institute.com/pdfs/article_DecodingToyotaProductionSystem.pdf) reports on four cultural beliefs or rules that, "guide the design, operation, and improvement of every activity, connection, and pathway for every product and service" (p. 98):

   A clear understanding of the one way work is to be done
   Direct pathways to send or receive communication from customers
   Simple and direct pathways for building products or delivering services
   Changes to work should be accomplished at the lowest possible level
       under the guidance of a mentor in accordance with the scientific method

10. Stringer, R. 2002. *Leadership and organizational climate.* Upper Saddle River, NJ: Prentice Hall. Chapter 1.

11. The other two factors—External Environment (i.e., the external political, economic, technological, social, and competitive factors that influence the organization) and Historical Forces (i.e., past practices and patterns of rewards and punishments, how crises were handled, memories of past leaders, and resource allocation)—are not under the control of the organization and are therefore less useful in efforts to influence changes in climate.

12. Womack, J.P., and Jones, D.T. 2005. *Lean solutions: How companies and customers can create value and wealth together.* New York: Free Press. Chapter 8.

13. Lareau, W. 2003. *Office kaizen: Transforming office operations into a strategic competitive advantage.* Milwaukee, WI: ASQ Quality Press. pp. 67–68.

14. Hospitals may also be unique in this regard, given the role that the hospital's medical staff (i.e., doctors) assumes in the decision-making process.

15. Of course, a spectacular failure can mean the end of LHE for the university. But Liker (Liker, J.K. 2004. *The Toyota Way: 14 management principles from the world's greatest manufacturer.* New York: McGraw-Hill. p. 305) confidently states that a carefully conducted Lean project by an individual with Lean expertise has about a 100% chance of making huge and visible improvements.

16. Typical improvements achieved through the application of Lean, based on results from more than 50 companies, are 70 to 90% reduction in machine setup time, 20 to 60% productivity improvement, 40 to 80% reduction in process time, and 30 to 70% reduction in inventory, as reported in Laraia, A., Moody, P., and Hall, R. 1999. *The kaizen blitz: Accelerating breakthroughs in productivity and performance.* New York: John Wiley & Sons. pp. 3–4; Allway, M., and Corbett, S. 2002. Shifting to lean service: Stealing a page from manufacturers' playbooks. *Journal of Organizational Excellence* 21: 46.

17. Laraia, A., Moody, P., and Hall, R. 1999. *The kaizen blitz: Accelerating break-throughs in productivity and performance*. New York: John Wiley & Sons.
18. Liker, J.K. 2004. *The Toyota Way: 14 management principles from the world's greatest manufacturer*. New York: McGraw-Hill. pp. 286–288.
19. See Lareau, W. 2003. *Office kaizen: Transforming office operations into a strategic competitive advantage*. Milwaukee, WI: ASQ Quality Press. pp. 68–69 for a more comprehensive list of criteria that can be used to determine the need to form an LHE Project Team.
20 Ibid, pp. 69–70.
21. These responsibilities are adapted from Tapping, D., and Shuker, T. 2003. *Value stream management for the lean office: Eight steps to planning, mapping, and sustaining lean improvements in administrative areas*. New York: Productivity Press. p. 21.
22. Lareau, W. 2003. *Office kaizen: Transforming office operations into a strategic competitive advantage*. Milwaukee, WI: ASQ Quality Press.
23. Shinkle, G., Gooding, R., and Smith, M. 2004. *Transforming strategy into success: How to implement a lean management system*. New York: Productivity Press. p. 35.
24. Laraia, A., Moody, P., and Hall, R. note in Chapter 4 of their book (*The kaizen blitz: Accelerating breakthroughs in productivity and performance*. New York: John Wiley & Sons. 1999) that volunteers will be critical to the success of Lean teams as they are first introduced. It is typical for team members to work long hours, work outside of traditional job specifications and boundaries, and be asked to endorse radical change.
25. Laraia, A., Moody, P., and Hall, R. 1999. *The kaizen blitz: Accelerating break-throughs in productivity and performance*. New York: John Wiley & Sons. Chapter 4.
26. Tapping, D., and Shuker, T. 2003. *Value stream management for the lean office: Eight steps to planning, mapping, and sustaining lean improvements in administrative areas*. New York: Productivity Press. pp. 20–21.
27. LHE training at the location where the process or service is being reviewed is strongly preferred over more traditional classroom training programs that occur away from where the process takes place.
28. Liker, J.K. 2004. *The Toyota way: 14 management principles from the world's greatest manufacturer*. New York: McGraw-Hill. pp. 202–203.
29. Laraia, A., Moody, P., and Hall, R. 1999. *The kaizen blitz: Accelerating break-throughs in productivity and performance*. New York: John Wiley & Sons. Chapter 4.

Chapter 5

What Do They Really Want?
Identifying What the Beneficiaries of Higher Education Value and Expect

Professor Maharris takes great pride in his teaching in the psychology department, most especially his teaching of undergraduate statistics, a required course in the five-course sequence required of majors. That is why he is taken aback by the admonishment he received from the department chair, who raised concerns about his failure to cover statistical concepts that students are expected to know in later courses in the sequence. The instructors of these next courses are forced to provide remedial work to get Dr. Maharris' students caught up, making it difficult for them to cover all the materials they are expected to cover before sending the student along to the next course in the sequence. Even some of the students who initially gave him very positive course evaluations are complaining on the university's survey of graduating seniors that Dr. Maharris did not teach them what they need to know to be successful.

After several months of hard work by many staff members, the Office of Information and Educational Technology (IET) introduces the updated version of the college's course management system. This upgrade has the IET staff very excited because the course management software is extremely flexible and adds significantly more options than most faculty members could imagine to support their academic courses. As the first calls and e-mails come in, the Director of IET is numb. Faculty members hate the upgraded system and they are making that fact known to their students, department

*chair, and dean. The expanded options are confusing and unneces-
sary, and faculty members must now fill in several additional fields
(one trade-off for the enhanced flexibility of the new course management software) when submitting course information.*

*The university president receives a call from the state representa-
tive who represents the district in which the university is located.
The representative informs the president that he is introducing
legislation that will make it illegal for the university to require that all
freshman students live on campus during their first year at school.
His constituencies are complaining that on-campus student housing
is substandard, expensive, and unfair to local landlords. As she listens
to the representative, the president is calculating in her head the
potential financial impact that the proposed legislation would have
on the university's budget.*

*The Director of the University Budget Office watched as enroll-
ments in summer credit courses flattened out and began a small but
consistent downward trend over the past 7 years. The traditional 6-
and 8-week summer sessions generate a significant portion of university revenues that help subsidize and support academic year programs
and services. A quick e-mail poll of the other state institutions reveals
similar declines in enrollment except for the 2-year community colleges throughout the state. Cutting the summer budget in response to
enrollment declines would free up some resources for the university,
but reducing the investment in summer courses may, in the long run,
further depress enrollments as fewer course sections are offered.*

What went wrong in each of these scenarios, and why was the university
employee surprised or perplexed? In all cases, a university office or member
designed a process or service around what they value regardless of whether
the beneficiary of that process or service has the same expectation of value.
Professor Maharris valued a fun and engaging classroom; his students and
colleagues valued adequate coverage of the defined course content. The
IET office valued a highly flexible and sophisticated course management
system; the users wanted a simple- and easy-to-use system. The university
president wanted a university-controlled housing environment that generated a predictable revenue stream; students and families wanted greater
choice and lower cost. The University Budget Office expects a certain net
revenue return from summer sessions; students are choosing lower cost and

more flexible summer options that allow them to save money by living at home and holding a summer job to help pay for their educational expenses. Overall, these examples depict a disconnect between the value that beneficiaries expect and what the university provides.

Simply stated, value is anything for which the beneficiary is willing to pay. In the context of LHE, any contribution to the process that makes it closer to what the beneficiary expects or desires adds value. Value is added when a process delivers the amount or level expected by the beneficiary, the quality the beneficiary expects, in as timely a manner as the beneficiary expects, where the beneficiary expects to receive it, and at a cost the beneficiary is willing to pay. Conversely, waste is anything that does not add value as defined by the beneficiary. Waste can include aspects of a process:

■ For which the beneficiary is unwilling to pay (e.g., high cost, substandard, on-campus housing).
■ That result from an inconsistent process (e.g., professors covering different material in a required course).
■ That overburden those involved in the process (e.g., the additional fields in the new course management system were unnecessary and unwanted by the end users).

The reduction or elimination of waste results in a process that is more "Lean" (as defined by the increased proportion of value-added steps or activities in the process), thereby bringing the process closer to meeting or exceeding the expectations of the beneficiary.

Determining expectations about value is the first principle of LHE: *Define the value of the process from the perspective of the beneficiaries of the process.* This chapter presents key concepts for identifying and delivering the value expected by those who benefit from university processes. In addition, the chapter includes techniques for hearing the "voice of the beneficiaries" in a university setting.

5.1 The Beneficiary Defines Value; The University Delivers Value

The critical starting point for LHE is defining value from the perspective of the beneficiaries; the university's goal should be to deliver that value.[1]

Beneficiaries may include current and prospective students and their families, faculty members, alumni, employers who hire graduates of the university, state regents and legislators, accrediting agencies, and others. Different beneficiaries may define value differently. At a macro level, one or more beneficiaries might define value as well-educated graduates prepared to enter and contribute to the workforce, students graduating within 4 years of full-time matriculation, applied research that improves quality of life and spurs economic development, basic scholarship that expands knowledge and understanding, and civic-minded and globally prepared citizens. Beneficiaries may also define value at a more micro level: engaging courses where much was learned, a simplified process for reviewing a questionable bursar charge, the timely routing of a grant application for approval of university matching funds, help with preparing a resume, receiving an e-mail about personally relevant scholarship or financial aid opportunities, a 24/7 clickable site for getting your office computer up and running after a virus attack. Overall, the beneficiaries of the process define the value they expect the university to provide.

This beneficiary-driven approach to defining value may be quite different from what exists at most universities. Historically, the faculty, college councils, chairs and deans, and other academic leaders or oversight bodies define value in all things academic because they are believed to know and act on behalf of what is best for higher education and indirectly through the way universities are designed.[2] For example, faculty argue that they, as disciplinary experts and "owners" of the university's academic courses and programs, are in the best position to determine degree requirements. Many faculty members and academic administrators bristle at the "university-as-a-business" model in higher education, rejecting the notion that they are service providers and students, as customers, should play any role in determining what the university experience should be. It is easy to understand why some feel it may be inappropriate for current students to decide what coursework or experiences they should successfully complete to graduate. But alumni and employers, key beneficiaries of higher education, may have important insights into the value of certain courses and experiences that would better prepare graduates for successful careers, fuller lives, and more.

The provider-driven approach to defining value is not much different in academic support areas (e.g., enrollment, financial aid, academic advising, counseling services) and nonacademic areas (e.g., purchasing, buildings and grounds, campus safety and parking, housing and dining services) of the university. The hierarchical administrative structure of higher education makes it difficult for students to provide input on their expectations of value for their university experience. Support staff, directors, associate deans, and associate vice presidents buffer opportunities for chairs, deans, and vice presidents to hear directly from students, and the directors and senior administrators of nonacademic and academic support services also have very little direct contact with students. Taken together, these forces have worked to create university organizations that are better designed to meet the expectations of value determined by the faculty and administration rather than the expectations of value for processes that are held by the multiple beneficiaries of higher education.

This provider-driven approach may be shifting, however. State legislators are tightening their control and oversight over higher education funding, selectively rewarding the programs and services that they value (e.g., 4-year graduation rates, degrees in high-need areas such as biotechnology and nanotechnology, research that is readily commercialized or stimulates economic investment in the state). Business leaders are withholding their support (e.g., gifts and contributions, lobbying state legislators on behalf of higher education) until they see improvements that they value: a business curriculum that is up-to-date and prepares a graduate to compete effectively in a global workplace, or an executive MBA program that is flexibly scheduled and tailored to the current challenges faced by today's organizations.[3] Prospective students and parents are more discerning about what value they expect: ease of transferability of courses from other schools, access to faculty and advisors, class sizes and availability, a semi-private residential experience, and a safe living and learning environment. Accrediting agencies, alumni, professional organizations, and other beneficiaries of higher education may have their own unique expectations of value. Importantly, faculty members, as "internal" beneficiaries of many university processes, will have expectations of value from the university that are critical to their professional success (e.g., accessing research materials through interlibrary loan or electronic access, approval of grant applications, scheduling classroom technology to support guest lecturers through streaming video).

Returning to the fictitious examples at the beginning of the chapter, it should be apparent that the beneficiaries of the processes were not asked to share their expectations of value. As excited as the IET staff were by the technological advances of the upgraded course management system, faculty valued ease of operation over flexibility. Their confusion and frustration with the new system spilled over into their classrooms and the lives of the students. The two ultimate customers of the system, faculty and students, did not get a new system that added value from their perspectives; instead, it added waste (i.e., overburdening them with having to enter unnecessary data fields). In the third example, the representative would not go to the trouble of proposing new legislation if on-campus housing provided the value expected by students and parents; what they expect from on-campus housing must be woefully absent for them to contact their representative. In the final example, it would appear that summer programs have not responded to shifting expectations of what students value. Cost and convenience have become more highly valued by students as the overall cost of higher education has climbed. Now, traditional summer sessions (6- and 8-week courses, four face-to-face lectures per week, scheduled in the middle of the day) offer limited to no value to the current generation of students who must work during the summer, or live at home during the summer to cut expenses, in order to afford college for the next academic year. The traditional summer schedule may have been convenient for the program administrators, and for faculty members who have well-prepared teaching materials for 6- and 8-week summer courses, but they did not provide the value expected by the students. In this case, the students chose to enroll in less costly and more flexible summer courses while living at home.

In the provocative book *On Q: Causing Quality in Higher Education,* Seymour passionately argues that universities must develop clear under-standings of what each "consumer constituency" (i.e., beneficiaries) values. Universities can accomplish this by broadening the historically limited set of consumer-constituencies, each of which represents individuals (or organized groups of individuals) affected by a university's processes. Each beneficiary must be seen as an important partner in defining value, and college and university leaders must understand, appreciate, and respond to their multi-consumer environments:

> *Although we don't have such rigid hierarchical structures in higher education as in many businesses we are not any better listeners. Professors are paid to lecture. Administrators are paid to develop and implement policies—top down. Directors of housing and computer services seem to issue memos at the same rate of corporate America. We all have something to say, and we keep searching for someone who will listen to it. It's part of our culture, too. When you think of it, students are the only ones on a college campus who are really encouraged to listen…. We have wonderful listening net-works—college classrooms, advisory boards, alumni groups, and so on. But we talk to them. We don't really listen.[4]*

5.2 Listening to the Beneficiaries of Higher Education: What Do They Value and Expect?

Chapter 4 discussed establishing an LHE Project Team to implement improvements in an important university process through the application of LHE principles and practices. One of the first steps by the team members as they begin their task is to identify all the key beneficiaries of the university process and thoroughly understand what value they expect from the process. This chapter section discusses how to identify the beneficiaries of the process that is the focus of the LHE initiative, and identify the expectations of value these beneficiaries hold.

5.2.1 Identify Who Benefits from the Process

Many individuals, groups of individuals, and organizations may benefit from one or more of the many processes that make up a university. Previous chapters have noted several beneficiaries: prospective students, current students, parents, faculty, staff, alumni, state legislators, accrediting agencies, and regional employers. A comprehensive list of beneficiaries is likely to be quite extensive, including:

- K–12 schools.
- Community members.
- Other colleges and universities.
- Local businesses.
- Vendors.
- Internal university offices.
- Granting agencies.
- Alumni chapters.
- Professional societies.

Different beneficiaries will be involved with different sets of university processes (e.g., the involvement of vendors may be limited to the bidding process and the accounts receivable process). Furthermore, different beneficiaries may bring different perspectives on what they value and expect from the same process (e.g., an employee enrolled in an online course may value 24/7 technical support, whereas the employer paying for the course may value transferability of knowledge and skills to the workplace). Importantly, the beneficiaries may be university colleagues and offices that are either "upstream" or "downstream" in the process (e.g., the process for sending funds to overseas study abroad programs would have the sponsoring language department "upstream" of the study abroad budget administrator and the treasurer's office responsible for currency exchange wire transfers "downstream" in the process). Given the potential for differences in expectations of value, it is essential that all relevant beneficiaries have an opportunity to share with the LHE Project Team what they value and expect from the process.

As an example, consider the relevant beneficiaries of a university's freshman orientation process, a multi-day series of programs and activities scheduled between freshman move-in and the first day of classes. Who are some of the beneficiaries of the freshman orientation who define the expectations of value for this process?

- New freshman students (interest in feeling prepared to begin their college experience).
- Faculty teaching freshman courses (interest in student readiness and motivation to learn).
- State legislators (interest in first-year retention and persistence to degree)
- Freshman parents (interest in a successful student transition).
- College advisors (interest in student academic progress).
- Regional accrediting agencies (interest in college experience and success).

While this is not an exhaustive list, it identifies a number of key beneficiaries who could play a role in defining the expectations of value for the freshman orientation process. These beneficiaries of the freshman orientation process should determine the value of this process—*not* the university employees responsible for overseeing the freshman orientation process.

5.2.2 Learn What Beneficiaries of Higher Education Value and Expect

Many tools and techniques are available to gather information from key groups or individuals who, as beneficiaries of the process, define the expectations of value essential for beginning the LHE initiative.[5] The choice of one or more options discussed below may depend on access to the beneficiaries and LHE team resources available (e.g., amount of time, research and statistical expertise, etc.).

Direct observation. Direct observation of the entire process is a critical part of every LHE effort. This is accomplished by shadowing beneficiaries and providers and noting every step and activity of the process that they experience. Physically observing a faculty member as she completes the university's internal grant approval process (e.g., finding and completing necessary paperwork, monitoring e-mail and phone correspondence, walking the grant application across campus for required signatures) provides insight into process steps that add value from the beneficiary's perspective (e.g., confirmation of the appropriate calculation of indirect costs). Importantly, it will also allow you to see what parts of the process do not add value from the beneficiary's perspective (requiring completion of internal forms that are incompatible with the materials already completed for the state or federal grant application). Experiencing the process in real-time alongside the beneficiary provides an opportunity to probe perceptions on the process and expectations of value that are (or are not) delivered. Direct observation is an essential part of learning what beneficiaries of higher education value and expect. Other options noted below can supplement—but should not replace—the use of direct observation.

Archival data. Archival information may already exist, providing insight into what the beneficiaries of university processes value and expect.[6] Responses to close-ended and open-ended items from archival survey results may shed some light on whether a process or service is working well from the perspective of the beneficiary. For example, students' poor ratings of faculty advising, coupled with open-ended comments (e.g., "I have the world's greatest advisor who actually e-mails me to make sure everything is going well and inviting me to stop by and catch up."), can highlight an area of concern and provide some sense of what students value and expect. Universities often have extensive amounts of archival data (surveys, accreditation reports, program reviews, performance metrics), but lack the resources to organize this information in a useful format and "push" it to those who can learn from it.[7] More informal archival data, including e-mails, letters, exit interviews, documented phone calls, and shared anecdotes from informal listening opportunities (e.g., an agenda-free breakfast meeting for faculty leaders hosted by the provost; the vice president for student affairs visiting with a table of students eating in a dining hall) may be available for review.[8] While the LHE team cannot probe existing archival responses, and archival data are unlikely to provide a complete understanding of beneficiary expectations of value, the existing data can be a very useful starting point and provide some initial direction for gathering additional information.

Focus groups, interviews, and surveys. Focus groups and interviews (in person or over the phone) provide structured opportunities for the LHE team to ask beneficiaries specific questions (and probe their responses) regarding their perceptions of the university process and whether it provides the value they expect. Paper-and-pencil or online surveys can be tailored to gather information from each beneficiary group; this can provide a very targeted understanding of the value each expects—and what they feel they now receive—from the university process that is the focus of the LHE initiative. As an example, the library staff at William Patterson College surveyed selected patrons to learn about their failed searches to find the information they needed. Their analysis led them to look for the root cause of the search failure (e.g., was it a catalog error, a retrieval error, a circulation error, etc.), and this data led the library staff to observe the search efforts of another group of users. That data identified that library error (e.g., poor signage) rather than user error caused more than half of the search failures, and specific steps were the taken to remedy the problems and improve patrons' access to the college's holdings.[9]

It may also be valuable to conduct focus groups, interviews, and surveys with potential beneficiaries who self-selected themselves out of the process. That is, collecting information from faculty candidates who declined offers to join the university, student applicants (and their parents) who chose not to be part of the university, alumni who have abruptly disengaged from their alma mater, and so on may provide extremely useful insights. Similarly, probing beyond the formal exit interview data to understand why former faculty, staff, and students left the university may provide equally important information about university processes. For example, the LHE team could arrange one focus group for faculty members who have recently organized and led education abroad workshops for undergraduate students, and conduct a second focus group with faculty members who have since stopped participating in education abroad experiences. The focus group facilitator can guide the discussions to obtain detailed information about the faculty members' experiences with existing processes that support education abroad trips, providing useful insights into what expectations of value they had from the process and whether those expectations were met. As a second example, the LHE team could ask new freshmen and their parents to complete a brief online survey comparing what they expected during the freshman move-in process to what actually occurred; the LHE team could also design a complementary survey for all university staff and faculty who worked or volunteered during freshman move-in on behalf of the university. Excellent practical advice for designing and conducting focus groups, interviews, and surveys is available.[10] In addition, most universities have faculty and staff who can serve as expert advisors on the development, administration, and interpretation of focus groups, interviews, and surveys.

Kano analysis. Kano analysis[11] is a structured technique that helps identify and prioritize what beneficiaries of a process value most (in contrast to designing processes around the priorities or convenience of a university office or employees). Specific questions are developed to confirm the relative importance of values or priorities identified by beneficiaries following an interpretation of information collected during previous focus groups, interviews, and surveys. For each identified value or need, beneficiaries are asked (1) how they would feel if this need or value was addressed and (2) how they would feel if it was not addressed. Based on the response choices provided by beneficiaries (I'd be very pleased; It's what I'd expect; I really don't care; or I'd be very disappointed), beneficiary needs and values can be classified as:

- *Dissatisfiers*: basic requirements that must be included as part of a process or beneficiaries will be dissatisfied.
- *Satisfiers*: aspects of a process that are important to beneficiaries and influence their feelings of satisfaction.
- *Delighters*: when unexpected features of a process add value through innovation and usefulness, and this additional value impresses beneficiaries.

For example, the Office of Student Financial Aid may conduct a kano analysis that assesses how part-time evening students (i.e., the beneficiaries) feel about extended hours for evening and weekend services. The Office of Student Financial Aid could convene a group of evening students and collect their responses to multiple pairs of questions (e.g., "How would you feel if there were extended evening hours one weeknight per week?" and "How would you feel if there were no extended evening hours on any weeknight?"). Their analyses of responses would allow the office to determine that offering no extended office hours on weeknights would be a significant "Dissatisfier" for students, having in-person office hours one or two nights per week would be a "Satisfier" for students, and offering online chat and phone-in options during extended office hours one or two nights a week would be a "Delighter" for students.

Data mining. Universities can exploit their information systems and databases to gain insights into what beneficiaries want (versus what they get). Existing databases may contain useful information for the discerning questioner. For example, a university's Office of Information Technology may use an online process for faculty, staff, and students to request service support for computer hardware and software issues (e.g., a malfunctioning printer, a server crash, disinfecting a computer hard drive, finding lost files). Records of these requests and their resolutions may provide some traditional measures of customer service (e.g., time to problem resolution, satisfaction with solution). In addition, they may provide useful information on the common problems experienced by the beneficiaries of information technology services. This would provide insights into how they might add more value that beneficiaries expect (e.g., laptop and desktop computers that are problem-free, that repair their own problems when they occur, or problems that are quickly, remotely, and completely solved by information technology services staff). In response, the Office of Information Technology could reduce the most common service support requests by prioritizing hardware solutions (e.g., installing dual hard drives with automatic system backup), preventive maintenance (e.g., monthly e-mail to beneficiaries that includes a clickable Web site that automates a hard drive tune-up and virus check), and training (e.g., "ten best tips" solutions for typical software problems encountered most often by university employees or students). Focusing on these beneficiary-driven priorities would allow the Office of Information Technology to offer higher levels of service expected and valued by faculty, staff, and students.

Literature/benchmarking. The professional literature may include research findings that speak to the values and expectations held by beneficiaries. Professional journals, reports from professional associations and survey organizations, and other sources of consumer survey or interview results offer national or regional findings that may generalize to local beneficiaries of higher education. For example, the National Survey of Student Engagement[12] gathers data from participating college and university students on a wide variety of topics, and the North American Association of Summer Schools[13] regularly conducts surveys of their member colleges and universities to share information on meeting the needs of students during the summer terms. Survey findings may provide insights into what experiences students value during their university experience (e.g., academic advising) and what expectations they have about the processes that support these experiences (e.g., the availability and competency of their advisor).

The Higher Education Research Institute[14] and other national organizations regularly assess faculty attitudes, experiences, and professional concerns that may shed some light on their values and expectations concerning institutional processes (e.g., self-reported levels of stress associated with institutional procedures and "red tape"). Similarly, state and national surveys of college parents and employers of college graduates may provide additional perspective on their values and expectations about the processes that comprise institutions of higher education. For example, a consortium of professional organizations and societies gathered employers' perspectives on the quality of preparation and work readiness of recent entrants to the U.S. workforce.[15] Overall, the professional literature may have useful information to supplement other sources of information on the values and expectations of the different beneficiaries served by higher education. However, one needs to be careful that the beneficiaries (e.g., student, faculty, parents) are the actual source of reported values and expectations rather than secondary reports provided by university staff.

Together, these sources can be used to provide converging evidence that offers a clear sense of the values and expectations that different beneficiaries hold for the university process under review by the LHE team.

5.2.3 Determine and Communicate What Beneficiaries of Higher Education Value and Expect

The beneficiaries of a higher education process can provide a large amount of information, collected across a variety of methods, for use in establishing the values and expectations held by this group. Consider the following information gathered as part of an LHE initiative focused on improving the undergraduate advising process:

- *Direct observation.* Shadowing a student as he scheduled and met with his faculty advisor highlighted the following challenges: It took considerable time to establish via e-mail an appointment slot that was convenient for both to meet; there was no comfortable place for the student to wait for his advising appointment; the faculty advisor had an outdated course transcript, requiring that part of the advising appointment be used to update the faculty member on past and current course work; the faculty advisor was not familiar with alternative course offerings outside his own department; and the bulk of the appointment time focused on course selection rather than career guidance.

■ *Results from broadly focused university-administered survey.* Some 73% of rising seniors indicated that they did not know who their advisor was; 85% responded that advising was a bureaucratic hurdle that added no value to the process of developing an academic schedule for the upcoming semester.

■ *Open-ended comment on the student survey.* "There was no way to call the college advisor directly. I had to call a general number and, after dealing with a frustrating voicemail menu, finally got to talk with a live person. But all this person could do was take a message because the advisor I needed was unavailable at the time. The advisor did call me back, but because I was in class, she got my voicemail. So I once again called the general number …."

■ *Student focus group.* "I couldn't believe that I got an e-mail from my advisor reminding me that it was time to meet and discuss how things were going and what classes I might take next semester. I was able to use her online calendar to schedule a meeting on one of the open times that worked for her and me. She also provided Web links in the e-mail to help me review my transcript, determine what courses I needed to graduate, and identify potential courses for the next semester that fit into my school and work calendars. She even provided links to get me thinking about service learning opportunities, research opportunities, and studying abroad. When I got to our meeting, I was totally prepared."

■ *Student interview.* "I waited with other students outside my faculty advisor's office for about 20 minutes during office hours, which is when we were told he was available for advising. Once it was my turn, it took about 60 seconds—he quickly reviewed the courses, said 'Looks good!,' and signed off. Because of the line of students outside, I didn't feel comfortable asking some of the questions I had about internships and graduate school. Maybe next time."

■ *Archival data.* "My husband and I were so impressed by Professor Bretchad, our son's advisor. She went out of her way to stay in contact with him throughout his first 2 years of school. Her concern and gentle guidance during the freshman and sophomore years kept him on track and thinking long term—not just about what he needs to take next semester. Our son has matured and assumed more responsibility for his advising; he was not quite ready for this when he first started school, and neither one of us are college graduates and nor could we offer much help. He enjoys his advising appointments because Dr. Bretchad knows him and really cares. Thanks!"

■ *Exit interview with former students.* "I transferred to another university because I felt lost and unable to get the help I needed about my courses and my career goals. At my new school, the advisors know me by name and really seem to care about my personal and professional goals. While I am taking more responsibility for my decisions, it is nice knowing that there is someone around who is more than happy to help."

■ *National survey results.* Some 17% of undergraduate students enrolled during the summer session are taking courses that they need so they can graduate on time. Only 10% of these students report that their advisor recommended summer session as a strategy for early graduation, or to free up time during the fall and spring semesters to do an internship.

■ *Faculty focus group.* "Advising is one of my least favorite parts of the job. Students rarely come for advising, and they are often unprepared and expect you to do all the work. I'm the one who has to give them the bad news that they still need to take a three-course sequence, which will require that they stay an extra semester beyond their own plans; I become the bad guy because they didn't come see me earlier. And I'm always afraid that I will give a student wrong advice about the general education requirements after getting chewed out by my department chair and the associate dean for not knowing that the requirements had been changed—again. I'm supposed to be an expert in urban planning, not college advising; no one ever got a merit increase for being a good advisor, but they failed to get merit by not publishing enough."

■ A review of college advising office records indicates that advising appointments are heavily skewed toward the end of the semester. Focus group participants suggest this is due to three reasons: (1) course offerings for the next semester are not available earlier in the semester, (2) students want to wait and see how they are doing in their current courses before planning for the next semester, and (3) the advising office prefers to use the first part of the semester to deal with other advising responsibilities (e.g., degree audits for graduating seniors).

■ *Kano analysis.* Rising juniors were asked a number of questions about how they would feel if certain aspects of the advising process were changed. Results indicated that dropping faculty advising and replacing it with professional college advisors would be a dissatisfier, late afternoon appointments would be a satisfier, and an evening online live chat with a faculty member and other students from the major (and allowing parents to participate) would be a delighter.

These data, rich in detail, would provide the LHE team with insights from multiple beneficiaries (i.e., students, parents, and former students) of the advising process as well as the perspective of the professional and faculty advisors who provide this service. Team members would review the collected information, and distill it down to a clear description of what beneficiaries of academic advising value and expect from the university. The team's responsibility for determining and communicating the beneficiaries' values and expectations will help ensure that the needs of the all-important beneficiaries are not diluted or displaced by the values and expectations of university offices or staff with a vested interest in the process (e.g., academic administrators, the college dean, professional advising staff). The general framework below can help the LHE team frame an initial, comprehensive statement of values and expectations that beneficiaries have for any university process.[16]

Providing exactly what is wanted adds value. More often than not, beneficiaries of higher education know what they want. The problem is that they rarely are asked; and if they are asked, their responses are not taken seriously. The data collected as part of the LHE initiative should give clear insights into what the beneficiaries want rather than what faculty and university administrators think beneficiaries want (or worse, unilaterally decide what beneficiaries need). Referring to the advising process above, what do the different beneficiaries of higher education want? What do they value? Students want easy access, expert review of their transcript, answers and advice about future course work, and career guidance. Parents want proactive efforts to reach their students, course scheduling advice to improve the probability of graduating in 4 years, and guidance on the availability of co-curricular activities that will distinguish their son or daughter when applying for jobs or graduate school. Employers and graduate program faculty want academic experiences that develop specific knowledge and skills that enhance the graduate's success in the workplace or graduate school, reducing their training and remediation expenses.

Delivering service where it is wanted adds value. The point or place of delivery of a process in higher education should be where the beneficiaries want it and not for the administrative convenience of the university. Continuing with the advising process, students may value advising services offered in their residence halls, offered through an online, interactive forum with their advisor, or offered in a group setting with other students who share similar interests and goals. Parents may want college advising to take place in the high school, during the student's junior and senior years, to ensure their student is academically prepared (e.g., successfully completed a set of courses that are typical of successful students in a certain major) or has fulfilled academic expectations in high school to avoid the need for remedial courses in college.

Offering service when it is wanted adds value. Beneficiaries of higher education may have preferences for when a university process is available. These preferences may differ dramatically from times currently provided by the university (often Monday through Friday from 8:00 a.m. to 5:00 p.m., excluding the lunch hour, holidays, and perhaps over university break periods; faculty advisors may not be available during the summer, given their 9-month academic year contracts). The beneficiaries of academic advising may value "just-in-time" processes—that is, I want them when I am ready for them, not at an earlier or later time. In the context of advising, students may want to meet with an advisor late in the evening or on weekends, immediately after attending an education abroad recruitment meeting to determine whether they could make such an experience work without delaying graduation, or during the summer when their lives are less hectic and they are sharing plans with their parents. Parents may want advising when they are visiting campus to see their son or daughter, or immediately after their college junior informs them that he or she is changing majors. Employers and graduate program faculty may want advising sessions very early in the student's college career, so that the student has the greatest opportunity to enroll in critical courses, gain internship experience, and become involved in important co-curricular experiences before course scheduling becomes less flexible.

Not wasting the beneficiary's time adds value. The total experience of beneficiaries of higher education includes the amount of time they waste and the hassle they experience, not just the tuition and fees charged by the university. Waiting on the phone, navigating through a nonintuitive call transfer system, waiting in lines, accessing a networked computer, waiting to hear back from a faculty or staff member, repeatedly providing the same information to each successive phone contact, waiting for business hours to begin, and walking across campus are aspects of a beneficiary's total experience that are often invisible to or ignored by the university. Just providing excellent advising service at the actual point of contact with the beneficiaries will not deliver what they value or expect if their comprehensive experience with the advising process is riddled with wasted time and perceptions of feeling hassled.

Solving the beneficiary's problem completely adds value. University beneficiaries value and expect processes that provide complete solutions to their needs or problems. The university process must meet all the above dimensions for it to be a complete solution: Provide exactly what is wanted, deliver value where it is wanted, offer value when it is wanted, and do not waste the beneficiary's time. Falling short on one dimension drags down the beneficiary's evaluation of the entire process, frustrating university employees and offices that have worked hard to do their part of the process as best as they can. The advising process will still get failing grades even with well-trained advisors with flexible schedules if the overall advising process wastes beneficiaries' time and is a hassling experience.

Solving the beneficiary's problem forever adds value. The ultimate measure of success of a university process is anticipating and meeting the needs and expectations of the beneficiaries once and for all. By solving a beneficiary's problem forever, the total number of problems facing the beneficiary is reduced, thus saving time and energy. A university that would commit to scheduling required and gateway courses 5 years into the future (i.e., specific to each semester, days of the week, and times of class meetings) would allow advisors to build multi-year schedules for students that accommodate work schedules, internships and practica, education abroad experiences, and so on. Changing a major or dropping (or failing) a course would require that the next advising appointment with a student focus on building a new course schedule. For students making good progress on their degrees, advising appointments could be shorter (or less frequent) and focus on issues of greater interest or value to the student (e.g., involvement in undergraduate research, identifying clubs and activities that provide relevant experiences to foster personal and professional growth, establishing a competitive profile for admission to graduate and professional schools). Solving the problem of a beneficiary forever is an ambitious goal, and provides both a direction and an endpoint for guiding the LHE team's efforts.

Using the information gathered by the LHE Project Team from the beneficiaries of the undergraduate advising process, this framework helps the team develop a preliminary statement of values and expectations that can guide their work:

■ Beneficiaries of academic advising value and expect personalized and integrated advising services that cover degree progress, course selection, maximizing the college experience, and career or graduate school guidance and preparation.

- Beneficiaries of academic advising value and expect "just-in-time" access to advising services, delivered when needed and with no waiting.
- Beneficiaries of academic advising value and expect "one stop shopping" that integrates advising services with course registration, enrollment in co-curricular options, etc.
- Beneficiaries of academic advising value and expect a multi-year course schedule plan accompanied by a university commitment to honor the plan (i.e., courses required by the major and enough sections of gateway courses to ensure degree progress).
- Beneficiaries of academic advising value and expect advising services in locations that are convenient for them.
- Beneficiaries of academic advising value and expect 100% accuracy in the information and recommendations they receive from advisors.

The LHE initiative would focus on providing the value and meeting the expectations determined by the beneficiaries (i.e., students, faculty members, parents, alumni, business leaders, vendors, legislators) for the university process selected for improvement. Meeting all the values and expectations may be impractical (24/7 advising by the student's faculty advisor) or unreachable in the short term (e.g., providing each student with a multi-year plan of coursework that the university is obliged to deliver). Nevertheless, they define, as a set, the ultimate level of performance to which the university process should aspire through the initial efforts of the LHE initiative and the subsequent, ongoing, continuous improvement efforts by the faculty and staff who are responsible for the process.

5.3 Establish Metrics for Assessing What Beneficiaries Value and Expect

To assess progress on the statement of values and expectations for a university process held by the beneficiaries, the LHE Project Team should establish corresponding performance metrics that accurately and reliably measure what the beneficiaries value and expect. Simply stated, if you cannot measure a process, it will be very hard to improve it.[17]

There is no predefined set of metrics for assessing the performance of all processes. The LHE Project Team should identify existing measures, or develop new measures, that adequately capture the extent to which the process adds value and meets the expectations of the beneficiaries, supports employees who are involved in providing the process or service, and uses university resources wisely. These metrics would provide agreed-upon quantitative measures that benchmark the current state of a process and identify realized improvements from the LHE initiative.

The following categories of performance metrics may provide a useful starting point for determining appropriate criteria for evaluating the performance of a process. This list of potential metrics includes those identified in previous Lean studies conducted across a wide variety of settings that may be appropriate for applications in higher education.[18] The categories may also prompt the development of additional process-specific performance metrics by LHE Project Team members.

Metrics related to the time required by the process. Examples of performance metrics in this area are cycle time (e.g., time between when a prospective student requests admissions information and when that information is received), lead time (e.g., the time between calling to schedule a sick visit and the time of the appointment), and changeover time (e.g., the amount of time to reset classroom technology and seating configurations between different academic courses). Metrics related to the time required by the process used in previous studies include:

■ *Process Time*. Process Time (also known as Value-Creating Time) measures the time it takes to complete a value-adding step of a process from beginning to end *without interruption*. Because Process Time may vary, it may be most useful to express it as a range or average. Example: The time it takes the Office of Diversity Initiatives to review a job posting/ad for compliance with federal, state, and university policies is 10 to 20 minutes (Average Process Time = 15 minutes).

■ *Total Time*. Total Time (also known as Lead Time) measures the actual *elapsed* time it takes to complete a process. Total Time is greater than Process Time due to work that sits in queues, having to wait for someone else's contribution to the process, interruptions, and other reasons. Because Total Time may vary, it may be most useful to express it as a range or average. Example: The time it takes the Office of Diversity Initiatives to provide a response on a submitted job posting/ad for compliance with federal, state, and university policies is 1 to 2 working days (Average Total Time = 1.5 days or 12 hours).

■ *Value-Added Time.* Value-Added Time measures the percent of the total elapsed time of a process that adds value that a beneficiary desires or expects. Value-Added Time is expressed as a percentage (Value-Added Time = [Aggregated times of steps in a process that add value ÷ Total Time] × 100). Example: In the Office of Diversity Initiatives example above, the average Value-Added Time would be 2% (15 minutes ÷ 720 minutes × 100).

■ *Changeover Time.* Changeover Time measures the amount of time it takes an employee to transition from one work activity to another to complete his or her steps in the process. Changeover Time can refer to time that is a physical part of the process (e.g., retrieving file folders; moving among computer screens, databases, software) as well as time lost due to the mental process of "getting back up to speed" when returning to an incomplete task. Example: If a dean requires 10 minutes to review meeting materials prior to meeting with the college council, then Changeover Time = 10 minutes.

Metrics related to the number of steps in the process. Examples of performance metrics in this area are the number of persons/contacts necessary to complete the service (e.g., how many individuals at the university are required to review and sign off on a grant application) and the physical distance required by the process (e.g., the total distance in feet a student must walk to collect the necessary approvals to drop a course). Metrics related to the number of steps in the process used in previous studies include:

■ *Number of Steps/Handoffs.* Number of Steps/Handoffs measures either the total number of distinct steps that are part of a process, the total number of individuals or groups who play a part in the process, or some combination of the two. Example: The personnel payment process at the University of New Orleans (see Chapter 3) included 33 distinct steps prior to the implementation of their Lean initiative.

■ *Total Distance.* Total Distance measures the total physical distance traveled by a person, product, or material as part of the delivery of the process. Example: Prior to implementation of Lean University™ initiatives (see Table 3.1 in Chapter 3), the travel path for work order requests at the University of Central Oklahoma was 1,265 feet.

Metrics related to the adequacy of resources for the process. Examples of performance metrics in this area focus on ratios of the availability of people, equipment, and facilities versus the demand for people, equipment, and facilities to complete a process. Metrics related to the adequacy of resources for the process used in previous studies include:

■ *Available Time.* Available Time measures the amount of time the employee, office, or university is open and available to perform the particular process. Available Time reflects the time during the workday that can be committed to the process after subtracting break times, attendance at meetings, training, time spent on behalf of professional associations, supervisory responsibilities, and so forth. Example: The full-time receptionist for the department of anthropology is at her desk from 8 a.m. until 5 p.m., excluding two 15-minute breaks and a 60-minute lunch (Available Time: 7.5 hours during "traditional" weekday business hours [i.e., no evening or weekend availability]).

■ *Reliability of Equipment.* Reliability of Equipment measures the percent of time that essential work-related equipment (hardware and software) is available when needed for a process. Reliability of Equipment also indicates the extent to which tools needed to support the process (e.g., fax machines, copiers, printers, databases, e-mail system, etc.) are poorly maintained, outdated, or absent. Example: Available Internet bandwidth for the university network is 65% of required capacity during key time periods due to the faculty's use of online learning components in the face-to-face classroom, thus limiting the updating of administrative systems to once daily during overnight hours.

■ *Staffing Capabilities.* Staffing Capabilities measures the number of individuals who are capable of completing the activity needed to support the process. Staffing Capabilities reflects the extent to which cross-training has prepared employees to support a process during absences or periods of high demand, or whether the process is delayed while a critical employee is absent, at training, or otherwise unavailable. Example: Spending and personnel request authorizations are delayed due to outreach and fund-raising activities that require the business dean to be out of the office 50% of the workweek.

Metrics related to the scheduling/delivery of the process. Examples of performance metrics in this area are "just-in-time" performance (e.g., the inclusion of up-to-date information in materials distributed to donors) and performance leveling (e.g., the extent to which ITS staff schedule computer repair/upgrade appointments throughout the week to provide a consistent flow of work for service technicians). Specific metrics used in previous studies include:

- *Accumulated Inventory.* Accumulated Inventory (also known as Batching Practices) measures the degree to which information or activity to support a process queues up, detracting from the flow of the process. By definition, Accumulated Inventory contributes to an increase in Total Time and a concomitant decline in Value-Added Time. The unit of measure for Accumulated Inventory will depend on the process being studied; it might include physical paperwork, pieces of mail in an outbox, projects underway but not yet completed, an accumulation of e-mails requiring action, and so on. Items may accumulate according to some "batching" method that specifies that the information or activity will be addressed on a regular schedule (i.e., done at some fixed interval) or level of pending work (i.e., when a certain amount of work has accumulated). Example: Research proposals requesting approval to use human subjects accumulate until the monthly meeting of the university's institutional review board committee.
- *On-Time Delivery.* On-Time Delivery measures the percentage of time a process is completed in a promised or established unit of time. The established unit of time for calculating On-Time Delivery will depend on the process studied (e.g., while the student is waiting, within one business day, etc.). Example: During peak periods of activity, university staff fail to prepare meeting rooms with requested tables and seating, technology support, and refreshments 13% of the time.

Metrics related to the quality of the process. Examples of performance metrics in this area are the frequency or percentage of errors (e.g., the number of times student records are misfiled or the percentage of misfiled records), the significance of errors (e.g., faculty turnover attributed to delays in providing promised startup package), and the extent to which rework is required (e.g., the number of faculty travel reimbursement requests that must be resubmitted because of mistakes or missing information). Specific metrics used in previous studies include:

- *Percent Complete and Accurate.* Percent Complete and Accurate measures how often required information, materials, and so on needed by employees to complete their steps or activities in the process are complete and accurate (i.e., arrive when needed, are up-to-date, and meet quality standards). Example: The posting of charges (e.g., tuition fees, bookstore purchases) and awards (e.g., financial aid, departmental award) is done according to different schedules by the various offices responsible for them, making it difficult for the university to provide students with the exact current balance on their bursar accounts.

- *Error Rate*. Error Rate measures the number of mistakes made per some fixed number of transactions, service requests, and so on. Error Rate measures the actual number of errors or mistakes, so it is possible to have more errors than the number of transactions/requests (i.e., when there are multiple errors made on a single transaction/request). Error Rate is calculated by dividing the number of total errors by the total opportunity for errors (four errors on three requests out of 100 service requests would result in an Error Rate of 4%). Example: Due to last-minute changes in assignments and payment rates, the Error Rate for each 100 summer teaching contracts issued is 6%.

Metrics related to outcomes of the process. Examples of performance metrics related to outcomes of the process are percent of target goal (e.g., number of library books re-shelved per allocated staff hour), reduction in problems (e.g., the decrease in classroom scheduling change requests), and measures of critical performance goals (e.g., percent of full-time freshmen successfully completing 30+ hours at end of spring semester). Specific metrics used in previous studies include:

- *Demand Rate*. Demand Rate measures the expected volume of activity for the process over some specified time period. Demand Rate reflects the existing beneficiary requirements for the process (i.e., providing the process when the beneficiary wants it), which may vary across the specified time period. Example: The Demand Rate for mandatory advising during the 4-week course registration period that occurs in the middle of the semester is 2,000 students.
- *Process Completion*. Process Completion is a measure of the achievement of the outcome expected by the process. Example: After the LHE implementation, the time Bowling Green State University students waited to be assigned a counselor for individualized mental health services was reduced to less than 1 day (see Table 3.5 in Chapter 3).

Metrics related to subjective evaluations of the process. Examples of performance metrics related to subjective evaluations of a process are targeted feedback measures (e.g., student completion of short assessment distributed at the time of appointment at writing skills center), survey data (e.g., faculty satisfaction with a new course approval process), focus groups (e.g., facilitator-led evaluation by representative clients of the office of capital planning), and interviews (e.g., phone surveys of parents on perceived quality of student support services). A specific metric found in previous studies is:

■ *Perceptual/Attitudinal Measures.* Beneficiary perceptions and attitudes, when quantified, may provide useful indices of how well (or poorly) the process works. Targeted assessments collected immediately after the beneficiary experiences the process (e.g., a short postcard-length survey that is completed and mailed immediately afterward), or specific items about the process included on existing annual surveys, can provide a direct assessment of what the student, parent, faculty member, and so on think about their experiences. Similarly, employee attitudes and perceptions in key areas (e.g., satisfaction, involvement, challenge, etc.) provide complementary process metrics from the employees' perspective.[19] Example: 78% of parents are either "very dissatisfied" or "dissatisfied" with the impersonal, menu-driven electronic phone attendant used for calls to the office of financial aid.

Metrics related to the cost of the process. Examples of performance metrics in this area are cost per unit of service (e.g., the total number of faculty and staff hours involved in a grade appeal), space usage (e.g., the square footage of lighted and air-conditioned office space required to deliver the service), and total costs (e.g., the discounted price of purchasing copier paper in bulk plus the costs of warehousing and moving the letterhead from warehouse to user). Specific metrics used in previous studies include:

■ *Time Savings.* Time Savings measures the decrease in the amount of time required by a process for either the beneficiary or provider of the process after the introduction of LHE solutions. Example: The Student Health Center at Bowling Green State University reduced the average time students spent in the waiting room for walk-in appointments by 3.2 minutes after implementing LHE Project Team recommendations (see Table 3.7 in Chapter 3).

■ *Salary/Cost Savings.* Salary/Cost Savings measures the decrease in financial cost required by a process for either the beneficiary or provider of the process after implementing LHE solutions. Example: The University of Central Oklahoma reduced the annual paper cost for its work order process by 92%, saving more than $14,000 per year (see Table 3.1 in Chapter 3).

■ *Cost per Unit.* Cost per Unit calculates the "total" costs (i.e., usually personnel costs and/or related direct expenses) required by a process for each process cycle completed or unit of service delivered. Example: The office of summer programs calculates that the average direct total cost (instructional salary and benefits, administrative salaries and benefits, and marketing and promotional expenses) to deliver one credit-hour of instruction to an undergraduate student during the summer term is $98.00.

Summary and recommendations. Overall, a large number of performance metrics are available. These examples can inspire LHE Project Teams to develop additional performance metrics that have greater relevance to the needs and expectations of the beneficiaries of the process targeted for improvement. Thus, performance metrics should differ across LHE initiatives, targeting key performance aspects of the process under review. The following recommendations are offered to help guide the selection and development of performance metrics.

■ *Performance metrics must represent the identified values and expectations of the process identified by the beneficiaries.* For example, if business owners value and expect the process of connecting their business needs to faculty expertise to be simple and quick, the number of phone call transfers within the university before connecting with the right faculty member provides a better metric of service than would the number of Web page hits.

■ *The LHE Project Team should identify multiple measures to provide broad coverage of the important values and expectations identified by all beneficiaries of the process.* By including process metrics that reflect the perspectives of beneficiaries, employees, and the university, trade-offs that improve the process from one perspective while harming it from an alternative perspective are more likely to be recognized and avoided. For example, hiring additional advisors during peak periods may improve student satisfaction with the advising process, but the additional personnel expense adds waste rather than resolving the root cause of problems that make the advising process suboptimal.

■ *Specific and focused measures will be more useful than general measures.* For example, faculty member ratings gathered using a mailed postcard immediately following the completion of the process for upgrading office computers is a more focused measure of service performance by the office of technology support service than a review of the number and content of help-desk calls.

■ *Direct measures are generally more useful than indirect measures.* For example, a measure of the actual time from receipt of gift to donor acknowledgment contact might be a more focused performance assessment of the development office's process for thanking donors for their charitable contributions than an analysis of annual repeat giving at levels equal to or larger than the previous year.

■ *Performance metrics can come from a variety of sources.* For example, data gathered by LHE Project Team members when creating a visual map of the process (e.g., Total Time) is an important and rich source of performance metrics. Other process metrics may require the review of archival data available in the university's records or databases (e.g., Error Rate). Still others may require additional data collection outside the mapping process or institutional records (e.g., Perceptual/Attitudinal Measures).

■ *Performance metrics can be collected that reflect the experiences of the providers (i.e., university employees involved in the process) to the extent they do not dilute or deflect attention from the needs and expectations of the beneficiaries.* For example, the amount of space needed to deliver a service should be viewed from the perspective of beneficiaries (i.e., wasted space increases costs and adds no value) rather than the perspective of the staff member who is part of the process (i.e., personal preferences for privacy or personally convenient storage).

Together, the LHE process metrics should provide a clear understanding of the performance of the current process, accurately describing the current state of the process in terms of the values and expectations of all beneficiaries.

5.4 Final Thoughts: Higher Education as Monastery or Market

In the competitive environment of every industry—including higher education—customers have options.[20]

Universities are a unique type of organization with important missions and responsibilities that differ from other profit, nonprofit, and governmental organizations. Faculty governance, academic freedom, lifetime tenure, sabbaticals, and many other features deemed central to their longevity and effectiveness make them unlike most other businesses and organizations.[21] These recognized differences may explain why, when universities apply business concepts, there is a vocal and often vitriolic response from some faculty and administrators. Arguments ensue, often laden with the "offensive" parallels drawn between the work of universities and the work of other organizations (e.g., students as customers, faculty as labor, academic courses and degrees as products, higher education as a commodity). At the same time, university trustees, higher education organizations and consultants, and community and business leaders may fume at the perceived inefficiency and ineffectiveness of universities at a time when other organizations are reinventing themselves to remain competitive in a dynamic marketplace.

The religious and monastic roots of higher education led to existing institutions guided by their faculty's collective wisdom, and the deliberative process prior to implementing change has protected universities from moving quickly in directions that are misguided trends or philosophically wrong. The monastery metaphor for higher education[22] suggests an internally focused enterprise that reflects the values and expectations of the faculty, who, through the administration they empower, determine the academic degrees, curriculum, and requirements based on their disciplinary and pedagogical expertise. It is their responsibility to set and uphold the standards for higher education with vigor and determination, which is occasionally at odds with recommendations or demands from university administration, students, employers, accrediting agencies, and state and federal bureaucracies. In contrast, the market metaphor presumes the power of the marketplace in co-determining the value and expectations included in higher education. Market forces are seen as playing an important role in influencing (but not determining) what academic degrees are offered, what the curriculum includes, and what requirements are needed for graduation. Under this model, faculty-led curriculum decisions consider student preparedness and interest in higher education, the knowledge and skills needed by graduates in the competitive global workplace, feedback from alumni, and standards established by accrediting, state, and federal agencies. Changes to the curriculum are considered on a regular basis in response to ever-changing market demands, and decisions are quickly reached and implemented.

Neither metaphor may accurately reflect the current—or future—states of universities. Most institutions are likely to share at least some aspects of both, placing them somewhere along a monastery–market continuum rather than being in one or the other mutually exclusive category. Whether or not your university identifies with higher education as a monastery or market, some universities have already accepted or embraced the market metaphor. For-profit institutions are certainly in this group, but the group includes nonprofit colleges and universities as well. Market-leaning institutions are tailoring their offerings of degrees or programs, when and where they are taught, and what materials they cover based on careful attention to an expanded marketplace of individuals who can benefit from higher education. These individuals include:

■ Prospective students seeking educational experiences that help them obtain and keep good jobs.
■ Employers investing in a workforce that will be successful in the global competitive marketplace.
■ Employees wanting academic credit for their life and work experiences as they begin or return to college.
■ Companies and agencies desiring more business-based credentialing of knowledge and skills for their employees rather than disciplinary academic degrees.
■ Legislators investing in an educated workforce to attract employers to their communities.

These and other forces (e.g., the expansion of higher education opportunities outside the United States) have expanded competition among universities for enrollments and revenue. For example, online and blended distance education options now permit universities to reach well beyond those students who are close to their campuses, and community colleges are offering the first 2 or 3 years of a bachelor's education on their campuses at affordable prices.

The critical point here is not whether either metaphor is correct. The point is that regardless of which metaphor you choose to embrace, students are more likely to attend (and faculty are more likely to join, and alumni, parents, legislators, and employers are more likely to support) universities that meet or exceed the values and expectations of their beneficiaries. LHE's focus on identifying the values and expectations of the beneficiaries of higher education improves processes regardless of where an institution places itself on the monastery–market continuum.

Endnotes

1. Womack, J.P., and Jones, D.T. 2003. *Lean thinking: Banish waste and create wealth in your corporation*. New York: Free Press. pp. 16–17.
2. Seymour, D. 1993. *On Q: Causing quality in higher education*. Phoenix, AZ: Oryx Press and the American Council on Education. Chapter 3.
3. The following three articles in *The Chronicle of Higher Education* provide some evidence that business schools are responding to demands from the marketplace to include more coursework on ethics, the environment, and social responsibility: Crawford, E. May 21, 2003. M.B.A. Students Want Programs to Put More Emphasis on Ethics, Survey Finds; Mangan, K. January 8, 2003. Accrediting Board Endorses Stronger Focus on Ethics in Business-School Curriculums; and Pulley, J. October 19, 2005. Business Schools Increasingly Provide Education in Social and Environmental Issues, Survey Finds.
4. Seymour, D. 1993. *On Q: Causing quality in higher education*. Phoenix, AZ: Oryx Press and the American Council on Education. p. 55.
5. See George, M.L., Rowlands, D., Price, M., and Maxey, J. 2005. *The lean six sigma toolbook*. New York: McGraw-Hill. Chapter 4.
6. In fact, it is often these data that trigger a response by the university administration to review and improve a university process. Unfortunately, ad hoc evaluation committees, divisionally focused (i.e., "siloed") responses, and response efforts lack authority, support, perspective, and a framework (such as LHE) for improvement.
7. It might be extremely helpful if university offices responsible for survey research organized their items and findings around university processes rather than vice presidential area, survey respondent, topical area, etc. Looking at five survey items that all point to a problem with an important university process (e.g., advising, registration, library borrowing privileges) would be powerful feedback for understanding whether the process is meeting the expectations of its constituents.
8. Seymour, D. 1993. *On Q: Causing quality in higher education*. Phoenix, AZ: Oryx Press and the American Council on Education. pp. 55–56.

9. Ciliberte, A. 1987. Material availability: A study of academic library performances. *College of Research Libraries* 48(6): 513–527. Described in Seymour, D. 1993. *On Q: Causing quality in higher education.* Phoenix, AZ: Oryx Press and the American Council on Education. p. 53.

10. Greenbaum, T. 2000. *Moderating focus groups: A practical guide for group facilitation.* Thousand Oaks, CA: Sage; Fowler, F., and Mangione, T. 1990. *Standardized survey interviewing.* Thousand Oaks, CA: Sage; Golden, A., and McDonald, S. 1987. *The group depth interview: Principles and practices.* Englewood Cliffs, NJ: Prentice Hall; Greenbaum, T. 1993. *The practical handbook and guide to focus group research.* Lexington, MA: Lexington; Krueger, R. 1993. *Focus Groups: Practical Guide for Applied Research.* Thousand Oaks, CA: Sage. 2nd edition.

11. George, M.L., Rowlands, D., Price, M., and Maxey, J. 2005. *The lean six sigma toolbook.* New York: McGraw-Hill. pp. 64–67. Chapter 4 of this book contains other alternatives for collecting the "voice of the customer" when designing or improving a product, service, or process.

12. Information about the National Survey of Student Engagement can be found at http://nsse.iub.edu/index.cfm.

13. The home page for the North American Association of Summer Schools is http://www.naass.org/index.htm.

14. For information about HERI, visit the Web site http://www.heri.ucla.edu/facoverview.php.

15. Are They Really Ready to Work? Employers' Perspectives on the Basic Knowledge and Applied Skills of New Entrants to the 21st Century U.S. Workforce. A 2006 consortium report by The Conference Board, Partnership for 21st Century Skills, Corporate Voices for Working Families, and the Society for Human Resource Management. New York: The Conference Board, Inc.

16. Womack, J.P., and Jones, D.T. 2005. *Lean solutions: How companies and customers can create value and wealth together.* New York: Free Press. p. 185.

17. This is one of many variants of the quote attributed to one of the great scientists of all time, Lord Kelvin, "You can only improve something if you can measure it."

18. Performance metrics were drawn heavily from the following excellent resources: Keyte, B., and Locher, D. 2004. *The complete lean enterprise: Value stream mapping for administrative and office processes.* New York: Productivity Press; Laraia, A., Moody, P., and Hall, R. 1999. *The kaizen blitz: Accelerating breakthroughs in productivity and performance.* New York: John Wiley & Sons; Womack, J.P., and Jones, D.T. 2005. *Lean solutions: How companies and customers can create value and wealth together.* New York: Free Press; Dennis, P. 2002. *Lean production simplified: A plain-language guide to the world's most powerful production system.* New York: Productivity Press; Tapping, D., and Shuker, T. 2003. *Value stream management for the lean office: Eight steps to planning, mapping, and sustaining lean improvements in administrative areas.* New York: Productivity Press.

19. For a good list of potential employee perceptions and attitudes to gather, see Cook, J., Hepworth, S., Wall, T., and Warr, P. 1981. *The experience of work: A compendium and review of 249 measures and their use.* New York: Academic Press.

20. Seymour, D. 1993. *On Q: Causing quality in higher education.* Phoenix, AZ: Oryx Press and the American Council on Education. p. 42.

21. Nonprofit training hospitals that share governance with the medical staff may provide the closest parallel to colleges and universities.

22. I thank my colleague Dean Richard Kennell for providing this helpful metaphor.

Chapter 6

Preparing Visual Maps for a Comprehensive Understanding of University Processes

The preparation of a comprehensive visual map[1] of the university process chosen for improvement that identifies all the steps required both by the provider (i.e., university representatives) and beneficiaries (e.g., students, faculty, alumni, parents, employers, legislators) is an essential task for the LHE Project Team. The visual map of the university process targeted by the LHE team shows the flow of people, documents and forms, products, information, and so on as it currently occurs at the university. This mapping task allows the LHE team to personally experience and thoroughly understand the process or service from beginning to end. The visual map becomes an indispensable tool for communicating the current process to all those who are involved in the LHE project (e.g., LHE Project Team members, employees who contribute to the process, administrators who oversee the process). Importantly, it provides a practical starting point for the LHE team to determine which steps add value to the process, and identifies those steps the LHE team could recommend eliminating or changing to reduce waste and improve flow. A subsequent "future state" visual map of the process would then be prepared to reflect all improvements proposed by the LHE Project Team.

This chapter discusses how LHE Project Teams can prepare visual maps of a university process. The first chapter section presents general guidelines for creating visual maps of university processes. The second section demonstrates the application of these guidelines using the "new course approval process" example from Chapter 1.

6.1 Preparing a Current State Visual Map

Armed with a set of performance metrics identified as important by the beneficiaries of the process selected for improvement, the LHE Project Team would begin the task of preparing a visual map of the process as currently experienced by beneficiaries and providers.

6.1.1 What to Include in the Visual Map

All visual maps of a process should include six basic components: perspectives from both the provision and beneficiary streams; identification of major steps of the process; flow of activity through the process; flow of information that supports the process; common visual format for representing the steps, activities, and flow of the process; and listing of performance metrics identified as important for evaluating the process.

Perspectives from both the provision and beneficiary streams. University processes have complementary streams that reflect the experiences of two important perspectives: (1) the provision stream, which reflects the experiences of those who provide or perform the process, and (2) the beneficiary stream, which reflects the experiences of those who benefit from the process.[2] The provision stream, represented by university employees or those contracted to work on behalf of the university, captures the flow of materials, information, priority setting, decision making, etc. on the part of the university representatives who are involved in providing the process. The beneficiary stream, which reflects the experiences of those who benefit from what the process offers, captures the experiences of the individual beneficiaries as they attempt to obtain the goods and services they value and expect. Both perspectives on the university process are important to understand. Historically, universities have focused on the internal perspective when improving a process, introducing changes that improve internal efficiency or reduce cost with no or little focus on the experience of the beneficiary. Any proposed LHE solution to improve the process based on one perspective only can lead to unintentional negative consequences for the other. For example, automated phone attendants reduce personnel costs for the university, but may frustrate callers who value a personal interaction or who cannot identify which branching option can address their need. LHE's focus on meeting the needs and expectations of the beneficiaries of the process requires that their perspective is critical for the LHE Project Team to understand and include alongside the perspective of the university provider. Therefore, the visual mapping activity by the LHE Project Team must incorporate the perspectives of both the provision and beneficiary streams.

Identification of major steps of the process. The visual map should depict on a single sheet of paper (e.g., 11 x 17 inches) all major steps or activities that comprise the process. LHE Project Team members should agree prior to the mapping task on the level of detail used to determine the number of steps to prevent the visual map from becoming too unwieldy. Series of minor steps or activities that occur in a short amount of time without interruption can be collapsed into a single step, creating a more manageable map. For example, in the earlier illustration of the freshman move-in process, a large number of activities that were part of unloading the car (e.g., wheel moving tub to building, wait for elevator, take elevator to correct floor, navigate hallway to room) were combined into a single "unloading the car" step on the visual map. If necessary, the distinct activities pooled as a single step on the map can be expanded later into greater detail as needed.[3] As a rule of thumb, a visual map of a process will include five to twenty major steps, with some steps including several meaningfully grouped activities.

Flow of activity through the process. The visual map should portray clearly the flow of steps and activities as part of the value-creating process. This information is gathered by having LHE Project Team members physically walk through the process stream as it is experienced by the person, document, application, etc. The LHE team will develop a clear sense of the flow (or lack thereof) in a process by understanding exactly what happens during the steps (e.g., work products are set aside or returned due to missing or incorrect information, a process is regularly interrupted to respond to an emergency or exception) and between steps (e.g., items to be processed accumulate until there are enough of them to warrant processing, forms are placed in an outbox that is emptied irregularly and infrequently). It is important for the LHE Project Team to observe first-hand as much of the current process as possible, because reports by students, families, and university employees involved are commonly inaccurate (indicating what should be happening rather than what is actually happening) and insufficient. Referring again to the freshman move-in process, the LHE Project Team would physically walk (where possible) the path of new freshmen and their families as they experience the process, beginning with the university's first communication about the move-in process through to the family's departure from campus on move-in day. Similarly, an LHE Project Team would follow the "travel approval and reimbursement" process from the preparation of the request form by the traveler followed by the physical flow of the form through the university process until the traveler receives reimbursement.

Flow of information that supports the process. The visual map should also capture the flow of information that currently takes place to support the process. This verbal, written, or electronic information may prompt the university employee or office to initiate the process, order materials, circumvent the standard steps in the process, acknowledge completion of the process, update records, and so forth. The LHE Project Team would document and evaluate the flow of information currently available to support the process: whether the information was accurate, whether the information was received at the time needed, whether the information was in a useful format, etc. In addition, the flow of information may shed some light on whether and how the information is actually used to support the process (e.g., the LHE team can use date-stamped physical and electronic information to determine the percentage of responses to beneficiaries that are provided within the promised 48 hours). For example, understanding how students report room repairs/reconfigurations to the maintenance staff of the residence hall during freshman move-in will help the LHE Project Team fully capture the perspective of students/families and staff.

Common visual format for representing the steps, activities, and flow of the process. All LHE project teams should use a common visual format when preparing maps of processes and services. In the absence of a comprehensive set of mapping icons for higher education (or, more generally, the service industry), a more simplified visual representation is recommended and followed throughout this book.[4] Specifically, visual mapping includes boxes to represent the major steps in the process from the perspectives of both provider and beneficiary, triangles are used to indicate waiting between steps, steps are shaded when noted as adding value to a process, and a simplified timeline is included. While this visual map format may provide a more limited gestalt of the entire process, it focuses effort by the LHE Project Team members on describing the process rather than developing and having to draw a specialized set of icons for higher education during the mapping process.

Listing of performance metrics identified as important for evaluating the process. The visual map of the process should prominently display the current levels of performance on the set of performance metrics identified as important to the needs and expectations of the beneficiaries. The visual mapping task will provide information used to calculate a number of the performance metrics. For example, the LHE Project Team might estimate Process Time (i.e., the time needed to complete a value-adding step from beginning to end without interruption) and Total Time (i.e., the total elapsed time needed to complete the step) for each of the major steps or activities in the current process. The LHE team can then calculate over-all measures of Process Time and Total Time (including "wait" time) for the entire provision stream. Other performance metrics will require analysis of data unavailable from the LHE Project Team's walk-through of the provision and beneficiary streams (e.g., Error Rate, Perceptual/Attitudinal Measures). The LHE team might identify still other performance metrics that are help-ful for identifying problems with the process and provide focus for potential LHE interventions. For example, the LHE Project Team might discover a con-voluted pathway along which a financial aid application form travels during the "financial aid request" process, leading to the inclusion of Total Distance as an additional performance metric for the process.

6.1.2 *General Steps and Suggestions When Preparing a Current State Process Map[5]*

Drawing a visual map of a current university process or service is relatively straightforward. Starting with a large, blank sheet of paper, each member of the LHE Project Team individually completes the following steps:

1. Begin with either the perspective of beneficiary or provider for the cur-rent process.
2. Identify the initial and final point of the process, typically beginning at the point where the process is initiated within the university and end-ing at the point where the university has completed the process. Steps or activities prior to or after the university process are not included (e.g., steps within an external granting agency that lead to their request that the university provide an annual accounting of an awarded grant).
3. Draw each intervening step or activity in the process, following the flow of the individual or material through the process. The LHE Project Team can represent activities completed without interruption by a single person or office as a single step of the process.

4. For each process step or activity, include information about what is occurring, the individuals involved, databases used, flow of information to support the step or activity, etc.

5. Observe and measure the Process Time and Total Time for each step or activity, where appropriate. If observation is not possible, obtain estimates from individuals involved in the process.

6. Observe and measure the waiting or "queue" times for each step or activity. If observation is not possible, obtain estimates from individuals involved in the process.

7. Document the types of communication that support the process.

8. Document whether the flow of individuals or materials from each step or activity to the next is requested ("pulled") by a specific individual or office or delivered ("pushed") independent of a request or verified need. For example, a mail run on the main campus by a staff member of the university's regional campus could stop only at offices that indicate there is mail waiting or stop at every location regardless of whether there is any mail.

9. Supplement the visual map with additional information that enriches the LHE Project Team's understanding of the process. This might include, for example, how individuals and offices handle exceptions to the process and their impact on the flow and overall effectiveness.

10. Repeat Steps 3 through 9 from the alternative perspective (i.e., provider or beneficiary) of the process.

11. Combine both provider and beneficiary streams into a single, comprehensive visual map of the process.

12. Compute and display performance metrics established by the LHE team that indicate the effectiveness of the university process as currently delivered.

Finally, the following suggestions are provided to help the LHE team during the visual mapping task.

Before beginning the mapping task, the LHE Project Team should familiarize itself with the overall process. Prior to mapping the individual steps and activities of the targeted process, the LHE Project Team should conduct a quick walk-through of the entire process to get an overall sense of the flow and sequence of steps and activities. This general overview will prepare LHE team members for what to expect during the more detailed walk-through. This overview will also help the LHE team determine the correct level of analysis when identifying the specific steps and activities in the process. For example, if the LHE team members' initial walk-through identifies more than 15 to 20 steps in the process, they can look for ways to collapse individual steps and activities into a grouped set represented as an individual step or activity to keep the mapping task from becoming too unwieldy. (The LHE Project Team can subsequently examine any of these combined steps or activities in greater detail should they wish to do so.) This quick walk-through will also help LHE team members identify where they can obtain data for the performance metrics (and possibly suggest additional performance metrics to gather as well).

The mapping process should begin at the initiation of the process and be continued "downstream" by the LHE Project Team until completed. The LHE team should follow the downstream flow from one step to the next, beginning with the first point of contact the beneficiary has and continuing through all the steps in provider and beneficiary streams in their actual order of occurrence until ending with the last point of contact.[6] By following the physical flow of the beneficiary or material (e.g., routing form, application form, requisition form) through the process, the LHE team will have a greater sense of flow, time delays, physical distances traveled, and so on than they would if steps were reviewed in an unnatural order because of convenience or ease of accessibility.

The LHE Project Team should walk and map the entire process together. It is important that each member of the LHE team have a comprehensive understanding of the existing process. Personal observation and first-hand knowledge will provide LHE team members with the rich perspective they need to diagnose the process and offer appropriate LHE solutions for reducing waste and improving flow. All LHE team members should have a common understanding of all the key steps and the flow of people, materials, and information, regardless of whether they are each assigned different responsibilities as part of the visual mapping task (i.e., different members are responsible for sketching the process map, collecting process metrics data, determining what additional info is needed, etc.).

The LHE Project Team should observe and question those involved in the process. LHE team members should observe the process as it occurs rather than hearing about it from self-reports of interested parties (e.g., university administrators and supervisors who oversee the process, employees and beneficiaries involved in the process or service). Individuals in the process may mis-remember what they do and how long each step takes, and motivational biases could result in unintentional (or intentional) inaccuracies in reports of what actually occurs during the process. However, honest estimates of Total Time, Process Time, Number of Transactions per Week, Percent Accuracy, and so on are preferable to waiting weeks or months for the retrieval of archival data or the extensive collection of new data. LHE team members should carefully observe the process in action, and ask questions to understand all the underlying steps and activities, information flow, dealing with exceptions, etc. This will provide the LHE team with a more accurate understanding of the process as it is done currently, and may shed some light on potential barriers and solutions when they are proposing LHE solutions to improve the process. LHE team members may wish to use the "Five Why" technique (i.e., asking "why" five times as follow-ups to the original question help dig more deeply into the root causes of certain steps and activities) when probing for more detail about the process.

The LHE Project Team should use "low-tech" tools to prepare the visual map. Drawing the visual map with pencil and paper during the walk-through of the current process will be more useful to the LHE team than a neatly organized computer drawing developed at a distance from the actual process. When the LHE team draws its visual map *in situ*, answers to questions and clarification regarding the flow of people, materials, and information changes and additional detail will result in improvements to the visual map. Pencils (with erasers) are ideally suited for this activity, keeping the LHE team focused on the process rather than fussing with software. Using the simplified mapping technique recommended above (i.e., using no or very few mapping icons) should make the visual mapping task even easier. The goal is to understand the process, not master the use of icons and supporting software.

The LHE Project Team should not rush the visual mapping task. The development of an accurate visual map of the current process is a critical, if not the most critical, step in the application of LHE. An incorrect, poorly detailed, or unintelligible visual map and accompanying performance metrics will fail to provide the LHE team with a foundational understanding of the current process. In turn, a poor understanding of the process will prevent the LHE Project Team from developing accurate LHE solutions to reduce waste and improve flow in the process. It is essential that the visual map be correct and complete and includes reasonable estimates on each of the performance metrics.

Overall, the visual mapping task captures the critical steps and flow of activity and effort from the perspectives of the provider (i.e., the individual employees performing activities and exerting effort as part of their roles in the process) and the beneficiary (i.e., the activities and effort required of the individual being served). The visual map provides a tool for helping individuals beyond the LHE team (e.g., process participants, university administrators, advisory boards) understand the complete process and enlist their advocacy and support for improvements. The accuracy of the comprehensive visual map of the current process, including the selected performance metrics, is essential in guiding the choice of LHE solutions to remove waste and improve flow in a revised future process.

6.2 Creating a Visual Map: The Approval Process for New Courses

The process for approving new courses is critically important to the vitality of higher education. New course offerings reflect the expanding knowledge within a discipline and the emergence of new interdisciplinary thought. New courses also provide students with the most current understanding of issues in preparation for work, graduate school, and civic responsibilities. The timely approval of new course offerings allows universities to maintain their academic leadership, attract stronger students, and meet the professional and personal needs of their graduates and the larger communities that they serve. Chapter 1 presented a brief description of a process for approving proposals for new undergraduate courses that could benefit from the formal application of LHE. This section returns to that hypothetical example to demonstrate the steps taken by an LHE Project Team to create a visual map of the process for reviewing proposals for new undergraduate courses as it currently exists.[7]

For purposes of discussion, assume that the university has endorsed this LHE initiative and appointed an LHE Project Team to spearhead it. The LHE team conducted interviews and focus groups with identified beneficiaries of the course approval process (e.g., faculty members, department chairs and curriculum committees, deans and representatives from college offices), who provided a comprehensive statement of what they value and expect from the new course approval process:

- The new course approval process should support university-wide standards for course requirements and prevent intercollegiate conflicts between course titles and content.
- The new course approval process should take no longer than 2 months to ensure a curriculum that is up-to-date and competitive.

■ The entire process from proposing a new course to the actual teaching of the course should take no longer than 5 months (i.e., a course proposed by July 1st can be offered the following spring semester).
■ The approval process should be simple and straightforward to avoid wasting the time of any individual involved in the process.
■ The new course request form should contain all relevant information and never be returned to an earlier step in the process for additional information.

Using the statement of values and expectations provided by the beneficiaries, the LHE Project Team identified four critical performance metrics to gather during the visual mapping task that would inform their evaluation of the current process for approving a new course:

■ *Total Time*: the actual elapsed time it takes from the initiation of the proposal for a new undergraduate course to the approval and creation of the course (and subsequent delivery of the course to students).
■ *Value-Added Time*: percent of time during the entire course approval process that can be identified as directly contributing to the review of the new course proposal.
■ *Percent Complete and Accurate*: percent of time that information in the proposal that is needed by those who approve new courses is complete and accurate.
■ *On-Time Delivery*: percent of time that final decisions on proposals for new courses are made within 2 months of initiating the process.

The LHE Project Team then met with "faculty sponsors" who have recently proposed new courses and department, college, and university representatives involved in the course approval process. Descriptions of the steps and activities of the faculty sponsors and university staff, along with the university's written course approval guidelines, served as an initial overview of the process and gave the LHE team a sense of the activities that occur and the flow of the steps from one person or office to the next. Based on this overview, the LHE team determined that the individual steps in their visual map would collapse some smaller steps and activities completed by an individual or office during the course approval process into a combined set (i.e., separating distinct activities performed by each person or office would have resulted in an unwieldy number of steps and activities and made the process difficult to follow). This overview also informed the

LHE team where it could obtain information for the identified performance metrics. Finally, the LHE team developed a list of questions to ask during the team members' planned walk-through of the entire course approval process to ensure their complete understanding.

LHE Project Team members next began their physical walk-through of the process, starting with faculty sponsors from various colleges who were proposing new courses for their departments and undergraduate majors (i.e., beneficiaries). The LHE team quickly realized that the steps for approving new courses differed significantly across college offices. (Not surprisingly, the LHE team discovered that the current course approval process did not mirror the written guidelines, and none of the individuals or offices involved in the process were aware of the work performed by others or, by extension, the complete process for approving new courses.) Therefore, the LHE team chose to limit its review of the course approval process to the College of Arts, and Sciences (i.e., the College of A&S submits the largest number of new course approval requests and its courses are more likely to affect curriculum offerings in other colleges). The LHE team examined the course approval routing form as it progressed from step to step, following the flow of written materials as well as oral and electronic communication between individuals and offices to support the current process. They also estimated the amount of time each step took, identifying the portion of that time that contributed value (from the perspective of the faculty sponsors) to the process. LHE team members were very careful to base their description of the process on their personal observations and archival routing forms to document accurately the actual process rather than on how it is supposed to work (or how individuals or offices describe it to place them in the best possible light). They did find some archival data that was very useful; for example, minutes from college and university meetings provided accurate records of when groups met, when new course proposals were discussed, and information on whether a proposal was returned for missing or limited information. The LHE team estimated average wait or queue times along with other performance metrics, and asked probing questions at each step in the approval process to improve the team's description of the flow of the current course approval process. Based on all the information gathered, team members drafted pencil-drawn visual maps that provided a clear and accurate depiction of the course approval process from the perspectives of both beneficiaries and providers.

6.2.1 Visual Map of Current Approval Process for New Courses

Beneficiary perspective. Figure 6.1 shows the visual map of approval process for a new undergraduate course from the perspective of the beneficiary (here, the faculty sponsor proposing the course). The visual map shows the LHE Project Team that the process requires only four steps (taking, on average, a total of just under 16 hours, with the bulk of that time spent preparing the original course proposal) on the part of the faculty sponsor. It also indicates, however, that the approval process for new courses requires faculty sponsors to wait for long periods (i.e., 90 workdays on average between when the faculty sponsor forwarded the proposal to his or her department chair and when the faculty sponsor spoke on behalf of his or her proposal to the Undergraduate Council).

Provider perspective. The LHE Project Team also mapped the provider stream (i.e., university offices and areas involved in the course approval process), which is shown in Figure 6.2. The LHE team identified more than ten offices or areas that review and endorse/approve proposals for new courses, including the library, the faculty sponsor's own department, the faculty sponsor's college, all other colleges, the university-wide undergraduate council, and the office of the provost. The LHE team also notes that the process is designed as a series of reviews, done sequentially rather than in parallel, and that the course proposal spends considerable time waiting in in-baskets, out-baskets, and campus mail.

Combined perspective. Figure 6.3 shows the comprehensive visual map for the approval process for new courses, combining both the beneficiary and provider streams. The combined map provides the LHE Project Team with a detailed overall understanding of the entire process for the first time, as no single individual or office had a firm grasp on the steps in the process outside their areas of interest or focus. The visual map of the combined process also provided the information needed by the LHE team to calculate the performance metrics selected to evaluate the university's current process for approving new courses:

■ *Total Time.* On average, the actual elapsed time from the initiation of the course proposal by faculty to the approval and creation of the course is 145 workdays (120 workdays required for all the steps in the university's process, and 25 days for the faculty member to create and revise the course proposal). The Total Time does not include delays due to revisions that occur infrequently (e.g., the 20% of the time that the

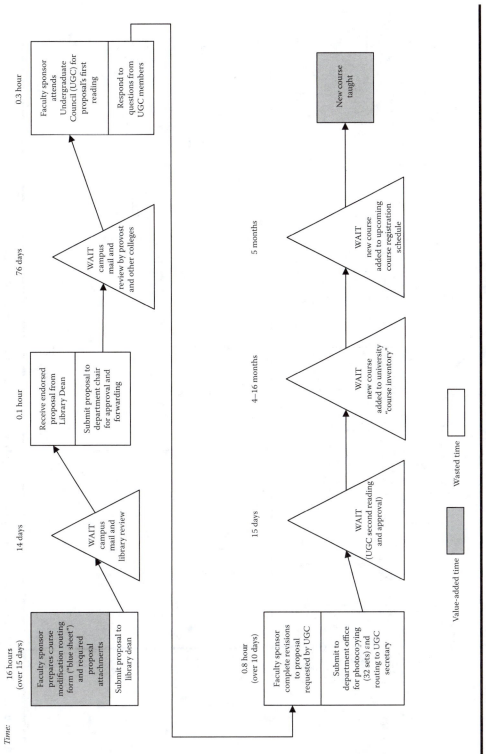

Figure 6.1   Visual map of current new course approval process: beneficiaries' perspective.

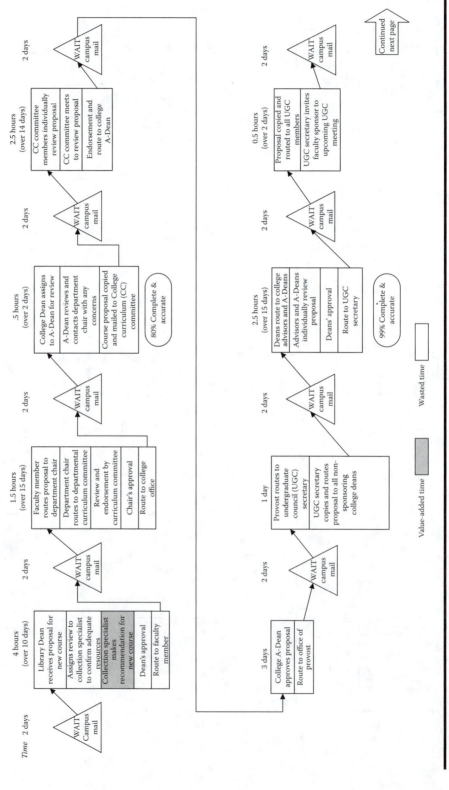

Figure 6.2a   Visual map of current new course approval process: providers' perspective.

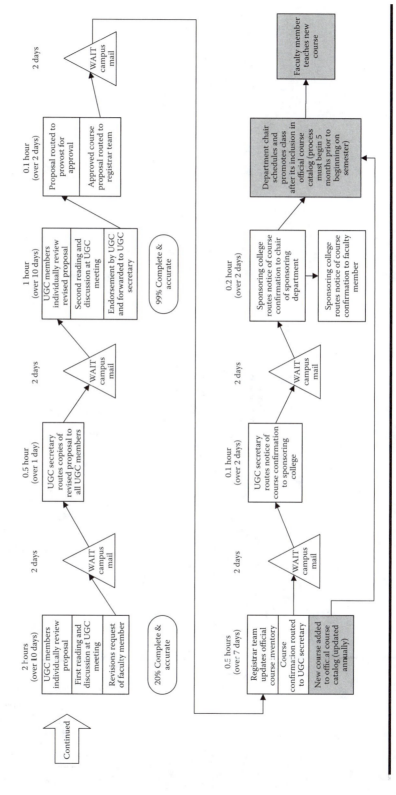

Figure 6.2b   Visual map of current new course approval process: providers' perspective.

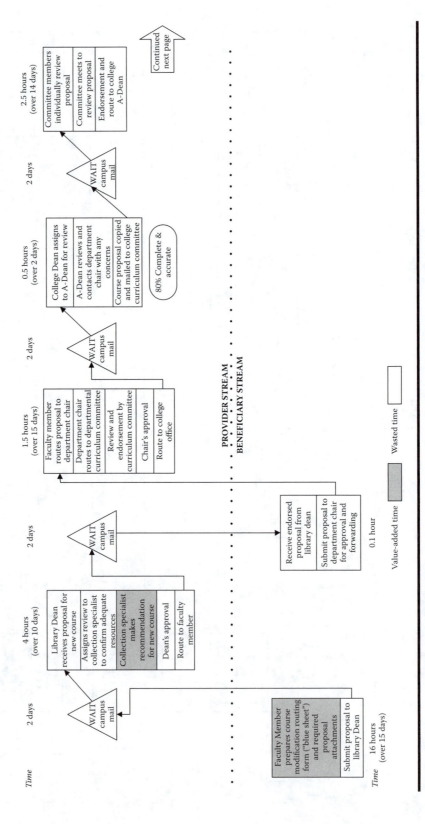

Figure 6.3a Visual map of current new course approval process: combined perspectives.

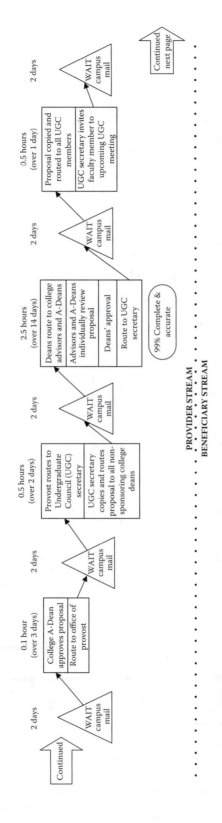

Figure 6.3b Visual map of current new course approval process: combined perspectives.

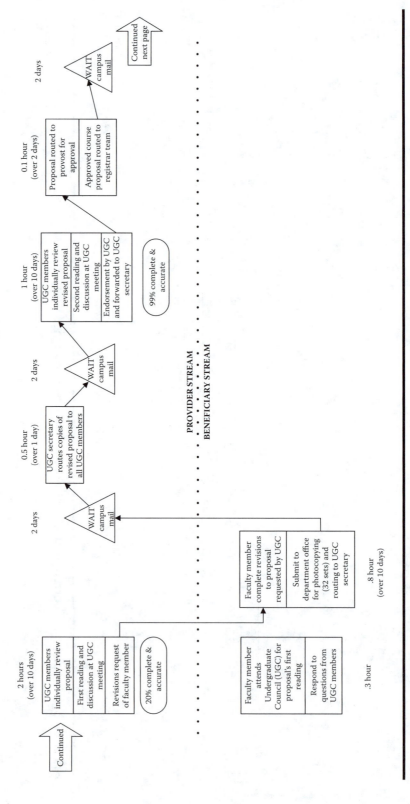

Figure 6.3c Visual map of current new course approval process: combined perspectives.

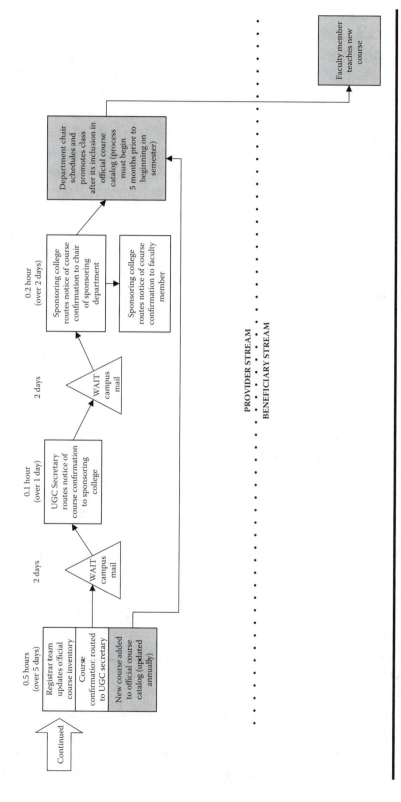

Figure 6.3d   Visual map of current new course approval process: combined perspectives.

college associate dean returns the proposal to the department chair for changes). It also does not take into account potential delays that occur with some frequency (e.g., full meeting agenda that delays the proposal to a later meeting, interruptions to the process when committees do not meet over semester and summer breaks, delays when key members of the process are out of the office and unable to complete their steps). The LHE Project Team was surprised to learn that approved courses must be listed in the official course catalog before being offered. To be listed in the course catalog, course information must be submitted 4 months prior to the release data of the new course catalog. Thus, the timing of when the newly approved course reaches the registrar's office is critically important, because missing the 4-month lead-time could result in a delay of more than a year before the course is included in the university's official catalog. Furthermore, the course registration process begins 5 months prior to the beginning of a semester; if new courses are not yet listed in the official course catalog, they cannot be included as scheduled course offerings. Taken together, the total time required from course proposal to course delivery takes no less than 50 weeks (i.e., 29 weeks for the course approval process plus 5 months for the course registration process) and may take more than 2 years (i.e., narrowly missing the deadline for inclusion in the university's official course catalog would add a 12-month delay).

■ *Value-Added Time.* The LHE Project Team identified only three steps (or parts of steps) that added value to the approval process: faculty time spent on proposal development, determination of the adequacy of library materials for course support by the library collection specialist, and inclusion of newly approved courses into the university's official course catalog. Together, these three activities take an average of approximately 20 hours. The remaining steps and activities add no value from the perspective of the beneficiary. For example, multiple levels of review and time spent correcting errors are considered "waste;" a well-designed process would complete work correctly the first time. The calculated Value-Added Time was less than 1%.

■ *Percent Complete and Accurate.* The LHE Project Team identified four steps in the approval process that provide indicators of completeness and accuracy: the review by the college's A-dean (80% pass rate), the review by deans from other colleges (99% pass rate), the first reading by the Undergraduate Council (20% pass rate), and the second reading by the Undergraduate Council (99% pass rate). The failure rate for the first reading by the Undergraduate Council is significant, indicating that four out of every five proposals require revisions. The visual map shows that this adds 25 additional days (or 17% of the Total Time) to the approval process.

▪ *On-Time Delivery*: The LHE Project Team confirmed that the current approval process for new courses approved 0% of new course proposals for inclusion in the curriculum within 2 months of the faculty member's initiation of the process.

In addition, the visual mapping process provided the LHE Team with several other insights:

▪ "Staffing Capabilities" may be a useful performance metric to include, based on answers to questions from staff members involved in the process. The LHE Project Team learned that the course approval process is delayed regularly when the sole person authorized to review/approve a specific step in the process is unavailable or does not see his or her step in the process as a high priority (e.g., the proposal sits for days in an in-basket while other seemingly more important issues are addressed). There is no indicator in the current process to show when this occurs, or its actual impact on Total Time.

▪ "Demand Rate" may be also be a useful performance metric, because the flow of course approval requests was uneven throughout the year.

▪ Faculty sponsors submitting requests for approval of a new course received very little feedback on the progress of their proposals.

Overall, the mapping exercise provided the LHE Project Team with a detailed understanding of the entire process that is currently used to approve new undergraduate courses. By understanding the process from the perspectives of the provider (i.e., university offices and staff) and the beneficiaries (i.e., faculty sponsors, their department, and their students), and measuring its performance using metrics that tap into the value provided by the process, the LHE team began to see opportunities to reduce waste and improve flow. In addition, the visual map allowed the LHE team to share the entire process with the individuals and offices involved, as well as with university administrators, in a clear and effective format. Chapter 8 continues this example and describes how the LHE team can eliminate or change steps and activities in the "current" map of the new course approval process to reduce waste and improve flow. This will result in a

proposed "future" map of the process that provides greater value to beneficiaries while at the same time reducing university resources wasted on the
approval process.

6.3 Summary

Creating a visual map of the current university process under review by
the LHE Project Team for improvement is a critically important task. First, it
provides a comprehensive and valid description of how the university currently accomplishes the process and, using performance metrics identified
as important by the process beneficiaries, evaluates how effective that university process is. This helps the LHE team and other university members
see, perhaps for the first time, how the process falls short of expectations,
despite the best efforts by individuals and offices involved to do their jobs
as well as they can. By seeing the entire process from the perspectives of
both provider and beneficiary, non-value activities and steps become immediately obvious and provide initial points of discussion for recommending
targeted improvements. Overall, the visual map with accompanying performance metrics provides a useful tool for the LHE team—composed of
members who have a vested interest in improving the process—to understand, diagnosis, recommend, and act. By applying the LHE tools discussed
in Chapter 7 to remove waste and improve flow, the LHE team can create
a "future state" process that better addresses the needs and expectations of
beneficiaries and uses university resources more efficiently. Equally important, the experience of mapping an important university process provides an
opportunity for the university to show that it values employees (e.g., becoming process owners and active contributors of LHE solutions) and invests in
its employees (e.g., expanding their understanding of the university, enriching their job skills, creating more motivating and satisfying work processes).
LHE, through the appointment of LHE Project Teams, gives individuals the
knowledge, tools, and authority to become owners of a process, who will
work to improve the process. Their ownership and expertise (i.e., training
in LHE tools and methods as well a deep understanding of the complete
process) dramatically increases the probability that the process will be
improved, will stay improved, and will be continually improved (in stark
contrast to consultants who fly in, get up to speed, recommend changes,
and fly out).

Before closing the chapter, a few comments on the example used to demonstrate the visual mapping task seem in order. The visual map of the process for proposing new academic courses, based on a real example, suggests a process with significant opportunity for improvement. The visual mapping of virtually *any* process at *any* college or university, including the other scenarios used in this book (i.e., freshman move-in, thank-you letters to donors, installing a laboratory pass-through door), will uncover significant amounts of waste and impediments to flow (carefully observing a service area or drawing a visual map of the process will prove this point). Some of these process streams occur within a single functional area of a university (e.g., the process of requesting internal travel support in the department of management), while others may span several functional areas (e.g., the new course approval process) or be university-wide (e.g., the process of designing and delivering first-year experience programs to new freshmen).[8] While all these processes differ, they have much in common. These processes fall short of delivering what their beneficiaries value and expect. Very few individuals or offices involved in the process have a grasp of the complete process. There is either no owner of the process, or the owner is far removed from the actual day-to-day operations of the process. Finally, the absence of good performance metrics means that even if process owners are in place, they would not know how well—or poorly—the process is working.

The identification of numerous "broken" processes may lead some individuals (especially beneficiaries who might be frustrated with the process) to speculate that university administrators or their staff are inept, uncaring, or both. LHE provides an alternative and simpler explanation: no one understands or owns the entire process. Administrators may make it clear to their staffs that the process is important (e.g., the provost pledges that proposals for new courses will be processed quickly within her office), and employees work diligently to perform their tasks (e.g., the goal of the secretary to undergraduate council is a 24-hour turnaround within the office of the provost). But ensuring that each step is done well does not mean that the entire process works well; in fact, many steps that are well done may be wasteful activities that add absolutely no value. Without an owner of the process, it may continue as is, or individual offices may make changes to their activities with the intention of improving the process (when in fact they may not). Despite these good intentions, individuals or offices that benefit from the process complain because what they value and expect is not being delivered by the process. The application of LHE, including the visual mapping step performed by the LHE Project Team, is designed specifically to address these concerns and challenges. The opportunities for LHE initiatives that eliminate waste, add value, and improve the flow of processes in higher education are numerous—at every university.

Endnotes

1. Lean practitioners commonly refer to the visual map as a "value stream map."
2. Womack, J.P., and Jones, D.T. 2005. *Lean solutions: How companies and customers can create value and wealth together.* New York: Free Press.
3. Keyte, B., and Locher, D. 2004. *The complete lean enterprise: Value stream mapping for administrative and office processes.* New York: Productivity Press. Chapter 5.
4. The mapping system used in this book is consistent with a more recent book by James Womack and Daniel Jones that explicitly expands Lean principles and practices beyond the shop floor in traditional manufacturing organizations; Womack, J.P., and Jones, D.T. 2005. *Lean solutions: How companies and customers can create value and wealth together.* New York: Free Press. A comparable adaptation to the visual mapping process has been used in healthcare settings with success; Miller, D., ed. 2005. *Going Lean in health care (Innovation Series #8).* Cambridge, MA: Institute for Healthcare Improvement.
5. Many of the tips for drawing the current process map are drawn from the following: Tapping, D., and Shuker, T. 2003. *Value stream management for the lean office: Eight steps to planning, mapping, and sustaining lean improvements in administrative areas.* New York: Productivity Press; Keyte, B., and Locher, D. 2004. *The complete lean enterprise: Value stream mapping for administrative and office processes.* New York: Productivity Press; Rother, M., and Shook, J., 1999. *Learning to see: Value stream mapping to add value and eliminate muda.* Brookline, MA: The Lean Enterprise Institute.
6. Mapping both the beneficiary and provision perspectives of processes from beginning to end is recommended (Womack, J.P., and Jones, D.T. 2005. *Lean solutions: How companies and customers can create value and wealth together.* New York: Free Press), given that it follows the actual experience of the beneficiary involved in the process. This downstream flow is in contrast to the mapping recommendation in Lean manufacturing, which typically states that you should map the process working backward from the customer's requirements (i.e., backward from the product ready for delivery at the shipping dock).
7. This example is developed using the actual steps and time estimates of the course approval process at my own university as it existed in 2007.
8. Still other processes may cross institutional barriers (e.g., a regional or statewide interlibrary loan process for consortial member institutions that involve processes at multiple colleges and universities).

Chapter 7

Eliminating Waste and Improving Flow

The completed visual map for the targeted higher education process, coupled with a clear understanding of what the beneficiaries of the process value and expect, provides the LHE Project Team members with critical information to begin their disciplined approach to identify and eliminate waste and improve flow. In contrast to internal or external consultants who might focus on the most visible problems (or problems aligned with their expertise or interest), LHE offers a systematic approach that builds on the team's personal familiarity and experiences to recognize and remove both visible and hidden waste and establish an uninterrupted flow across the entire process. The visual map of the process as it currently exists allows LHE Project Team members to see the wide variety of waste that adds no value from the perspective of the beneficiary and disrupts the smooth flow of the process. The LHE team can then propose a set of LHE solutions that follows from a set of Lean practices and techniques with demonstrated success in eliminating waste and improving flow to create a future process that provides greater value to the beneficiaries, makes better use of the talents of employees, and reduces costs for the university.

7.1 Identifying Waste in University Processes

Waste is any step or activity in a process that consumes resources but adds no value, as seen from the perspective of the beneficiary of the process.[1]

Most individuals would agree that some waste is present in many, if not all, university processes; what is surprising is the vast amount of waste that exists. Research findings across a variety of manufacturing companies estimate that the typical business process is 90% to 95% waste and 5% to 10% work that brings value to the consumer of the process.[2] Estimates of the waste in service industries such as health care, air transportation, and retail sales are similarly high.[3] There is no reason to assume that the level of waste in the processes of higher education differs from these estimates. It is not uncommon to see students walking across campus to wait in lines, employees correcting errors that are brought to their attention, delays in sharing and acting on information by senior and mid-level university administrators, and different offices across campus entering and checking the same information more than once. The freshman move-in process (see Chapter 2) estimated that the percentage of time wasted during the move-in process was approximately 70% and 80% for students and their families and university staff and volunteers, respectively. The applications of LHE presented in Chapter 3 provide further support for the high levels of waste found in the processes at a number of universities prior to the implementation of Lean principles and practices. Together, these findings affirm perceptions of legislators, trustees, parents, students, faculty, staff, and administrators that significant amounts of waste are present in university processes.

A student visit to a campus health center provides an example of one ubiquitous form of waste, the "waste of waiting." A student typically waits for an appointment, waits in the health center's waiting room, waits for the health professional to arrive in the treatment room, waits for lab work, waits for their prescriptions, and waits to check out. The healthcare providers also wait for student records to be located, wait for results from a lab test, and wait for prescription payment approval from the student's healthcare insurer. In none of these instances does the required waiting add value to the medical assessment and treatment received by the student. Furthermore, the waiting does not reduce the workload of the healthcare providers; in fact, more resources are consumed to accommodate the waste of waiting (e.g., the need for a larger waiting room, staff time to manage the movement of waiting students, staff time to contact students with lab results). Finally, the waiting time required by students during their visits to the campus health center ignores the value of their time, which the health center staff may neglect to see as real opportunity costs to students. Overall, the waste of waiting (not to mention other forms of waste likely to be part of this process, i.e., waste of correcting errors, waste of movement) adds no value to the process from the perspective of the student, and consumes resources that contribute to the overall cost of the health center visit. In the end, this hidden cost is passed along to students and their families. This last point cannot be overstated: students, faculty, parents, business leaders, legislators, and other beneficiaries of university processes pay for the additional costs associated with every process laden with waste, and this waste adds absolutely nothing of value to the processes that beneficiaries need. The following quote underscores the importance of eliminating waste from every university process:

> *Often, waste is obvious and visible to everyone. This is apparent whenever paperwork cannot be found or is incorrect.... More often, waste is not visible or noticeable as it eats away at profits beneath the surface of everyday work. The requirement for an extra signature here, a delayed response to a phone inquiry there, two people doing the same work on different systems with different numbers, poorly run meetings, and project teams floundering without direction are all waste.... In all too many cases, [these and other wastes] are accepted as "the way it is" or "part of the cost of doing business" or "people will be people." This is not the attitude that world-class organizations tolerate.... No well-informed customer would willingly agree to pay for such foolishness if they had a choice.[4]*

The ultimate goal of LHE is the total elimination of waste. Resources that are freed up by eliminating waste can be reinvested by the university in other high-priority processes to increase the value to the level expected (or desired) by those they serve. In addition, eliminating waste provides a strategic competitive advantage: eliminating waste will improve the quality of the university experience, enhancing the institution's ability to recruit more and better students, recruiting better faculty and supporting their success, improving the university's reputation, and strengthening support from the legislature more quickly than a "competitor" university. Finally, waste poisons the work environment. The direct impact of waste on university employees (e.g., complaints from students and families, correcting errors, inability to complete work efficiently) can be emotionally exhausting and stressful, taking much of the fun and satisfaction out of the work people do.[5]

7.1.1 Types of Waste

Various frameworks are available for identifying the types of waste that pollute work processes. A list of seven to ten categories evolved from Lean's early work in manufacturing, modified over time to accommodate Lean's expansion to the nonmanufacturing sector.[6] Alternative frameworks for waste have been developed for specific applications of Lean. For example, the University of Central Oklahoma created the acronym "DOWNTIME" to represent the types of waste in transactional services.[7] As the applications of Lean principles and practices have matured to encompass a broader range of services, Lareau[8] developed a more elaborated framework that organizes waste into four general categories that described 26 specific types of waste. This latter framework provides a useful guide for learning to identify waste, and is presented below with examples relevant to higher education.

People waste. *People waste* refers to the category of wastes that occurs when universities fail to capitalize fully on the knowledge, skills, and abilities of employees and workgroups. Five specific types of people waste can be identified.

1. *Waste of goal misalignment.* The waste of goal misalignment occurs when people work at cross-purposes. Some examples of the waste of goal misalignment include
   - Implementing across-the-board budget cuts due to low enrollment, which results in cutbacks in the admissions office.
   - Faculty members focusing on graduate education when the dean is advocating for greater emphasis on undergraduate education.
   - Establishing divisional goals that are inconsistent with overall university-wide initiatives.
   - Failing to support online students in different time zones, or evening students who are unable to access student support services offered during "normal business hours."
   - Placing holds on student accounts for unpaid library fines, which result in a loss of state subsidy due to late registrations.
2. *Waste of incorrect assignment.* The waste of incorrect assignment occurs when time and effort are spent on unnecessary or inappropriate tasks. Some examples of the waste of incorrect assignment include
   - Completing historically required reports that are filed away immediately without review or action.

- Maintaining full office coverage and traditional work assignments during holiday closures when student services are not in high demand.
- Requesting scholarship applicants to document life experiences, gather reference letters, and write personal statements for scholarship applications that are not used when making scholarship decisions.
- Requiring faculty to provide curriculum vitae information multiple times and in different formats on request for internal and external purposes.
- Academic units and colleges preparing overly detailed and expensively designed reports for on- and off-campus presentations and audiences.

3. *Waste of waiting.* The waste of waiting occurs whenever a process is halted or slowed down while waiting for people, information, actions, or resources. Some examples of the waste of waiting include
   - Department chairs waiting for sequential signatures from various offices before being able to extend a job offer to the chosen candidate for a position.
   - Faculty members waiting for maintenance repairs to their grant-funded research laboratories.
   - Students waiting in lines to register or pay a bursar bill.
   - University administrators waiting for a meeting to begin.
   - Waiting to retrieve information from systems that are unavailable 24/7 or have slow response times.

4. *Waste of motion.* The waste of motion occurs when there is unnecessary movement of people, machines, or materials that do not contribute to the successful completion of the process. Some examples of the waste of motion include
   - University staff walking to and from office machines (e.g., copiers, printers, fax machines).
   - Requiring students to visit multiple locations to complete a request or transaction.
   - University administrators manually transferring/updating files across multiple devices.
   - Requiring faculty to obtain written approval signatures from various offices on grant applications.
   - Students visiting multiple offices for authorized signatures to drop a course.

5. *Waste of nonoptimal processing.* The waste of nonoptimal processing occurs when work is performed in a less efficient and effective manner than should be expected by failing to draw upon the physical skills,

talents, creativity, and ideas of employees or those it serves. Some examples of the waste of nonoptimal processing include

- Providing slow and error-prone services to students due to inadequate training of regular and seasonal employees.
- University staff creating memos and reports "from scratch" without relying on established templates, or lacking computer and PDA solutions to improve their efficiency and effectiveness.
- Limiting the responsibility and authority of highly skilled and motivated university staff to complete their jobs.
- Failing to ensure that university meetings start and end on time, and adhere to a clear agenda.
- University officials failing to draw on faculty and staff expertise for ad hoc assignments.

Process waste. *Process waste* refers to the cluster of wastes that occurs due to shortcomings in the design or implementation of university processes. Twelve specific types of process waste can be identified.

1. *Waste of ineffective control.* The waste of ineffective control occurs when direct supervision or monitoring of performance fails to have a sustainable, long-term impact on overall job performance. Some examples of the waste of ineffective control include
   - Varying levels of performance by custodial workers corresponding to the presence or absence of their supervisors.
   - Failing to establish, communicate, and monitor specific performance goals for admission office staff.
   - Failing to gather evaluations of service in offices that provide frontline contact with students.
   - Conducting perfunctory performance reviews with staff simply to fulfill a university requirement.
   - Inconsistency over time in the performance criteria (and their standards) expected of the office of sponsored research.
2. *Waste of variability.* The waste of variability occurs when university time and effort are spent to compensate for or correct an unexpected outcome of a process. Some examples of the waste of variability include
   - Tracking down a travel and entertainment reimbursement check that was mailed to an old address.

- Parents reaching a different contact person when calling the bursar, each unfamiliar with the history of and progress made in response to an earlier call.
- Departmental and college advisors conferring with the study abroad office to ensure that recently updated academic credits taken overseas will transfer appropriately to a student's transcript.
- Discussing the impact of unpredictable changes in immigration regulations on international student eligibility for matriculation, course and credit registration, and internship and employment options.
- Offering financial incentives for faculty to participate on university priorities, which run afoul of the institution's existing overload compensation policy.

3. *Waste of tampering.* The waste of tampering occurs when a process is changed arbitrarily without full knowledge of the "upstream and downstream" ramifications of the action. Some examples of the waste of tampering include
   - A new mandate by the business office that requires that reimbursed cab fares (including tip) be accompanied by a signed and dated official receipt provided by the cab service.
   - The treasurer's office requirement that reimbursement for international expenses be submitted using the daily currency exchange rate conversion for each purchase to prevent the university from overpaying due to fluctuations in exchange rates.
   - Establishing planned reductions in library purchases of journals and books independently of the new course approval process that assumes reasonable investments in library holdings.
   - Department chairs reducing the number of undergraduate offerings that fulfill general education requirements to meet the needs of an expanding graduate program.
   - Establishing new minimum health insurance coverage standards that exceed those of existing parent policies that cover many students.

4. *Waste of nonstrategic effort.* The waste of nonstrategic effort occurs when time and effort are invested in activities that satisfy short-term goals and needs of internal members of the university (i.e., process providers) at the expense of individuals served by the process (i.e., process beneficiaries). Some examples of waste of nonstrategic effort include
   - Maintaining 8 a.m. to 5 p.m. weekday office hours in the advising office for the convenience of staff scheduling rather than the needs of evening students.

- Building course schedules around faculty teaching preferences.
- Canceling upper-division courses that are needed for graduation due to minimum enrollment guidelines.
- Requiring consistent teaching, scholarship, and service workload assignments for all faculty members.
- Installing new enterprise systems that satisfy the information needs of the senior administration while burdening units that support students and faculty.

5. *Waste of unreliable processes.* The waste of unreliable processes occurs when time and effort are required to correct unpredictable outcomes of the process that are (initially) due to unknown causes. Some examples of the waste of unreliable processes include
   - Failing to inform new department chairs that they are required to pre-order computers for new faculty members 3 months in advance.
   - The director of sponsored programs delegating a task to a part-time employee who misses a deadline to submit a required form necessary for receiving a federal grant extension.
   - A dean failing to sign summer contracts before leaving to attend a national conference, resulting in summer faculty being paid in a later pay period than expected.
   - Delaying an offer of employment to a new faculty member due to the department chair's noncompliance with a recently adopted university requirement to submit a "new faculty success plan."
   - Miscoding and incorrectly categorizing revenues and expenditures during the transition to a new financial management system.

6. *Waste of nonstandardization.* The waste of nonstandardization occurs when resources are needed to compensate and correct for processes that are completed in an arbitrary and unpredictable way because standards are ignored. Some examples of the waste of nonstandardization are
   - The payroll office spending time to investigate faculty complaints about allegations of uncompensated work that are eventually attributed to the incorrect processing of supplemental pay contracts.
   - Students required to attend summer session to complete unmet graduation requirements due to incorrect advice from their faculty advisors.
   - An advancement office staff member misunderstanding the final date by which an end-of-year gift from alumni can be processed to receive the charitable gift deduction for the current year.

- Incurring the cost of a second mailing to conference attendees that includes campus parking information and passes that were left out of the original mailing.
- Incurring the cost of an emergency purchase of an HVAC compressor unit because of the failure to follow maintenance guidelines required during seasonal switchover.

7. *Waste of suboptimization.* The waste of suboptimization occurs when competing or duplicative processes in the university consume unnecessary time and energy to the detriment of the outcome of the process. Some examples of the waste of suboptimization include
   - Duplicate reporting of a computer problem through both an online problem report center and a phone call to the building's tech support specialist.
   - Individual academic departments preparing news releases because of a work backlog at the university's centralized office of public relations.
   - Individual colleges maintaining their own alumni databases rather than contributing to a centralized database.
   - Retaining duplicate (and often incomplete) faculty files within academic units and college offices in addition to official files maintained by the office of the provost.
   - Requesting academic units to prepare ad hoc reports on summer contracts and course enrollments that could be generated centrally through the university's registration system.

8. *Waste of poor scheduling.* The waste of poor scheduling occurs when time and effort are required to compensate for poorly/incorrectly scheduled or coordinated activities. Some examples of the waste of poor scheduling include
   - Failing to establish vacation blackout periods for the registrar's staff during a planned major upgrade to the university's course registration system.
   - Individual colleges establishing local enrollment targets without regard for their impact on overall university enrollment management goals.
   - Scheduling the fall semester opening date of residence halls for domestic students that ignores the week earlier arrival required of new international students.
   - Posting tuition and fee charges to student accounts earlier than the graduate college timeline for awarding of graduate assistantships that include tuition and fee waivers.

- Postponing a second-round campus interview with the final candidate for chief academic officer due to the general unavailability of faculty members and faculty senate officers during the summer.

9. *Waste of work-arounds.* The waste of work-arounds occurs when time and effort are invested in informal processes (e.g., "shadow systems") that duplicate or compete with established university processes. Some examples of the waste of work-arounds include
   - Academic unit budget directors creating unique spreadsheets to monitor budget balances that are difficult to gather from the university's financial management system.
   - Individual colleges and academic units maintaining their own databases to track donors.
   - Students receiving unexpected bursar charges because the off-campus program office had not updated its locally developed student fee sheet.
   - Student employees regularly conducting physical inventories of storeroom supplies in response to a cumbersome online inventory management system.
   - Permitting faculty to record and store student test and homework grades using any self-chosen method because the university-provided course management software is difficult to use from home.

10. *Waste of uneven flow.* The waste of uneven flow occurs when extra resources are needed to cope with the irregular demand or fluctuating schedules caused by backlogs or "pinch points" in a university process. Some examples of the waste of unevenness are
    - Excessive staffing throughout the freshman move-in process to respond to unpredictable periods of high volume.
    - Overpurchasing beverages and food for events due to unpredictable attendance.
    - Modifying course staffing because of underenrolled or overenrolled classes.
    - Incurring high utility costs for classroom and administrative buildings during off-peak and weekend hours.
    - Managing the preparation of multiple mandated reports that are all due at the same time.

11. *Waste of checking.* The waste of checking occurs when steps in a process are reviewed or duplicated because they cannot be trusted to be done correctly the first time. Some examples of the waste of checking include

- Regular personal or electronic monitoring of employees by supervisors.
- Requiring that feedback on an academic course proposal be solicited from various offices that have no feedback to provide.
- Multiple proofreading requests for documents prior to their production and distribution.
- Independent calculations of travel reimbursement requests by the traveler, local budget administrator, and centralized business office.
- Requiring second level supervisor concurrence, in addition to direct supervisor approval and employee signature, for use of vacation, sick, or personal leave time.

12. *Waste of correcting errors.* The waste of correcting errors occurs when an activity or step in a process must be repeated to correct a mistake or resolve a problem. Some examples of the waste of correcting errors include
    - Alumni Affairs delaying a mailing to alumni because of outdated mailing labels.
    - Senior leadership groups revisiting their recently approved policy in response to unexpected consequences or reactions.
    - Revising student bursar bills due to fee waivers that were received late and not posted.
    - Re-advertising faculty openings (and delaying the hiring process) due to mistakes in the content or placement of the original job posting.
    - Constant recruiting and hiring of campus food service workers because of high rates of turnover due to poor performance or attendance.

Information waste. *Information waste* refers to the category of wastes that occurs when available information is deficient for supporting university processes. Five specific types of information waste can be identified.

1. *Waste of information translation.* The waste of information translation occurs when data, formats, and reports for individuals and offices are modified by individuals at different steps in the process. Some examples of the waste of information translation include
   - Budget directors importing uniquely formatted expense ledgers from different overseas study abroad sites for centralized budget reconciliation.

   – Evaluating courses and grades from high school and community college transcripts to determine appropriate transfer credits.
   – Adjusting compensation and benefits data collected from various institutions to provide comparative "apples-to-apples" benchmarking data.
   – Reformatting spreadsheet and data files from academic units using different computer platforms and software prior to aggregation.
   – Aggregation of college-, university-, and state-level performance metrics required for inclusion in accreditation self-study reports.
2. *Waste of missing information.* The waste of missing information occurs when additional university resources are needed to compensate for the absence of information critical to the process. Some examples of the waste of missing information include
   – University building and utility maintenance staff physically responding to complaints about building air-handling systems in the absence of centrally available monitoring data.
   – Allocating local capital improvement funds without the benefit of an up-to-date compilation of campus-wide needs.
   – Investing in student retention initiatives without a thorough understanding of the major "drivers" of students' decisions to leave.
   – The campus bookstore overbuying or underbuying course textbooks in the absence of up-to-date course enrollment information.
   – The university budget director responding to multiple phone calls and e-mails requesting the unstated method for calculating salary savings as required in an upcoming report.
3. *Waste of information loss due to hand-offs.* The waste of information loss due to hand-offs occurs when information or materials are not well integrated across different parts of a university process. Some examples of waste of information loss due to hand-offs include
   – Using different ad hoc decision rules in academic units, colleges, and the alumni office when entering recent graduate records into the university's alumni database.
   – Condensing or eliminating details on capital planning projects as they move forward for prioritization and approval by the university leadership.
   – Searching separate databases (e.g., bursar, financial aid, registration, student employment) when projecting and packaging student financial aid.

 – Designing and delivering first-year orientation programs through a loose confederation of representatives from academic affairs and student affairs.
 – Inadequate documentation of decision rules for investing in competing strategic priorities.

4. *Waste of irrelevant information.* The waste of irrelevant information occurs when the process is overburdened with unnecessary information that adds no value or results in inappropriate decisions or actions. Some examples of the waste of irrelevant information include
 – Senior leadership teams proposing solutions to poorly understood problems on the basis of an inadequate analysis of information.
 – Detailed weekly enrollment and budget reports requiring significant effort to compile, although only summary metrics are reviewed by leaders.
 – Overwhelming program review committees with large volumes of unsifted data that are forwarded by the academic units under review.
 – Confusing parents with bursar bills that include itemized transactions lacking explanatory detail.
 – Distributing university-wide enrollment and retention data to every college and program using a "generic" internal mailing list.

5. *Waste of inaccurate information.* The waste of inaccurate information occurs when time and effort are needed to correct information or mitigate the consequences of using incorrect information as part of a process. Some examples of the waste of inaccurate information include
 – Requiring early study abroad enrollment projections for budget planning well before students make a commitment to participate in the program.
 – Recording inaccurate student financial aid information that results in incorrect student billings and prevents students from participating in available work study programs.
 – Inaccurate information provided by faculty members on book orders that delays the availability of course materials to students and unnecessary book returns/reorders by the university bookstore.
 – Inaccurate information on course enrollments provided by the course registration system that requires unnecessary manual verification of enrollments by staff and mistaken decisions to open and close course sections.
 – Out-of-date donor records, which requires staff to look up current addresses for mailings returned to the university as undeliverable.

Asset waste. *Asset waste* refers to the cluster of wastes that occurs when the university does not use its resources (human, facilities, and materials) in the most effective manner. Four specific types of asset waste can be identified.

1. *Waste of overproduction and inventory.* The waste of overproduction and inventory occurs when there is an oversupply of resources stockpiled for a process, when steps or products are completed before they can be used at the next point in the process, or the output of the process exceeds what is needed. Some examples of the waste of overproduction and inventory include
   - Academic units submitting large batches of graduate student applications that overwhelm the graduate college's ability to process them as quickly as expected by each unit's graduate admissions committee.
   - Bulk campus-wide purchasing of copier paper requiring climate-controlled storage and on-demand redistribution by university staff.
   - Discarding local stockpiles of university travel reimbursement and other forms when updates are issued.
   - Distributing documents to committee members prior to meetings and bringing duplicate printed sets of the documents to the meeting.
   - Discarding bulk printings of admissions and academic program brochures that are quickly outdated due to personnel and programmatic changes.
2. *Waste of unnecessary transport.* The waste of unnecessary transport occurs when materials, information, and people travel greater distances or more often than needed. Some examples of the waste of unnecessary transport include
   - Physically retrieving older credit and noncredit course registration records stored at an off-site location when requested to verify the completion of coursework.
   - Scheduling meetings in locations convenient for the committee chair that require considerable travel for the committee members.
   - Transporting plant bedding mulch to multiple locations throughout the campus from a remote bulk storage location.
   - Faculty and staff walking from their offices to a centralized location for printing, duplicating, and faxing.
   - Assigning available research and office space across campus to accommodate expanding academic units.

3. *Waste of fixed assets.* The waste of fixed assets occurs when land, physical plant facilities, and equipment are used inefficiently. Some examples of the waste of fixed assets include
   - Withholding revenue-generating campus rooms from the available inventory to accommodate possible last-minute needs of the university's senior leadership.
   - Incurring increased utility, security, and cleaning expenses by distributing the small number of evening classes across multiple academic classroom buildings.
   - Permanently assigning research space to individual faculty members.
   - Holding university-sponsored workshops and events in rented community facilities because of lower cost, accessible parking, and better customer service.
   - Maintaining a large classroom inventory to meet high-demand teaching times based on faculty preferences.
4. *Waste of overburdening people, equipment, and facilities.* The waste of overburdening people, equipment, and facilities taxes people beyond their physical, psychological, and emotional limits and physical resources beyond their natural and safe limits. Some examples of the waste of overburdening people, equipment, and facilities include
   - Diverting capital improvement funds from high-priority projects to cover repair costs for residence halls well beyond their life expectancy.
   - University employees acting in unsafe manners to complete facility repairs quickly or inexpensively.
   - Understaffing reception and help desks during peak periods.
   - Faculty are mandated to assume more extensive advising responsibilities without a concomitant reduction in other responsibilities.
   - Students declining to pursue a grade appeal because they perceive the process to be long, unclear, and contentious.

7.1.2 Summary

Every university process includes waste. Some waste can be easily identified and removed, but much of the waste is well hidden within the process, making it difficult to find and eliminate.[9] From the perspective of offices or individuals who are beneficiaries of a process, waste adds time and cost for which they are expected to pay. The waste of waiting—for unreturned phone calls, for an appointment with an advisor, for approval to teach a new course, for approval to do research with human subjects—does nothing to provide beneficiaries of the process with what they want and consumes their uncompensated time and energy. The waste of motion—when employees are busily searching for files, filling out forms, moving from desk to file cabinet to copying machine and back again—gives the illusion of hard work and effectiveness. But if their actions add no value to the process, and are simply responses to other types of waste (e.g., reentering information on online forms that is already available within the system), they are pure waste. The waste of correction—having to repeat a process because of an error made the first time—requires beneficiaries to experience the original waste-ridden process yet again. In addition, this waste consumes precious university resources that could be reinvested in more important activities that enhance the success of the institution. Finally, waste can contribute to a toxic work environment. Employees recognize waste for what it is, and with neither a voice nor course of action for removing it, find it difficult to be and feel successful.[10] Furthermore, beneficiaries of the process recognize waste, and are equally frustrated—they are wasting their valuable time and are ultimately paying for the additional costs that all types of waste contribute to the process.

The framework and definitions of waste presented above can serve as a useful tool for helping LHE Project Team members recognize waste where it occurs. The examples provided for each of the twenty-six specific types of waste in four general categories (people, process, information, and asset waste) underscore the ubiquitous nature of waste, and the direct and indirect costs of this waste to the beneficiaries of the process, the faculty and staff involved in the process, and to the university. By reviewing the framework and examples, LHE Project Team members may be more able to identify and evaluate waste in the "current state" description of the process that is the focus of the LHE initiative underway. Overall, this framework can provide a common vocabulary for all those involved and serves as a tool to help LHE team members recognize the many forms of waste present in higher education processes. It is not important that LHE team members correctly classify the waste they observe into one of the 26 types of waste, or whether additional types of waste unique to higher education are missing from this extensive framework. What is important is that LHE team members have a practical "mental model" that is useful for recognizing incidences of waste where they occur, identifying their root causes, and implementing LHE solutions to eliminate them. Eliminating waste will mean more value to the beneficiary, satisfaction and pride to university employees, and increased effectiveness for the university.

7.2 Eliminating Waste from University Processes

7.2.1 Identifying the Root Causes of Waste

LHE views waste as pervasive symptoms of less-than-effective processes (and, by extension, less-than-effective universities). Identifying and understanding the root causes of these wastes will assist the LHE Project Team in diagnosing the underlying source of the waste and implementing the precise solution to eliminate the waste permanently, contributing to the overall success of the LHE initiative.[11] Choosing, or creating, the best solution clearly depends on the correct diagnosis of the problem. Getting to the root causes of waste is important to the success of LHE.

One very valuable Lean tool that can help identify root causes of waste is the "Five Why" technique. Where waste is identified, LHE Project Team members can ask employees the question "why" this waste occurred and listen to the answer, repeating the question up to five times to gain insight into the potential root cause of this particular type of waste. The following exchange demonstrates how the "Five Why" technique can help determine the root cause of the waste of correction that surfaced in the university's travel reimbursement process:

> **Why** *did you return the travel reimbursement form to the traveler?*
> The total amount listed was incorrect.
> **Why** *was the total amount listed incorrect?*
> The per diem rate for meals was calculated incorrectly.
> **Why** *was the per diem rate calculated incorrectly?*
> The reimbursement rate from the wrong year was used.
> **Why** *was the reimbursement rate from the wrong year used?*
> The traveler did not have the current form that included the per diem rate for meals.
> **Why** *did the traveler not have the current per diem rate form?*
> The new per diem rate was announced but the new form was not distributed.

The root causes of waste may reflect a number of core challenges: lack of training, inadequacies in current systems and business practices, outdated tools and technology, poor office layout, failure to establish standardized work, failure to specify roles and responsibilities, failure to specify and monitor critical measures of performance, and more.[12] Identifying these root causes will help the LHE Project Team recommend targeted solutions (in this example, to the travel reimbursement process) specific to the underlying causes of waste. An LHE solution has a greater likelihood of success of permanently eradicating waste and improving flow when its true underlying cause is also identified and eliminated.

7.2.2 LHE Solutions for Eliminating Waste

Once identified, the LHE Project Team can propose recommendations to immediately remove or reduce many instances of waste found in a process. However, even when identified, not all waste can be eliminated easily.[13] For example, the LHE team may uncover that, as part of a student scholarship application process, students complete numerous scholarship applications that overlap considerably in the types of student information collected. Each independent application requires students to provide highly redundant information across the different application forms. The LHE team can propose eliminating this "waste of irrelevant information" by introducing a common scholarship application. The core of this common application, completed once by students, contains the majority of information needed to process applications for a wide variety of available scholarships; student can then complete supplementary sections of the form that are specific to required criteria by one or more of the scholarships for which they choose to apply. In contrast, some university processes may include clear examples of waste that are an integral activity or effort in the process with no immediate possibility for reducing or removing it. For example, a university process for appealing a campus parking violation may require that a form be completed describing the circumstance and basis for appeal, which is then discussed by a university-wide appeals committee at its next scheduled committee meeting. Because it is impractical to have the committee meet on a daily basis to discuss the appeal in a timely manner (i.e., significantly reducing the "waste of waiting"), the completed appeal will languish until the next meeting of the committee. Thus, while the goal of LHE is to reduce or eliminate all waste from a process, some types of waste may be less amenable to elimination or reduction (but can be revisited in the future).

Solutions for eliminating or reducing waste are unlimited. Specific solutions will depend on the knowledge and experiences of LHE Project Team members, the unique characteristics of the university process, the history and culture of the university, available communication and information technologies, knowledge of the existing Lean literature, and the creativity of LHE team members. As such, there is no comprehensive set of prescriptive LHE solutions guaranteed to reduce or eliminate certain forms of waste in every situation. Many solutions for eliminating waste come from successful interventions shared by Lean practitioners in published writings, on community-of-interest Web sites, and so on. Other solutions come from the growing list of *in situ* insights and recommendations of university employees and the representative members of cross-functional LHE Project Teams (see Chapter 3). For example, the visual mapping process for student visits at the BGSU student health center found that medical professionals were spending unnecessary time escorting students to the lab (e.g., for blood work) and pharmacy (e.g., to have prescriptions filled) because students were assumed to have difficulty finding their way around the center. The LHE team addressed this "waste of motion" by providing simple and visible wayfinding instructions (e.g., color-painted footprints or different-colored striping of hallway walls to show the direct path to each location). Adopting the general Lean practice of clear visual systems,[14] the LHE team proposed a novel solution for this situation to reduce the waste of motion by health professionals, allowing them to spend more time providing medical services more quickly to waiting clients.

Decades of Lean practice provide a large set of solutions that has been implemented to reduce or eliminate waste.[15] These LHE solutions are listed in Table 7.1. Some solutions may be appropriate for reducing or eliminating waste in all four categories (i.e., people, process, information, and asset waste). For example, *"Establish employee goals for identifying and implementing ongoing process improvements"* could help reduce or eliminate all four categories of waste as well as improve flow in university processes. Other potential LHE solutions may specifically target one of the four general categories of waste. For example, *"Eliminate temporary holding areas or storage locations"* is a solution that addresses the waste of unnecessary transport, a specific type of asset waste. Other solutions may be appropriate for eliminating or reducing several different types of waste. As an example, *"Implement error-proofing systems that reduce the physical and mental burden of constantly checking for common errors"* can reduce the waste of incorrect assignment (i.e., a specific type of people waste), waste of checking (i.e., a specific type of process waste), and waste of overburdening people, equipment, and facilities (i.e., a specific type of asset waste). For all these reasons, it is difficult to develop comprehensive lists of solutions for each specific type or category of waste. Thus, Table 7.1 presents an extensive, but by no means exhaustive, list of solutions to reduce or eliminate waste, organized around the four general categories of waste. This table may

Table 7.1 Potential Solutions for Eliminating or Reducing People, Process, Information, and Asset Waste

Potential Solution for Reducing or Eliminating Waste	People Waste	Process Waste	Information Waste	Asset Waste
Establish employee goals for identifying and implementing ongoing process improvements	X	X	X	X
Prioritize major university processes, and relocate/co-locate their supporting individuals and/or offices to minimize distances traveled and use staff skills and limited space more effectively	X	X	X	X
Create ad hoc teams to quickly address unanticipated and anticipated changes in demand, process bottlenecks, duplication of effort, information errors, and production timeliness/quality problems	X	X	X	X
Require workgroups to track and review errors daily, taking corrective actions as needed (e.g., standardized successive checking, error proofing, creating job aids) to prevent their occurrence the following day	X	X	X	X
Create and enforce standardized work (using group-developed and management approved "best-practices" protocol, clear visual and written job aids, etc.) for workgroup members to ensure that all steps and activities in the process are completed without interruption in a reliable and effective manner (i.e., specifying what they should do, how they should do it, and when they should do it)	X	X	X	X
Use visual display systems in workplace to post publicly "real-time" (e.g., every hour) group performance relative to expected standards that identify what types of problems (backlogs, errors) are occurring and where they need to be addressed in the process	X	X	X	X

Table 7.1   (continued) Potential Solutions for Eliminating or Reducing People, Process, Information, and Asset Waste

Potential Solution for Reducing or Eliminating Waste	People Waste	Process Waste	Information Waste	Asset Waste
Involve employees in problem and solution identification to reach better, consensus-driven decisions	X	X	X	X
Have employees conduct "Five Why" technique after a process error is identified	X	X	X	X
Develop suggestion programs that actively pursue employee recommendations to eliminate waste (and improve flow) in processes	X	X	X	X
Mandate employee training programs in areas critical to university success (e.g., determining and meeting the values and expectations of beneficiaries, the importance of cross-functional processes to university success, LHE training on reducing waste and improving flow in university processes, establishing and using performance metrics to improve processes)	X	X	X	X
Establish a daily management system where tasks planned for the day are reviewed and approved as consistent with goals	X	X	X	
Create, distribute, and require standardized templates for forms, memos, reports, presentations, and other common methods of communication	X	X	X	
Establish standards for clear, simple, and inexpensive communication (e.g., presentations, reports, spreadsheets) that focus on information content needed by beneficiaries rather than excessive formatting, design, and delivery	X	X	X	

—continued

Table 7.1 (continued) Potential Solutions for Eliminating or Reducing People, Process, Information, and Asset Waste

Potential Solution for Reducing or Eliminating Waste	People Waste	Process Waste	Information Waste	Asset Waste
Cross-train employees with broader skill sets and share them across workgroups and functional areas to provide support for processes that are understaffed (employees are absent or appropriately involved in other activities) or experience a sudden fluctuation in demand	X	X		X
Require equipment/machine operators to perform basic maintenance, freeing up maintenance staff for more involved maintenance activities (e.g., equipment overhauls and upgrades)	X	X		X
Ensure that equipment, supplies, space, etc. are available to staff	X	X		X
Reduce as much as possible the number of times products, inventory, materials, are moved	X	X		X
Use "spaghetti diagrams" to create physical workplace map of provider or beneficiary movement throughout the process to identify wasted unnecessary motion	X	X		X
Implement error-proofing systems that reduce the physical and mental burden of constantly checking for common errors	X	X		X
Centralize locations of shared office equipment to minimize motion	X	X		X
Purchase additional printers, copiers, fax machines, etc. for individual workstations to reduce motion	X	X		X
Purchase machines that do not need to be "attended," thus allowing employees to do other tasks while printer, copier, fax machine, etc. are cycling	X	X		X

Table 7.1 (continued) Potential Solutions for Eliminating or Reducing People, Process, Information, and Asset Waste

Potential Solution for Reducing or Eliminating Waste	People Waste	Process Waste	Information Waste	Asset Waste
Clearing computers, desktops, and workplaces of materials that are not needed	X		X	X
Level workload and workflow throughout day/week to synchronize with the availability of staff resources required to provide the process	X	X		
Review all steps in process and eliminate unnecessary signatures	X	X		
Create self-contained work "cells" that can accommodate reduced or higher levels of staffing in quick response to demand for products and services	X	X		
Arrange files (physical, desktop icons and files) based on frequency of use	X	X		
Establish more frequent delivery runs among departments or offices, based on amount of time or accumulated material/information, to reduce waiting time for goods, information, materials, etc.	X	X		
Include all offices that are part of the process or service when deciding about changes in software, technology, etc. to achieve the best decision from the perspective of the beneficiary	X	X		
Create and post visual job aids in the workplace	X	X		
Create alignment of quantifiable and measurable goals that cascade from the highest to lowest levels of the university	X		X	
Establish contingency plans that put unexpected idle time to good use (training, error proofing, workplace organization, maintenance, LHE rapid improvement workshops)	X			X

—continued

Table 7.1 (continued) Potential Solutions for Eliminating or Reducing People, Process, Information, and Asset Waste

Potential Solution for Reducing or Eliminating Waste	People Waste	Process Waste	Information Waste	Asset Waste
Reduce as much as possible the distance over which products, materials, information, etc. are moved throughout the process		X	X	X
Eliminate unnecessary and/or inaccurate information used by employees		X	X	X
Establish clear objective performance metrics and expected standards of performance for workgroups that align with the needs or demands of beneficiaries		X	X	
Standardize physical and electronic filing systems to provide ease of locating, sharing, and storing of information		X	X	
Employ a "5S" system (Sort and remove items, Set in order, Shine and clean equipment, Standardize where equipment is placed, and Sustain orderliness over time) to create and maintain a clean and orderly workplace		X		X
Establish work flow sequence and/or amount of work (e.g., lot size) sent "downstream" to other individuals and offices that is appropriate for the overall efficiency of the process		X		X
Establish signal devices that trigger the initiation of a process as needed by the beneficiary or other "downstream" offices and individuals		X		X
Limit consideration of any new technology to that which is reliable, well tested, and improves the process from the perspective of the beneficiary		X		X
Produce or deliver only enough to meet the needs of the "downstream" beneficiary		X		X

Table 7.1   (continued) Potential Solutions for Eliminating or Reducing People, Process, Information, and Asset Waste

Potential Solution for Reducing or Eliminating Waste	People Waste	Process Waste	Information Waste	Asset Waste
Ensure that work is delivered to the next step in the process when it is ready to be received		X		X
Adjust delivery schedules among departments and offices based on the needs of processes rather than a fixed, arbitrary timetable		X		X
Reduce batch sizes of products, accumulated requests, etc. so that they are performed in a more frequent and timely fashion		X		
Build in quality expectations and accountability at the source (i.e., the employee who performs that activity or step in the process)		X		
Create self-contained work "cells" by combining separate functional process steps		X		
Implement the temporary or permanent use of quality circles and Six Sigma strategies to confront difficult quality issues		X		
Reduce the required setup or transition time that takes place when switching from one step or activity to another		X		
Adopt and commit to a long-term philosophy that places the needs and expectations of beneficiaries, staff, and mission ahead of short-term financial goals (e.g., "Never make an incorrect decision or ship a defective part.")		X		
Color code as much as possible		X		

—continued

Table 7.1 (continued) Potential Solutions for Eliminating or Reducing People, Process, Information, and Asset Waste

Potential Solution for Reducing or Eliminating Waste	People Waste	Process Waste	Information Waste	Asset Waste
Establish and follow standard format (e.g., single sheet of A3 size paper) for sharing key background information and recommendations with decision makers			X	
Enlist or assign responsibility for determining information needs to employees who have significant roles in that process			X	
Continually collect information from current and prospective internal and external beneficiaries about what they want or expect from a process			X	
Establish a preventive maintenance program				X
Apply methods for workplace organization and tool layout to eliminate unnecessary space needs and reduce physical exertion				X
Eliminate temporary holding areas or storage locations				X

provide a useful point of departure for LHE Project Team members, stimulating their thinking to develop new solutions tailored to their unique setting and circumstances to reduce or eliminate waste in the targeted process.

The overlapping lists of suggestions for reducing or eliminating people, process, information, and asset waste presented here provide a sense of the breadth of possible LHE solutions available. These solutions can be used individually, combined together to create new and novel solutions, and used to help stimulate additional, alternative solutions to improve processes within higher education. Some solutions can be implemented easily, while other solutions will introduce significant change to the current process. Additional solutions to reduce or eliminate waste will come from the creativity and ingenuity of LHE Project Team members. Experience has shown that a well-designed LHE team, including cross-functional team members with hands-on experience in the process being examined, will craft unique solutions that are well-suited for their specific situation.

7.3 Improving Flow in University Processes

Flow occurs when the steps or activities of a process occur without interruption across individuals and offices. Unfortunately, many of our everyday experiences lack flow: obtaining a driver's license, visiting the doctor's office, waiting for an airport shuttle bus to fill before it leaves the terminal, refinancing a mortgage, dropping off a child at summer camp, and applying for a job. The ubiquitous presence of poor flow—treating us as groups rather than individuals, a belief that waiting is acceptable, failing to focus on poor handoffs between individuals and offices that provide a service—have resigned us to accept processes as they are. In stark contrast, a top priority of universities that adopt LHE is to bring smooth flow to all processes, providing a competitive advantage over other institutions that results in more satisfied beneficiaries as well as increased efficiency and effectiveness. LHE strives to provide "continuous flow,"[16] where a request for a process initiated by a single beneficiary (e.g., student, faculty member, parent) triggers an immediate start to the process, which then proceeds smoothly and without interruption until the process is completed and the expectations of the beneficiary have been met. The antithesis of continuous flow is "batch and queue," where beneficiaries wait while their individual requests are bundled into small or large batches and then move unpredictably as a group through each step or activity to the next through the process. Even when the size of the batch is small, the university pays little or no attention to creating a smooth flow between individuals and offices across the steps or activities of the process.

There is no shortage of opportunities for converting university processes from batch and queue to continuous flow. For example, the placement testing and course registration process for incoming freshmen is frequently a batch process: Freshmen complete placement tests in batches, placement tests are scored in batches, and freshmen then wait in batches for an appointment with an advisor to select their courses. The university staff and offices supporting these batched activities are conscientious and hardworking. They recognize the importance of moving their own batched step or activity through the process quickly and accurately; failure to do so will create significant bottlenecks that delay employees and offices downstream from performing their jobs (e.g., a delay in scoring placement tests will delay advisor appointments for course registration). But even when the batch process is completed as designed, the beneficiaries (i.e., new freshmen and their families) are required to start, stop, and wait as each batched step or activity makes its way through the process. From the perspective of the beneficiary—the most important perspective in LHE—the process does not flow and falls short of what they value and expect. Many other university processes provide additional examples of poor flow: admissions and financial aid applications, preregistration advising, student grade and disciplinary appeals, prioritizing and funding local capital improvements, accumulated in-basket items, monthly budget reconciliation and reports, and thank-you letters to donors.

Teaching, one of the primary processes at a university, provides a provocative example for the rethinking of flow in higher education. The current model of starting and finishing courses at certain times during the year reflects batch processing. Historically, a common beginning and ending date may have been necessary for face-to-face instruction and the most effective use of faculty and facilities. The advent of online learning with Web-based (and Web-centric) courses may provide a technological opportunity that allows for improved flow (and providing what current and prospective students value and expect). Continuous flow would be found in flexibly scheduled courses that allow a student to enroll at almost any point in time and work at his or her own pace toward the completion of course requirements. Students would begin based on their own needs and finish once they demonstrate that they have fulfilled the learning objectives. Continuous flow in the teaching process would deliver great value for nontraditional learners such as shift workers, parents of young children, full-time employees who travel, and other students whose schedules are constrained by time and location. Of course, the shift from batch and queue to continuous flow would redefine some traditional aspects of a faculty member's job as well as the historic notion of fixed academic semesters. Open minds and an open dialogue would set the stage for discussions that redefine expectations of faculty who participate in these online alternatives (e.g., focusing on the number of credit hours of instruction offered during the year rather than the number of courses taught during each semester), assess completion of learning objectives, and create a transcript without semesters.

Overall, the continuous flow of financial transactions, hiring faculty, purchasing goods and services, scheduling classes, approving academic workshops, and many more university processes can be improved through both the reduction and elimination of waste as well as specific efforts to create smooth, uninterrupted flow. It is worth noting that LHE Project Team efforts to improve flow are likely to surface additional forms of waste in the process that batch and queue often hide. For example, the failure of employees who fail to complete their step or activity in a continuous flow process will have immediate and important consequences for every downstream person or office, resulting in efforts to diagnose and correct the causes of this failure.

7.3.1 LHE Solutions to Improve Flow

LHE Project Teams can use three general techniques to understand and diagnose the causes of poor flow prior to implementing solutions designed to improve or create continuous flow.[17] First, LHE team members should carefully follow the person (or form, application, request, proposal, etc.) as it physically travels through the steps or activities of the process. By never losing sight of its movement from the beginning to the end of the process, the LHE team will be able to pinpoint with accuracy when and where flow is interrupted. Second, LHE team members should disregard the traditional constraints on flow imposed by existing job responsibilities, department or functional turf issues, and employee classification and contract requirements when contemplating possibilities for eliminating impediments to continuous flow. One useful alternative is for the LHE team to begin with a blank sheet of paper and draw a continuously flowing process rather than reformulating the existing process step by step. Finally, the LHE team should thoroughly review and rethink each step or activity, all communication and information loops, technology expectations, and work equipment and layout issues that have the potential to impede continuous flow in any new or revised alternative. For example, many specific types of waste discussed earlier in this chapter interrupt continuous flow (waiting, checking, inaccurate information, unnecessary transport, etc.). Together, these three techniques can aid LHE teams as they work to understand and diagnose flow.

Decades of Lean practice have also identified a number of potential tools that help move university processes toward the goal of smooth, continuous flow.[18]

Timeprint performance measures. Timeprint performance measures provide objective estimates of times required of individual steps or activities in a process. Understanding these metrics helps the LHE Project Team members focus their improvement efforts on those steps and activities that most impede continuous flow, and introduces changes that synchronize the available capacity of the process with corresponding demand. That is, knowing the time required to provide one uninterrupted unit of service (e.g., college advising appointment) or individual product (e.g., transcript request) for a beneficiary allows the LHE team to determine whether the process "pipeline" can accommodate expected demand and, if not, what steps or activities should be modified or what additional resources are needed to deliver continuous flow. Space limitation precludes a detailed description of all timeprint performance indicators.[19] Some commonly used measures include *interval time* (the actual time needed to complete a single process), *cycle time* (the theoretical time available to complete a single process without interruption, commonly referred to as "takt" time), and *beneficiary lead-time* (the time that elapses between a beneficiary requesting a process and having that need met). For example, the LHE team may calculate an average cycle time of 90 minutes for a student employee at the university library to sort and shelve 10 linear feet of books and journals returned by patrons. In reality, the interval time for this activity may typically require 150 minutes of student labor due to waste and poor flow (e.g., patrons interrupt student workers with requests during the sorting and shelving of materials, student workers self-determine their sorting method and their travel path when shelving materials). Furthermore, the LHE team may calculate a beneficiary lead-time of 6 hours (i.e., the time between when a book or journal is returned and shelved). These timeprint performance measures can be used to identify shortcomings in the process that impede continuous flow, thereby reducing interval time (requiring fewer student hours to sort and shelve materials) and beneficiary lead-time (ensuring library materials are available as soon as possible to minimize the time library patrons spend searching for unshelved materials identified as available for loan). As a second example, the LHE team can determine if available resources are adequate for providing a continuous flow based on known need or demand. If twice as many materials are returned on Monday than on any other day of the week, staffing levels for student employees to sort and shelve should be increased that day to provide a continuous flow of returned materials to the library stacks and avoid backlogs.

Just in Time. Just in Time (JIT) facilitates a smooth flow in a process when any upstream step in the process is performed at exactly the right time and in the right amount as needed by the next person or office in the process. For example, budget administrators receive monthly electronic or print budget reports even though they may prefer budget information on more personalized schedules (e.g., after there has been activity in a low-activity account; every 3 months for the first three quarters of the budget year and then every month as the budget year comes to a close). JIT can be used to meet the needs of the next person or office downstream, minimize inventories (which need to be moved and stored, take up space, and may become outdated), and prevent process bottlenecks (by not overwhelming the next person or office downstream with more work than it wants or can handle). JIT solutions usually include some combination of creating "pull systems" and introducing "demand leveling."

Pull systems. Most university processes produce services or goods according to some planned schedule based on projected (i.e., *not* actual) demand or when it is convenient for university employees (i.e., *not* beneficiaries) to do so. For example,

- Student employees are asked to assemble and stockpile packets of information—even if those packets may not be needed before the materials become out-of-date or obsolete.
- University painters unnecessarily paint additional rooms in an academic building because they are already there anyway—even if other spaces in other buildings are left waiting to have their high-priority painting completed.
- The university bookstore intentionally over-orders logo wear items because of the price break on larger orders—even if storage space is a problem and there is no guarantee that the item will remain in fashion for an extended period of time.
- An advisor contacts advisees to come in for advising appointments during hours that are blocked out at times convenient for the advisor's schedule—even if the times are inconvenient for the student.

These hypothetical scenarios that keep employees busy and maximize the use of equipment and space, often in the name of efficiency, reflect "push systems." Push systems are antithetical to pure flow, when services and goods are delivered only when, exactly when, and in the exact amount needed. Unfortunately, most processes operate as "push systems," where people, materials, and information are forwarded to the next downstream person or office without regard to their need or readiness. In contrast, pull systems respond to requests of exactly what is needed (no more, no less, and no sooner) by the downstream person or office. Creating pull systems helps prioritize work to provide exactly what the next step in the process requires, creating a smooth flow matched to the actual demand as "pulled" by the final beneficiary of the process. In addition, visual tools are often included to serve as a signal or authorization from the downstream individual or office of their need or readiness for work. For example, wall racks that hold exactly two student case folders can be built for each medical provider in the student health center. This visual system would set a goal of having one folder in the rack (i.e., one student waiting for the medical provider). The absence of a folder would indicate that the medical providers are ready to "pull" another case for them to see, whereas the presence of two folders would direct the staff to "push" no more cases to this provider at this time. This JIT system would minimize waiting time for students that might occur if student cases were assigned on a rotating (or even more arbitrary) basis to each medical provider.

As a second example, prepared stacks of university public relations material sent to local public libraries could include a self-addressed postcard inserted three-fourths of the way into the pile. When the postcard comes to the top of the pile, it can be placed in the mail by library staff to serve as a signal to the university's public relations office to send replacement materials to the library as they are needed. As a final example, custodial supply closets can be stocked at appropriate levels by including a removable tag on each cleaning supply item. The custodians remove item tags as they withdraw supplies, placing the tag in a transparent envelope attached to the closet door. The custodial supervisors collect these tags during their visits each shift, with the tags providing the exact amount of supplies needed (i.e., no missing supplies, no excess inventory).

Demand leveling. Matching the availability of university resources with the needs of beneficiaries provides processes when needed and without wait. Demand leveling removes the variability of demand over time as it flows through a process; the process can then accommodate this predictable flow of work in a smooth and efficient manner. Demand leveling prevents the process from providing beneficiaries with what they need before they need it as well as overwhelming the process with requests that cannot be met (creating a backlog or queue that delays the completion of later steps and activities). By calculating workload flow over some appropriate time (e.g., day, week, month), the LHE Project Team can identify peaks and valleys of activity and implement demand leveling to provide a smoother, more continuous flow of activity at all times. For example, promoting walk-in appointments at the student counseling center during a less busy time of day (or day of the week) will direct demand away from peak time periods where the staff is overwhelmed and toward time periods where staffing levels are underutilized. As a second example, the LHE team could provide incentives (e.g., smaller class sizes, discount on course textbooks) to entice students to sign up for scheduled morning courses when classrooms are in greater supply, reducing the need for adding additional classroom spaces during peak early and late afternoon periods.

Theoretically, JIT would have the university's internal or external printing services print a single application form each time the admissions office receives an inquiry,[20] dining services would order a food item just as it is needed, and college advisors would be on call for only those hours where they are needed. In practice, JIT is more difficult to achieve, requiring some compromise. For example, pull systems permit some limited stockpiling of resources (staff hours, physical materials) beyond immediate demand and the ability to meet it. Thus, small lots of admission applications are available, dining services maintains a small inventory of food items, and full-time advisors are hired based on an accurate projection of demand (i.e., the number of enrolled students). These are imperfect solutions because overproduction and inventory is waste (it takes up space while being stored, it requires transport from storage to the location where it is used, it can be lost or damaged in storage, and it can become out of date). But realistic accommodations are likely in the early stages of LHE to ensure that a process provides what is expected by the beneficiaries until additional LHE solutions can be found and applied to further improve flow.

Working to pacemaker. The time to complete the individual steps or activities directly influences the flow of a process. The "pacemaker" is the step or activity that takes the longest time, and serves to control how smooth the overall flow will be. Specifically, steps or activities that *precede* the pacemaker and are completed more quickly than the pacemaker will queue up behind the slower pacemaker step or activity; steps or activities that *follow* the pacemaker and are completed more quickly than the pacemaker must wait for the pacemaker to pass along work. For example, the admissions process for transfer students includes a number of steps: admissions application, transcript review for course transfer, academic advising, course registration, financial aid packaging, obtaining student ID card, e-mail/course management system access, and so on. The step or activity that takes the longest time (after removing as much waste as possible) becomes the pacemaker and controls how quickly student applications can flow through the admissions process. If the pacemaker cannot be divided into smaller steps or activities to reduce the amount of time required to complete it (and thus speed up the flow of the process), the flow of steps before and after the pacemaker step would be adjusted (e.g., by having one individual take combined responsibility for several short steps that require a combined amount of time equal to the pacemaker). Matching all steps and activities in the admissions process to the time required by the pacemaker helps create "one person" flow: Applicants or their applications flow smoothly, one at a time, to the next step or activity in the process at the exact time it is ready to help.

Mistake proofing. Mistake proofing improves flow by preventing mistakes (e.g., incomplete or incorrect information on forms, missing attachments or approvals, calculation errors) that interrupt a process or compound errors as people, materials, or information move to the next downstream person or office activity. Mistake proofing eliminates the need for re-work (e.g., returning it to the previous step or activity for correction, performing additional and unplanned work to correct the problem) that interrupts flow, and avoids waste associated with the unnecessary quality control checks in the process.[21] Standardized work is an example of a mistake-proofing technique that prescribes clear standards for how a step or activity should be performed based on best practices, trains employees to error-free performance, and implements methods to prevent deviations in performance from flowing downstream.[22] An example of mistake proofing is using an online travel reimbursement template that cannot be submitted until all required information is provided (available from drop down menus) and which automatically calculates reimbursement totals. A second example is providing a structured interview guide for financial aid counselors who receive calls from parents requesting adjustments to their students' financial aid packages, assuring that all relevant information for the appeal is gathered and processed quickly.

Co-locating steps and activities and establishing work cells. Co-locating steps and activities and establishing work cells permit the smooth and efficient completion of an entire process within a contained physical area. The visual map developed by an LHE Project Team can provide great insights into the current physical flow of people, materials, or information across sequential steps and activities in the process, suggesting ways to bring them more closely together to improve flow. Implementing cross-functional work cells (i.e., a self-contained workgroup that is completely responsible for an entire process) supports an uninterrupted flow by reducing or eliminating many types of waste: overproduction and inventory, transport, correcting errors, and information loss due to hand-offs. Work cells are staffed to accommodate typical levels of demand by beneficiaries, but their size or number can be increased as needed to provide continuous flow during predictable and temporary peak periods. One example of co-locating activities is offering all necessary services together in a single location during the new freshman move-in process to assist students and their families with their needs (e.g., bursar payments, financial aid questions, health insurance, course scheduling changes) in a "one-stop-shop" approach. One example of an effective work cell is where each staff member in the research service office is able to provide complete services (budget development, proposal review, Institutional Review Board approval, compliance requirements) for any faculty member submitting a research grant proposal.

5S program. A 5S program, introduced earlier as a solution to reduce waste in processes, can help LHE Project Teams improve flow. A clean and orderly workplace helps smooth out each employee's contribution to the process:

- *Sort and remove.* The workplace is free of distracting and error-causing clutter (e.g., the employee's desk is cleared of irrelevant materials, which might be included by mistake in the current step or activity of the process).
- *Set in order.* Work materials are set out in an order that enhances flow (e.g., forms are laid out from left to right in the order in which they are assembled into a packet).
- *Shine and clean equipment.* Equipment is in working order and well maintained (e.g., desktop computer programs and the hard drive organization for finding and saving files are easily understood and match the task at hand).
- *Standardize.* Shared equipment is always returned to its proper location immediately after it is used (e.g., student files are withdrawn as they are needed and immediately replaced).
- *Sustain orderliness over time.* There is a commitment to maintaining a clean and orderly workplace (e.g., a checklist for cleaning and organizing the workplace is available, and it is used each week during the first available 30-minute block when there is no pressing demand for service).

For example, the department for sociology's undergraduate advising office could use 5S to create individual file drawers corresponding to the type of beneficiaries served (e.g., prospective undergraduate student visiting campus, sociology majors and minors, non-majors and minors). Hanging folders are organized based on the most "popular" items requested/provided; the same framework is used to design their Web page, desktop icons, and intranet filing system. Additional materials for assembling personalized packets of materials are nearby and readily available, and a multipurpose printer/scanner/copier/fax will allow the office to gather, copy, send, etc. additional information as needed. As file drawer materials are depleted, a reorder request form comes to the surface to automatically trigger a request to replenish materials.

Visual control systems. Visual control systems are clear and public displays that provide, at a glance, information on how process steps and activities should be completed by individuals and offices, as well as feedback on whether or not the work outcomes of any step or activity deviate from established standard.[23] One example of a visual control system to encourage employees to follow agreed-upon best practices is posting a visual description of how work should be done along with an exemplar of work that was completed correctly. The system can also highlight deviation from standards by posting a visual indication of the cumulative number of currently completed transactions for the day alongside the number of completed transactions expected at that point in time. This information of deviation from schedule can trigger assistance and troubleshooting support to avoid falling behind schedule or getting ahead of schedule, both of which can create bottlenecks that impede the flow of processes.

As a second example, a visual control system can be designed to assist student employees who do room setup for events held in the student union. Specific diagrams for each room setup can be provided (including a clear listing of the types and numbers of tables, chairs, etc.), with nearly invisible floor markings in each room corresponding to markings on the diagram provided to the setup crew. The space scheduling office can have a visual posting of each room setup, including the time that setup should be started and completed, which crew is responsible, and spaces for the crew to indicate that the setup task has been started and completed. The supervisor and other crews can easily track when a setup is falling behind schedule, reallocating resources to get back on track. A final example is attaching silhouettes of required office equipment in appropriate locations so that the tools needed to complete the step or activity are always available and easy to locate.

FIFO Lanes. It is very difficult to match perfectly the flow in any process (i.e., the upstream person completes her task at the exact time the downstream person becomes available to receive it). "First In, First Out" (FIFO) Lanes improve flow even when intractable waste due to waiting cannot be eliminated from a process by creating a storage buffer for small amounts of work in process without creating extensive waiting or excessive inventory. FIFO Lanes ensure that people, information, and materials that are first to enter the process are also the first to be completed by the next individual or office downstream. The FIFO Lane might allow for a maximum capacity of three people or forms, providing a visual control that alerts all employees involved in the process when unacceptable amounts of waiting are occurring and need to be addressed (e.g., through an automatic reassignment of employees who are cross-trained to assist this step or activity in the process). Thus, when upstream employees in the process observe the signal that the FIFO Lane is beyond acceptable capacity, they stop performing their step or activity (which is only adding to the queue) and assist the downstream person until the FIFO Lane is once again within established limits. An application of a FIFO Lane might be the on-site registration process for a noncredit conference where attendees are completing registration forms, making payment, preparing name badges, applying for continuing education units, receiving conference materials, and so forth. The LHE Project Team might implement a FIFO Lane that allows registrants to flow smoothly through each station of the process in the order in which they arrived, and a predetermined queue at any step would automatically trigger assistance from the staff working in the immediately preceding upstream step. A second example is developing a FIFO Lane for processing charitable donations by the advancement office. An inbox system would be created so that the first donation received becomes the first donation to be entered into the system, the first to receive a thank-you letter and gift receipt, and the first donor profile updated (i.e., making sure that the inbox is processed from the bottom of the pile rather than the top). When materials accumulating in any inbox begin to exceed the predetermined limits (e.g., limiting the number of available slots in the inbox so that an "overflow" signal is sent when all the slots are full), employees at the immediately preceding upstream step or activity stop their work and help reduce the queue to an acceptable level. As a final example, employees involved in the "primary care" process (i.e., sick visits) at the student health center may decide that the in-house lab should be set up as a FIFO Lane, with an understanding that no more than three students should be in the lab queue waiting for their lab work to be completed. When the lab technician signals that the FIFO Lane is overloaded, one of the assigned upstream medical professionals (i.e., nurse practitioner or medical doctor) stops his or her work and assists the lab technician until the FIFO Lane is back to acceptable levels. By shifting resources to correct an overload of the FIFO Lane, student flow through the primary care process can continue.

Changeover time reduction. Chapter 5 introduced changeover time as a performance metric reflecting the amount of time needed by employees to transition from one work step or activity to another in order to complete their contributions to a process.[24] Changeover time can include the time needed to make a physical change in equipment (e.g., changing from white to colored paper in the copier machine; reconfiguring a printer to print addressed envelopes; toggling back and forth between computer programs) and the investment of time needed to resume a step or activity that was set aside temporarily (e.g., resuming an analysis of a budget after waiting several days for confirmation on information contained in the spreadsheet; returning to a course modification from 3 months ago that was just returned with concerns that need to be addressed; re-reviewing documents and arguments for a policy discussion that was deferred to a later date because of time constraints). Both the number of changeovers and the time required to complete each physical or mental changeover are disruptive to process flow. LHE Project Teams can look for ways to reduce changeover time to improve process flow.

As an example, the LHE Project Team may discover that advancement office staff regularly open and close multiple databases (donor, alumni, current students, public records) throughout the day because having multiple databases open bogs down their computers. This results in a significant changeover time (verification and sign-in to the secured server each time a database is accessed) and leads them to update records in batches (i.e., accumulate changes needed to a data set and make them all the next time the data set is open). With a goal of creating one person flow, the LHE team identifies several alternatives to minimize or eliminate the number and length of changeover times: purchasing more powerful computers that allow multiple programs to run simultaneously without diminishing processing speed, providing staff with multiple computers or dual monitors, writing an interface that integrates updates between different databases, or purchasing a single, integrated software system.[25] Work computers could also be programmed to have multiple startup screens, each uniquely designed to provide simple navigation for a specific step or activity in a process. In this situation, changeover time would be minimized to a simple toggling between startup screens rather than reopening programs, searching more complicated file structures, selecting items from a larger list of potential templates, and so forth.

Buffer and safety resources. Generally, any inventory or work in progress that accumulates between steps and activities in a process is viewed as waste that contributes to poor flow. However, when it is difficult to implement demand leveling, or inefficiencies in a process could significantly disrupt—or bring to a halt—the flow of a process, buffer and safety resources may be needed to support continuous flow.[26] Buffer and safety resources can include human resources (e.g., hiring temporary employees and retirees, asking employees to work overtime, "borrowing" employees from another part of the university) as well as physical resources (strategic but modest buildups of inventories and supplies) that can be drawn on quickly (i.e., limited approval is needed) by individuals in the process to keep a critical process flowing. An example of a buffer and safety resource is a standing commitment by managers in the financial aid office to assist with parent/student phone calls and appointments when there is a sudden and unpredicted demand for service. A second example is a small amount of additional buffer stock of printed admission materials centrally located in the office of admissions in the event of an unanticipated surge of requests for materials.

Overall, there are a number of existing strategies for LHE Project Teams to consider in achieving smooth and continuous flows in university processes. LHE teams or individuals involved in the process may suggest additional strategies that are tailored to the unique circumstances that are impeding flow. The ultimate goal is for a process to reach "one person" or "one piece" flow, where the requests or needs of beneficiaries are fulfilled as quickly (i.e., cycle or takt time) and accurately as possible, benefiting both the beneficiaries of the process and the university (e.g., improved productivity, reduced inventory costs).[27]

7.3.2 The Interplay of Waste and Flow

Although discussed in discrete sections, the reciprocal interplay between solutions for reducing or eliminating waste and solutions for improving flow is important and leads to more holistic improvements to university processes. The LHE Project Team's assessment of the current state of a university's process will help identify people, process, information, and asset waste to target for reduction or elimination. Several types of waste (e.g., waste of waiting; waste of uneven flow) will offer clear opportunities for improving the smooth and continuous flow of that process. For example, the traffic queues during freshman move-in day, an obvious waste of waiting, can be attributed in part to the mismatch between when students arrive and the university resources available at that time. By taking steps to level the number of students arriving each hour throughout the day (e.g., by establishing a reserved check in time for students), flow can be improved dramatically. Then, as timeprint performance measures for improved flow are identified (e.g., the expectation that 50 move-ins are completed every hour), additional sources of waste hidden by the poorly flowing process will surface (e.g., the locations where students were required to park during unloading had not been considered, thus resulting in transporting their belongings over longer distances than necessary and lengthening unnecessarily the move-in time). The interplay between newly uncovered sources of waste and poor flow will be ongoing, and the LHE team will be expected to consider these future opportunities in a continuous process improvement plan put in place before disbanding the LHE team. This underscores the important Lean principle: *Pursue perfection through a combination of continuous improvement and radical transformation.* As solutions to improve smooth and continuous flow are implemented, additional forms of waste surface, creating a recurring cycle of continuous improvement to the process for the ultimate benefit of those who are the beneficiaries of the process.

7.4 Summary

The goal of LHE is to eliminate waste and improve flow, so that every step and activity contributes to what the beneficiaries of a process value and expect. Over the years, Lean practitioners have identified, described, and cataloged many types of waste in processes, providing a helpful framework for recognizing hidden waste that permeates every process. Lean practitioners also identified methods for diagnosing common shortcomings that interrupt or impede smooth and continuous flow in processes. These diagnostic tools, as well as the compilation of potential solutions for eliminating waste and improving flow, provide helpful direction for the implementation of LHE interventions designed to diagnose and improve critical processes in higher education. Together, they serve as established guides for LHE Project Teams, who may choose to use some of these methods and tools separately or in combination, adapting them for unique situations within higher education, or using them to stimulate new and novel approaches for diagnosing waste and flow and creating LHE solutions that improve processes. The absence of an overly prescriptive approach to diagnosing and improving higher education processes allows the experiences and ingenuity of LHE Project Team members to introduce tailored approaches for implementing successful LHE interventions.

Endnotes

1. Tapping, D., and Shuker, T. 2003. *Value stream management for the lean office: Eight steps to planning, mapping, and sustaining Lean improvements in administrative areas.* New York: Productivity Press. p. 45.

2. Liker, J.K. 2004. *The Toyota Way: 14 management principles from the world's greatest manufacturer.* New York: McGraw-Hill. p. 87; Dennis, P. 2002. *Lean production simplified: A plain-language guide to the world's most powerful production system.* New York: Productivity Press. p. 21.

3. See Womack, J.P., and Jones, D.T. 2003. *Lean thinking: Banish waste and create wealth in your corporation.* New York: Free Press for numerous examples.

4. Lareau, W. 2003. *Office kaizen: Transforming office operations into a strategic competitive advantage.* Milwaukee, WI: ASQ Quality Press. pp. 20–21.

5. Thompson, J. 1997. *The lean office: How to use just-in-time techniques to streamline your office.* Toronto, Canada: Productive Publications.

6. These categories are The Waste of Overproduction, The Waste of Waiting, The Waste of Transport, The Waste of Overprocessing (or Incorrect Processing), The Waste of Inventory, The Waste of Motion, The Waste of Correction, The Waste of Knowledge Disconnection, The Waste of Overburdening People or Equipment, and The Waste of Unevenness. See Tapping, D., and Shuker, T., 2003. *Value stream management for the lean office: Eight steps to planning, mapping, and sustaining lean improvements in administrative areas.* New York: Productivity Press; Keyte, B., and Locher, D. 2004. *The complete lean enterprise: Value stream mapping for administrative and office processes.* New York: Productivity Press; Dennis, P. 2002. *Lean production simplified a plain-language guide to the world's most powerful production system.* New York: Productivity Press; Imai, M. 1997. *Gemba kaizen: A commonsense, low-cost approach to management.* New York: McGraw-Hill; Thompson, J. 1997. *The lean office: How to use just-in-time techniques to streamline your office.* Toronto, Canada: Productive Publications; Laraia, A., Moody, P., and Hall, R. 1999. *The kaizen blitz: Accelerating breakthroughs in productivity and performance.* New York: John Wiley & Sons; Liker, J.K. 2004. *The Toyota Way: 14 management principles from the world's greatest manufacturer.* New York: McGraw-Hill.

7. D: Defects, O: Overproduction, W: Waiting, N: Not utilizing people, T: Transportation/travel, I: Inventory, M: Motion, and E: Extra processing. From Moore, M., and Kusler, 2007. continuous improvement in action—a university lean experience. In *National Consortium for Continuous Improvement in Higher Education.* New Orleans, LA.

8. Lareau, W. 2003. *Office kaizen: Transforming office operations into a strategic competitive advantage.* Milwaukee, WI: ASQ Quality Press.

9. A wonderful metaphor I heard referenced in another context on public radio (and whose speaker name I missed so I am unable to give credit) is a piece of steak we eat for dinner. Some of the waste of fat is quite visible and easily trimmed by the butcher from the edges of the steak, but additional fat is marbleized throughout the steak itself, making it hard to see or remove.

10. Tapping, D., and Shuker, T. 2003. *Value stream management for the lean office: Eight steps to planning, mapping, and sustaining lean improvements in administrative areas.* New York: Productivity Press. p. 45.

11. Keyte, B., and Locher, D. 2004. *The complete lean enterprise: Value stream mapping for administrative and office processes.* New York: Productivity Press. Chapter 7.

12. Keyte, B., and Locher, D. 2004. *The complete lean enterprise: Value stream mapping for administrative and office processes.* New York: Productivity Press. Chapter 7.

13. Womack and Jones (Womack, J.P., and Jones, D.T. 2003. *Lean thinking: Banish waste and create wealth in your corporation.* New York: Free Press. p. 38) discuss how the steps and activities in any process provided fall into one of three categories: (a) steps or activities that add value from the perspective of the beneficiary of the process; (b) steps or activities that add no value from the perspective of the beneficiary of the process, but cannot be eliminated easily (if at all); and (c) steps or activities that add no value from the perspective of the beneficiary of the process, and can be eliminated immediately.

14. The solution implemented here was a combination of two general solution recommendations: the use of color coding and the use of clear visual systems to guide behavior.

15. Potential solutions for reducing or eliminating waste are drawn from a wide variety of sources, including Lareau, W. 2003. *Office kaizen: Transforming office operations into a strategic competitive advantage.* Milwaukee, WI: ASQ Quality Press; Tapping, D., and Shuker, T. 2003. *Value stream management for the lean office: Eight steps to planning, mapping, and sustaining lean improvements in administrative areas.* New York: Productivity Press; Keyte, B., and Locher, D., 2004. *The complete lean enterprise: Value stream mapping for administrative and office processes.* New York: Productivity Press; Dennis, P. 2002. *Lean production simplified a plain-language guide to the world's most powerful production system.* New York: Productivity Press; Imai, M. 1997. *Gemba kaizen: A commonsense, low-cost approach to management.* New York: McGraw-Hill; Thompson, J. 1997. *The lean office: How to use just-in-time techniques to streamline your office.* Toronto, Canada: Productive Publications; Laraia, A., Moody, P., and Hall, R. 1999. *The kaizen blitz: Accelerating breakthroughs in productivity and performance.* New York: John Wiley & Sons; Liker, J.K. 2004. *The Toyota Way: 14 management principles from the world's greatest manufacturer.* New York: McGraw-Hill.

16. Also referred to as "one item flow" when a physical good is being produced, or "one person" flow.

17. Womack, J.P., and Jones, D.T. 2003. *Lean thinking: Banish waste and create wealth in your corporation.* New York: Free Press. Chapter 3.

18. Potential solutions for improving flow are drawn from a wide variety of sources, including Lareau, W. 2003. *Office kaizen: Transforming office operations into a strategic competitive advantage.* Milwaukee, WI: ASQ Quality Press; Tapping, D., and Shuker, T. 2003. *Value stream management for the lean office: Eight steps to planning, mapping, and sustaining lean improvements in administrative areas.* New York: Productivity Press;

Keyte, B., and Locher, D. 2004. *The complete lean enterprise: Value stream mapping for administrative and office processes.* New York: Productivity Press; Dennis, P. 2002. *Lean production simplified a plain-language guide to the world's most powerful production system.* New York: Productivity Press; Imai, M. 1997. *Gemba kaizen: A commonsense, low-cost approach to management.* New York: McGraw-Hill; Thompson, J. *The lean office: How to use just-in-time techniques to streamline your office.* Toronto, Canada: Productive Publications; Laraia, A., Moody, P., and Hall, R. 1999. *The kaizen blitz: Accelerating breakthroughs in productivity and performance.* New York: John Wiley & Sons; Liker, J.K. 2004. *The Toyota Way: 14 management principles from the world's greatest manufacturer.* New York: McGraw-Hill.

19. For an excellent discussion, see Laraia, A., Moody, P., and Hall, R. 1999. *The kaizen blitz: Accelerating breakthroughs in productivity and performance.* New York: John Wiley & Sons. Chapter 5; Tapping, D., and Shuker, T. 2003. *Value stream management for the lean office: Eight steps to planning, mapping, and sustaining lean improvements in administrative areas.* New York: Productivity Press. pp. 76–78.

20. With the availability of better and better local printing capabilities, however, this might not seem to be an impossible option. Printing materials could be personally tailored for each particular applicant based on his or her interests, background, etc. For example, if the applicant was interested in a degree in business, the application could collect relevant information that could be used by advisors and faculty members in the college to tailor the printed material for their recruitment of this particular student. Information about scholarships and financial aid could also be individually tailored based on the applicant's background or circumstances.

21. Mistake proofing also prevents errors from being passed along to the ultimate beneficiaries of the process, falling short of their expectations. Fixing mistakes after the process is completed, often in an expedited fashion, creates further perturbations to the flow of a process.

22. Dennis, P. 2002. *Lean production simplified a plain-language guide to the world's most powerful production system.* New York: Productivity Press. Chapters 3 and 4.

23. Liker, J.K. 2004. *The Toyota Way: 14 management principles from the world's greatest manufacturer.* New York: McGraw-Hill. p. 152.

24. It can also reflect the time required to change over physical equipment (e.g., changing tooling that produced one part to produce another) or entire production lines (e.g., producing one model automobile to another), although these types of changeovers are much less common in higher education.

25. An alternative solution would be to eliminate some of the tasks that came through this process, by allowing alumni to update their own information or permitting development officers to update certain donor information.

26. Tapping, D., and Shuker, T. 2003. *Value stream management for the lean office: Eight steps to planning, mapping, and sustaining lean improvements in administrative areas.* New York: Productivity Press. pp. 87–88.
27. Liker, J.K. 2004. *The Toyota Way: 14 management principles from the world's greatest manufacturer.* New York: McGraw-Hill. pp. 95–97.

Chapter 8

Implementing LHE Solutions and Sustaining Improvements

Lean [Higher Education] implementation is simple in concept, challenging to implement, and even more challenging to sustain.[1]

The comprehensive visual map of the current process chosen for improvement (i.e., the LHE initiative), created by the LHE Project Team, provides an objective look at the steps and activities that occur and insights into sources of waste and poor flow. Performance metrics chosen to reflect what beneficiaries value and expect help direct the LHE team's attention toward specific recommendations that can be implemented to reduce or eliminate waste and contribute to smooth flow.

8.1 Identifying and Implementing LHE Solutions

The LHE Project Team will generally follow a standard set of steps in its efforts to identify and implement LHE solutions to create an improved process for the future. First, the LHE Project Team prepares its preliminary evaluation of the current process that was selected for the LHE initiative, prioritizing specific areas that promise significant and achievable reduction in waste and improvement in flow. Next, LHE Specialist Teams are formed to address each of the prioritized areas identified, drawing on the expertise and energies of individuals beyond the original LHE Project Team. LHE solutions proposed by the LHE Specialist Teams are then gathered and reviewed by LHE Project Team members, who combine the solutions to propose a new visual map depicting a revised future process with less waste, improved flow, and greater alignment with what beneficiaries value and expect. After gaining approval and support from the university (e.g., Office of LHE, the senior leadership team), LHE Implementation Teams are appointed, representing a mix of individuals involved in the LHE initiative and others who are integral to the process, to carry out the specific LHE solutions that will lead to a new, improved process. Importantly, these steps to identify and implement LHE solutions can and should be completed quickly, and can easily be accomplished as part of a 3- to 5-day LHE rapid improvement workshop (or Kaizen event).

8.1.1 Preliminary Evaluation of the Current Process

Up to this point in time, the LHE Project Team has concentrated on producing a clear and accurate *description* of the current state of the university process that is the focus of the LHE initiative (although LHE team members may have made personal note of potential LHE solutions during this time). This description includes the identification of each step or activity in the process from both the provider and beneficiary perspectives, estimates (based on observation, archival data, or expert judgment) of the time needed to accomplish each step or activity, and information on selected metrics of performance (e.g., quantity, quality, timeliness, satisfaction indices) for evaluating the current level of performance. This information, consolidated into the visual map of the current process steps and activities, is shared with all LHE team members.

The LHE Project Team now shifts its collective efforts to *evaluation* of the current state of the university process. The meeting space should include an enlarged visual map of the process posted or projected onto a wall and around which all Team members can gather. Using self-adhesive notes (e.g., Post-it™ notes), LHE team members individually identify incidences of waste and poor flow. Two general questions may help challenge team members to think critically about each step or activity in the process:

■ Would the beneficiaries of this process be willing to pay for this step or activity if they knew about it? That is, does it add value from their perspective and should it keep being done, or is it waste that makes no contribution to what they value and expect from the process and should be eliminated?

■ Does the process flow smoothly and continuously across all steps and activities without interruptions or bottlenecks, delivering what beneficiaries value and expect? That is, does each step or activity contribute to individualized "one person" or "one piece" flow until the beneficiary's needs are met, or do they contribute to a jerky and erratic process with periods of stopping and waiting?

LHE Project Team members post their handwritten notes next to the specific steps or activities where they observe waste and impediments to flow. LHE team members are invited to "piggyback" on the types of waste or impediments to flow posted by other members, including additional areas of opportunity for improving the current process. This LHE team activity will generate a substantial number of incidences of waste and poor flow across the different steps or activities. While not specifically required to do so at this time (because it will be done more formally later on), LHE team members are free to post potential LHE solutions to reduce waste and improve flow that come to mind to ensure that they are not lost during their work.

8.1.2 Prioritization of Incidences of Waste and Poor Flow for Further Focus

The preliminary evaluation of the current process will identify many incidences of waste and poor flow that could be addressed. However, concurrently addressing every incidence could quickly overwhelm the resources of both the LHE Project Team and the university. Therefore, the LHE team prioritizes its energies on key incidences of waste and poor flow that can be expected to lead to significant improvement in the process. The LHE team accomplishes this by identifying those posted incidences (or clusters of incidences) that have a more significant impact on the performance of the process (as determined by the identified performance metrics) and, if resolved, will result in greater gains in what the beneficiaries value and expect. That is, the LHE team should not select incidences to address because they are the easiest to resolve (i.e., the proverbial "low hanging fruit") or by the frequency of notes posted. Instead, the LHE team should select incidences of waste and poor flow that interfere the most with the process's or service's ability to deliver the value that is expected by the beneficiaries, that is, those that create the biggest problems for students, faculty members, parents, employers, or others who are served. The following set of questions might help the LHE team prioritize among the incidences of waste and poor flow that will be the focus for identifying LHE solutions to improve the process:[2]

- ■ Would LHE solutions that resolve these incidences of waste and poor flow have a noticeable impact on the primary beneficiary(ies) of this process?
- ■ Would LHE solutions that resolve these incidences of waste and poor flow significantly improve the process as measured on the key performance metrics selected?
- ■ Would LHE solutions that resolve these incidences of waste and poor flow provide immediate or long-term savings to the university to reinvest in further improving other critical processes?
- ■ Would LHE solutions that resolve these incidences of waste and poor flow in this critical process be consistent with the strategic objectives of the university or the division in which the LHE initiative resides?

This prioritization step will define the ongoing scope of this LHE initiative, deferring other possible but less pressing opportunities for subsequent continuous improvement efforts by individuals involved in this process or service or a follow-up LHE initiative. For example, an LHE Project Team's preliminary evaluation of the university's summer orientation and registration process for new freshmen might identify a number of incidences of waste and poor flow. The LHE team's review showed that the majority of comments by the team (i.e., self-adhesive notes by the LHE team posted on the wall-size visual map) focused on the waste of unnecessary transport (i.e., students and parents walking back and forth across campus to various required sessions) and the waste of waiting (i.e., students and parents waiting in lines to meet with academic advisors, financial aid counselors, student employment staff), both of which interfered with smooth, continuous flow. These incidences detracted from what students and parents expected from the process (e.g., provide the process in one location and do not waste my time). The LHE team also calculated that these two types of waste contributed over 3 hours to the 12-hour (1.5 day) process (i.e., 25% non-value-added time, a key performance metric chosen for this process), yet added no discernible value from the perspective of students, parents, or university employees who are part of the process. In light of this, the LHE team reached a consensus decision to limit the scope of the LHE initiative moving forward to that of reducing or eliminating both waste of unnecessary transport and waste of waiting from the summer orientation and registration process.

Overall, the prioritization of incidences of waste and poor flow for more detailed analysis by the LHE Project Team helps ensure that the team's time commitment and available resources are not overextended, and that their efforts always begin from the perspective of the beneficiary of the process. However, when a preliminary evaluation of a process identifies an incidence of waste or poor flow that can be resolved simply and does not distract the LHE Project Team from its identified priorities, the team should implement the LHE solution immediately. Under certain circumstances, addressing some "low hanging fruit" may be helpful for building LHE team confidence and obtaining some early buy-in and credibility for LHE from the broader university community. For example, removing an unnecessary signature or eliminating requests for information that is available elsewhere can create some energy around the LHE initiative. Returning to the summer orientation and registration process example above, the LHE team may have recognized that the simple co-location of several tables in the display area of university departments and services would greatly improve the flow of students and families visiting this area. Implementing this change immediately (quite literally) improves the process for students and parents and places no continuing demand on the time and energy of the LHE Project Team.

8.1.3 Formulate LHE Specialist Teams for In-Depth Review of Prioritized Areas

Prioritized incidences of waste and poor flow are subject to in-depth review under the leadership of the LHE Project Team. LHE Specialist Teams are formed to address one or more clusters of waste and poor flow, providing more in-depth analysis of the area so that the most appropriate LHE solutions can be identified for implementation. An LHE Project Team member volunteers or is appointed to serve as the leader/facilitator for each of the new specialist teams; preferably, this individual will have some experience from previous LHE initiatives and demonstrated skills in facilitation and communication. Individuals beyond the original LHE Project Team are invited to join the LHE Specialist Teams based on their knowledge and experience with different aspects of the process, their area of expertise (e.g., technology, records management, information systems), past experience with LHE initiatives, or personal interest in LHE. These new members bring fresh perspectives and energy to the review of prioritized areas of waste or poor flow while expanding the number of individuals familiar with LHE and creating broader buy-in for any LHE solutions proposed.[3]

Newly formed LHE Specialist Teams would receive essential training on key LHE principles and practices to ensure a consistent language and framework across individuals for approaching their assignment. Additional "just-in-time" training would be provided as needed; for example, more detailed training on demand leveling could be provided if the LHE Specialist Team members felt that this specific LHE solution held promise to reduce waste and improve flow in their prioritized area of review of the process. Each LHE Specialist Team then uses the work completed by the original LHE Project Team as a starting point for its own in-depth review. Team members are given the opportunity to observe the complete process first-hand and quickly collect any additional data needed to fully understand the steps or activities of the process directly relevant to the prioritized area of waste or poor flow they were assigned. The framework for conceptualizing waste, as well as impediments to flow (Chapter 7), may provide insights or a more finely detailed understanding of the contributing causes of waste and poor flow. Additionally, the LHE Specialist Team might wish to visit other universities or organizations that have implemented Lean principles and practices to reduce waste and improve flow in identical or highly similar processes. For example, hospitals that have introduced "same-day appointments" with medical specialists through demand leveling, cross-training, and JIT practices may be a useful model for reducing waiting times for counseling center appointments, advising appointments, and so on. Manufacturing, service, and government organizations that have applied Lean principles and practices to their administrative office functions may be excellent models for improving administrative and support functions at universities.

8.1.4 LHE Specialist Teams Recommend LHE Solutions to Improve the Future Process

Each LHE Specialist Team recommends specific LHE solutions that result in incremental or radical changes to reduce or eliminate waste (e.g., eliminate unnecessary signatures, create self-contained work cells, implement standardized work) and create smooth and continuous flow (e.g., JIT delivery, mistake proofing, FIFO lanes) for both their prioritized area and the proposed future process overall. While available compilations of LHE solutions for removing waste and improving flow (see Chapter 7) can provide useful recommendations and should be considered, the LHE Specialist Teams may invent alternative solutions that are uniquely appropriate for improving this particular process. In addition, the LHE Specialist Team can use this opportunity to suggest other, higher-level system improvements to the university process, such as quantifying consumer expectations or creating new performance metrics. The following seven suggestions may serve as useful guidelines for the LHE Specialist Team as it contemplates solutions to remove waste and improve flow.[4]

Don't be constrained by the current way a process or service is provided. Significant reductions in waste and improvements in flow that deliver the value beneficiaries expected from the process may require an entirely different design. The LHE Specialist Team should not limit itself to proposing incremental change to an existing process if radical transformation is needed. As an example, the admissions process for new freshman students (submitting applications, transcripts, ACT/SAT test scores by a certain date, having applications reviewed on a regular schedule by multiple admission team members, mailing acceptance/rejection letters weekly) cannot accommodate students who wish to enroll immediately in flexibly scheduled courses offered online. In addition, the process does not allow the possible competitive advantage of extending an admissions offer and financial aid package to a prospective student at the end of a 4-hour campus tour. Transforming the admissions process to "one person" flow is essential to accomplishing this process expectation, a flow that is inconsistent with the existing (and traditional) batch-and-queue approach to admissions decisions. Each step in a new "one person" flow process would require radical change to eliminate waste and improve flow so that a personalized offer of acceptance is available in less than 4 hours for any prospective student.

Don't accept excuses or explanations for why the process is as it is. Because most university processes were not designed following LHE principles and practices, they are likely to be laden with waste and poor flow. Yet employees and managers involved with the process may argue that the process is as good as it can be, and certain forms of waste or poor flow are necessary. The LHE Specialist Team can use the "Five Why" technique to surface the root causes of waste and poor flow, and select targeted LHE solutions that resolve them. For example, the bursar's office may have a full-time employee dedicated to handling billing errors for students, and office leadership deems this an essential position for resolving student (and parent) problems. In contrast, the LHE Specialist Team would correctly view as wasteful any resources spent on correcting errors and instead focus on identifying and eliminating the causes of the errors. Not only would this immediately benefit students and parents (no errors means no phone calls to correct them), but also the staff member can be reassigned to new activities that add even more value for students and parents (an option not possible before because of limited personnel resources).

Don't look for expensive and complex solutions. LHE solutions to reduce waste and improve flow are often cost-free or inexpensive, and simple solutions are easier to introduce and more likely to be followed than complex ones. For example, investing in tracking and scheduling software is expensive and requires dedicated staffing away from where the process takes place to enter information; in addition, it quickly becomes inaccurate when information is missing or entered inaccurately. Instead, a simple whiteboard provides an effective visual system at the place where the process occurs for monitoring workflow and identifying bottlenecks and other problems quickly, at substantial savings to the university (i.e., monitoring becomes a responsibility of the employees involved in the process rather than a support employee outside the actual workflow).

Don't be afraid to think big. Look for opportunities to remove waste and improve flow that exceed the expectations of the beneficiary of the process to give the university an unparalleled advantage over the competition. Radical change is typical in LHE and often necessary to introduce significant improvements (followed by incremental changes through ongoing continuous improvement). For example, a student health center could implement modest changes to the appointment scheduling process and the appointment visit scheduled 1 or 2 days later. Greater reduction in waste and improvement in flow would come from guaranteeing same-day appointments for any student, accomplished by introducing LHE solutions that level the demand for services throughout the day, and then match the allocation of effort by the medical staff with this more predictable demand for service by students. A university that offers same-day appointments for every important service—student health, psychological counseling, study skills tutoring, academic advising, student legal services—will quickly distinguish itself from those institutions that make students wait.

Don't expect perfection. Implement the best LHE solution available, and commit to monitoring key performance metrics and supporting continuous improvement over time. Time spent searching for *the* perfect solution is a lost opportunity to provide a better process today. For example, a university's process for soliciting and prioritizing capital planning requests (e.g., proposals to build or remodel facilities) involves proposals by individual academic and administrative offices, cost estimation by university architects, management discussion and review, and more. Developing a comprehensive process that is free of waste with continuous and smooth flow that fully satisfies the expectations of all beneficiaries is daunting. Yet implementing LHE solutions that focus on reducing waste and improving flow in those steps or activities of the process that are most critical to individual academic units will have an immediate positive impact. Additional solutions can be implemented over time, consistent with LHE's commitment to ongoing continuous improvement, delivering the value expected to more beneficiaries of the process.

Don't be (or let others be) overly critical. Avoid focusing only on the potential faults of the proposed LHE solutions that the LHE Specialist Team carefully vetted. Communicate how the solutions will reduce waste and improve flow, countering any tendency to be overly suspicious and critical of change (especially radical change). For example, the recommendation to use nonprofessional staff to receive and catalog new library holdings may raise potential concerns about accuracy, fostering some sentiment to continue to have the professional staff maintain complete control over acquisitions. However, carefully trained nonprofessional staff may be quite capable of cataloging 90% of the typical new acquisitions without any problem; the professional staff could then focus on the remaining 10% of new materials that are more challenging (and professionally stimulating). This resolves concerns surrounding cataloging accuracy and frees up the professional staff to offer new or expanded professional services to library patrons. Overall, while maintaining their openness to potential concerns, the LHE Specialist Team is trusted to have carefully considered the potential impact of any proposed solution before recommending its implementation.

Don't ignore input from the entire team when developing solutions. It is important to create a climate of equality among members so that good LHE solutions are not stifled, because the ideas of five team members will create more potentially important LHE solutions than the ideas of one team member. The LHE Specialist Team should set aside university status and rank as they work together. All team members bring unique perspectives and experiences to understanding and improving the process, which can result in a broader set of suggestions for reducing waste and improving flow. For example, front office staff with direct student contact can offer practical solutions to the face-to-face bursar payment process that may be as useful as (and perhaps even better than) university employees at higher levels who have limited direct contact with students.

8.1.5 Consolidation and Prioritization of LHE Solutions

The LHE Project Team reconvenes to integrate the findings and recommendations of the individual LHE Specialist Teams. The individual LHE Specialist Teams share potential LHE solutions related to their specific charge. Together, the teams discuss and incorporate proposed solutions into a visual map of the future process following LHE efforts, reflecting reductions in waste and improvements in flow. Both timeprint performance measures (time required by specific activities or steps) and overall performance metrics critical to assessing the success of the process should be estimated, illustrating how various mixes of potential solutions can reduce the time required for the future process, the number of activities or steps required, improvements in the accuracy or quality of the process, and other key metrics. The assimilation of LHE solutions may stimulate further solutions to improve the process. Multiple alternative views for a proposed future process are likely, each offering a mix of LHE solutions that differ in terms of their ease of implementation, cost, impact, and so on. The following considerations can help the LHE Project Team choose among LHE solutions:[5]

- *What does the beneficiary really want?* Meeting or exceeding the expectations valued by the beneficiaries of the process is the first principle of LHE. Thus, it should play an important role in choosing from among many LHE solutions.
- *Which steps or activities generate the greatest waste?* Steps or activities that contribute the greatest amounts of waste are prime targets for the first round of LHE solutions. Eliminating or reducing these steps or activities should yield the greatest gains for the process.
- *Where are the greatest impediments to smooth and continuous flow?* LHE solutions that remove the largest obstacles that interrupt flow can provide immediate improvement to the beneficiaries of process. Even when continuous flow is not possible, LHE solutions that best manage interruptions and help balance the workload of employees to level out peak periods (i.e., avoid bottlenecks) may bring greater value to those served by the process.

Taking into consideration the questions raised above, along with cost, the ease of implementation and the impact of the individual LHE solutions will assist the LHE Project Team in designing a proposed "future" visual map of the revised process. Once LHE solutions are selected, a visual map of the proposed process should be drawn. Team members should then "walk through" the proposed new process, confirming the removal of waste and improvement in flow as planned. Together, the LHE Project Team and the LHE Specialist Teams outline their plan of action for implementing the LHE solutions, anticipating any potential barriers to success (e.g., cultural resistance, resource limitations, technical challenges) and estimating expected improvements in the key performance metrics used to evaluate the process.

8.1.6 *Obtain Endorsement of Proposed Future State Changes*

Members of the LHE Specialist Teams and the original LHE Project Team meet with university officials to present their work and obtain the university's endorsement to implement proposed changes to the process targeted for improvement. The presentation should be an exemplar of a "Lean" meeting: the right people in attendance, clear written objectives for the meeting, well-prepared participants, effective use of visual aids, informed decision making, and starting and ending the meeting on time.[6]

Invited to the meeting are the managers and directors who have responsibility for the current process, senior leaders representing the vice presidential area(s) that oversee the process, and representatives from the Executive Steering Committee of the Office of LHE. The Director of the Office of LHE (assuming such an office exists), or a member of the LHE Executive Steering Committee, serves as facilitator. Multiple representatives of the LHE Specialist Teams and LHE Project Team should participate in the presentation. The focused agenda for the meeting includes an update by the teams on their LHE efforts, obtaining leadership's endorsement to implement proposed changes to the process, and reaffirmation of the university's commitment to LHE principles and practices.

A common method of reporting out the work of the LHE Team is the "A3 Report," a visual aid limited to one side of a single piece of 11 inch × 17 inch paper.[7] This report would include

- A one-sentence summary of the process and why it was chosen for improvement
- A visual (preferred) or narrative description of the current process, including key performance metrics and critical examples of existing waste and poor flow
- Prioritized recommendations (and cost estimates, if needed) of LHE solutions to remove waste and improve flow across the critical steps and activities in the process

- A visual (preferred) or narrative description of the proposed future process, including expected improvements on the key performance metrics
- A brief implementation plan with timeline
- The names of members from the original LHE Project Team and the LHE Specialist Teams

Multiple representatives from the LHE teams provide a brief oral presentation to supplement and enrich the written report and respond to questions. Representatives should be prepared to answer the following key questions:

- Why did the LHE initiative focus on this university process?
- How does this initiative relate to the university's strategic objectives?
- How will the proposed LHE solutions improve the process to deliver what beneficiaries value and expect? How will solutions affect members of the university who complete the steps and activities of the process?
- Will the proposed LHE solutions lead to improvements on all key performance metrics?
- What resources (e.g., personnel time, expended dollars, cost for carrying and storing inventory) will be saved through the elimination of waste and improved flow?

Anecdotal data may help impress upon the university leaders present the need for improving the current process, and the hard data represented in the performance metrics attest to the validity of the proposed LHE solutions. The presentation should be focused and brief (i.e., 30 to 60 minutes).

University managers and senior leaders should acquire a clear understanding of the LHE teams' plan and rationale, affirming that the implementation of LHE solutions is consistent with the overall strategy and goal of the university to improve all processes for the express benefit of the beneficiaries it serves. Consistent with a university-wide climate committed to LHE, leadership's approval to proceed with most (if not all) of the proposed high-priority LHE solutions should be given immediately or within 72 hours of the presentation.

Team members should be recognized and thanked for their work. At some later point in time, two members representing the original LHE Project Team and the LHE Specialist Team(s) should be invited to make an even briefer presentation to the university president and his or her cabinet regarding the LHE initiative.

8.1.7 Implementing LHE Solutions: The LHE Implementation Team

The LHE Project Team leader, with the team's representative from the university's LHE Steering Committee, establishes an LHE Implementation Team. The Implementation Team selects members from the original LHE Project Team and the LHE Specialist Teams, with the possible recruitment of additional members based on specialized expertise related to the approved LHE solutions. The LHE Implementation Team should determine whether to introduce the approved LHE solutions simultaneously into the process, or whether a planned order of implementation is needed to ensure success. For example, LHE solutions designed to improve the flow of processing transfer student applications may require that university employees first have access to the required tools and information (i.e., desktop scanners and reconfigured computers that can easily retrieve and organize student information) needed to support changes in the steps and activities that will be introduced to improve flow.

Implementation of LHE solutions should be done with speed and intention. The LHE Implementation Team should develop a written implementation plan that prioritizes the introduction of LHE solutions into the process, establishes dates when each solution is targeted to begin and end, and assigns responsibility for each solution to one or more individuals from the LHE Implementation Team. A "milestone" or Gantt chart can document assignments and the expected timetable, providing a visual update of progress on implementation. Depending on the number of solutions and the complexity of the process or service, the time needed for the LHE Implementation Team to design, introduce, evaluate, and strengthen the solutions to remove waste and improve flow in the process typically can be completed in 1 to 5 days.[8] If the number of LHE solutions is quite large, the team members may choose to divide themselves into subteams with responsibilities for different components of the process in an effort to implement all LHE solutions within the same timeframe.[9] With their focus on the specific LHE solution(s) assigned, LHE Implementation Team members begin their work in the physical work location where the LHE solution is to be implemented.

LHE Implementation Team members use simple methods to begin the initial introduction of the solution: flipchart drawings of the new proposed flow; rough mockups of new forms, Web pages, or wall charts required by the revised process; taped outlines on the floor to relocate workstations or equipment; and prototypes of new tools and equipment proposed by the solution. (The team does not waste time on computer-produced flowcharts, desktop publishing of materials, or permanent electrical and telecommunication connections because additional changes are expected.) Proposed solutions to reduce waste and improve flow are shared with university employees connected to the process, and their feedback and suggestions are weighted heavily. Team members walk through the revised process with the employees who perform the tasks and activities, fine-tuning their efforts based on feedback from each step and activity. As quickly as possible and with the support of university leaders, the LHE Implementation Team rolls out the revised university process and monitors its early performance. Incremental improvements are introduced quickly in response to unanticipated problems by members of the LHE Implementation Team, relying on their skills and expertise regarding the process and their new knowledge of LHE. Once the LHE Implementation Team feels that the revised process has achieved its expected level of performance (using established performance metrics), changes to the process are formalized through an established workflow layout; standardized work, equipment, and materials; and simplified written and visual job instructions for training that are available for every step and activity. These efforts serve to document and standardize the LHE-improved process so that it will perform reliably and with an expectation of success, fully recognizing that further efforts to improve the process should continue as part of the university's ongoing commitment to continuous improvement.

8.1.8 General Recommendations for LHE Implementation

The following recommendations can help ensure the successful implementation of LHE solutions.[10]

Develop a standard process for all LHE implementation efforts. Consistency across LHE implementations will ensure that critical steps (e.g., training of team members, clarification of expectations) are included and employees who regularly participate on LHE Implementation Teams have a predictable experience. The common use of agendas (planned activities and their allocated times), A3 reports (standardized summary of proposed LHE solutions), and Gantt or milestone charts (targets with expected time of completion), each tailored to the project scope and allotted time for the implementation of LHE solutions, can provide a common structure and direction for the LHE Implementation Team's efforts.

Include the right people on the LHE Implementation Team. The success of LHE solutions is contingent upon the talent and motivation of

LHE Implementation Team members. The team should include a good representation of university employees involved in the process. LHE Implementation Team members should be familiar with different parts of the process and/or have specialized expertise (e.g., database management) critical to implementing LHE solutions. Where possible, several team members should have previous experience in LHE implementation that adds to the core competence of the team. Finally, team members should have an interest in, and commitment to, the application of LHE principles and practices.

Identify and communicate the objectives of the LHE implementation effort. Members of the LHE Implementation Team, the LHE Project Team leader, and senior leaders and managers must have a clear understanding of the scope of their assignment, the expected outcomes and timetable, and the accepted metrics for measuring success. The Implementation Team should develop a sense of ownership and accountability for the effective implementation of LHE solutions.

Communicate regularly and broadly. There should be many formal and informal opportunities for LHE Implementation Team members to communicate with each other (e.g., time set aside at the beginning and end of each day). There should also be opportunities for team members to communicate with university colleagues who are not on the LHE Implementation Team but are "upstream" or "downstream" contributors to the process.

Be flexible when the unplanned occurs. The complexities of implementing significant changes in complex processes and services make it probable that unplanned outcomes are to be expected. The team leader can help LHE Implementation Team members reframe these unanticipated consequences as opportunities to better understand the process and the university. Keeping the overall goal of LHE implementation in mind and using tools to understand the causes of unplanned outcomes (e.g., "Five Whys" Technique; PDCA cycle) can help the team adapt to unforeseen circumstances.

Do not let a problem derail LHE implementation. Unforeseen circumstances (e.g., a crisis that requires LHE Implementation Team members to leave temporarily, bad weather, etc.) may make it impossible for the team to implement LHE solutions according to their original timetable. Accept this temporary disruption and reschedule a time when the team will return to complete its task.

Be prepared to make mistakes (and learn from them). Expectations that the implementation of LHE solutions must be perfect are unrealistic and should not delay or, worse yet, halt initial efforts to remove waste and improve flow in the process. The LHE Implementation Team, university

leaders, and university employees who are part of the process should understand that LHE includes procedures for identifying and resolving unplanned
outcomes early. Careful planning, "beta" testing of proposed LHE solutions,
and ongoing monitoring of the revised process will safeguard against any
significant adverse effects on those served by the process.

The visible presence of leaders is important. Senior university leaders, champions of university-wide LHE efforts, and senior leaders from the
division with oversight responsibility for the process undergoing the LHE
intervention should visit the LHE Implementation Team to observe and
encourage their efforts. This expands their understanding of LHE and provides opportunities to address any concerns directly, and garners additional
institutional support for the LHE initiative.

Recognize the efforts of the LHE Implementation Team. The university should create opportunities to recognize the efforts and contributions
of LHE Implementation Team members. Recognition might include opportunities to present their work to senior leaders, letters of thanks and com-
mendation, and planned celebrations at the successful completion of LHE
Implementation. Public recognition also reinforces the importance of LHE to
the larger university community.

8.2 Sustaining the Gain: Institutionalizing the New Process

*Despite the efforts and the success of initial projects, the first six
to eight months of achievement were hard to see in terms of real
change in the way the business worked. Many projects that had
yielded spectacular results quickly faded, and much momentum
was lost. Old practices reemerged and erased some of the new ways
the teams had developed. The age-old problem of people under stress
reverting to what they knew and felt comfortable with are hard to
overcome. It's so easy to go back to the old way of doing things.[11]*

Successful implementation of LHE solutions is a significant accomplishment
for the university and the beneficiaries of the improved process. As LHE
initiatives to remove waste and improve flow are completed across the institution, the impact of LHE will become noticeable to an increasing audience
within and outside the university (and well beyond those university members who contributed to the LHE initiative). Critically important to the long-
term success of LHE, however, is the institutionalization of LHE solutions

to university processes to sustain achieved performance improvements. As is the case with other large-scale change initiatives for improving organizations, entropic forces create a tension or pull to revert to the historic (and more familiar) steps and activities found in the former "current state" visual map. Several forces may contribute to the slow decay or outright abandonment of LHE solutions. For example, leaders may reflexively return to the old way of doing things at the first sign of possible failure or unplanned outcomes by the new process, partly because they know it works (despite significant waste and poor flow) and partly because they are more comfortable with it. As a second example, significant changes to processes may dramatically redesign the day-to-day jobs of university employees involved in the process, threatening the personal power and reputation of employees gained through their knowledge and experience with the old process. This can be particularly stressful to managers who oversee the process, given the significant levels of responsibility and autonomy that are shifted to employees as part of the newly designed process. Returning to the old way of doing things would restore the former balance of power within the system. As a final example, declining interest in LHE by senior leaders as they shift their attention to other issues telegraphs to everyone that LHE is yet another business fad that has run its course, and levels of interest and support drop concomitantly throughout the university. By one estimate, approximately half of these change initiatives never take root beyond their initial implementation and simply wither away, including early initiatives in world-recognized Lean organizations.[12] Thus, it is important that LHE initiatives include a comprehensive strategy to sustain improvements to the process achieved through the application of LHE beyond their initial implementation.

As discussed in Chapter 4, the right workplace climate and leadership practices can create an environment that is open to the introduction of LHE principles and practices. These contextual influences remain important to the sustainability of LHE solutions over time. This section describes a variety of practical actions to take, or tools to use, to help stabilize and strengthen the newly improved process or service and contribute to a climate that embraces LHE.

8.2.1 Communicate, Communicate, Communicate

Regular and clear communication is essential throughout the LHE initiative. Most university employees are unfamiliar with LHE principles and practices, and only some of the employees involved in the university process were actively involved in the LHE initiative. In addition, change can be difficult for some employees to embrace, especially those worried about how it will impact their job security. Finally, change may be difficult to accept at some universities because the current climate implies that someone did not do his or her job well and will be held accountable for the "broken" process (as contrasted with an LHE climate, where an error is a learning opportunity used to make processes even better). Therefore, a comprehensive communication plan should be developed that shares information broadly and promotes buy-in and support for LHE. General features of the communication plan should include the following:

- *Communication should flow throughout the LHE initiative.*
  Communication about the LHE initiative should begin at the earliest stages of the project (e.g., communication that an LHE initiative is being considered and why) through the ongoing evaluation of the implemented LHE solutions. In addition to project-specific communication, an overall communication plan is needed to share general information about LHE (e.g., What is LHE? Why has the university embraced LHE?).
- *Communication should demonstrate clear support from senior leadership.* University-distributed communication should include clear and consistent leadership support for LHE. This support should come from leaders who immediately oversee the area pursuing an LHE initiative as well as senior leaders who may have less day-to-day contact with LHE initiatives (although it is advised to have all senior leaders involved in a LHE initiative at some point). Communication might include, for example, statements of support, planned investments based on recommendations from LHE Specialist Teams, and recognition of team members and successful LHE implementations.
- *Communication content should be appropriately targeted to audience.* The content and format of the communication should vary depending on the purpose and audience. For example, communication to university employees who are part of the process chosen for the LHE initiative would require substantial detail available in an interactive format, whereas communication to the university's board of trustees might include a quarterly written summary of LHE initiatives underway across the institution.
- *Communication should flow in all directions.* One of the features of LHE is its inclusiveness. University employees are encouraged to initiate communication, make suggestions about how to improve a process,

share information back and forth with LHE team members, and make presentations to senior leaders. It is also important for senior and mid-level leaders to initiate communication about LHE initiatives, openly discuss solutions with LHE team members, and express their support for and appreciation of those involved in LHE initiatives.

■ *Communication should support the LHE climate and motivate participation in LHE initiatives.* Communication systems can be a powerful force for shaping employee attitudes and behavior. The effective use of communication can help establish and reinforce the new university climate that endorses LHE principles and practices. Communication can also recognize and reward employees who participate in LHE initiatives, providing some additional influence on attitudes and involvement in LHE.

8.2.2 Tie LHE to University Strategy

Reinforcing the linkage between LHE and university strategy can help strengthen and sustain support for processes improved through specific LHE initiatives. University leaders with direct or oversight responsibility for the process must communicate to employees how the recently introduced changes contribute to the success of the unit, division, and university. Employees who understand how the expected performance gains from the improved process contribute to the larger strategy may invest more time and energy to ensure its success. For example, LHE implemented solutions that decrease the time needed to process freshman admission applications allow the university to extend offers before its competitors, yielding a higher acceptance rate and a more academically qualified incoming class. Thus, the LHE-improved process provides a strategic competitive advantage that strengthens enrollment, reduces the university's investment in remediation efforts, and supports academic rigor inside and outside the classroom. As a second example, removing waste and improving flow in the processing of work orders to schedule facility repairs will reduce faculty and staff time required to submit and follow up on their request, allowing them to spend more of their time on things that add value to the institution. Furthermore, the reduced administrative time allows the maintenance staff and supervisors to spend more hours completing work order requests. This, in turn, reduces any backlog in requests (some of which had the potential of becoming bigger problems) and increases the overall quality of buildings and grounds, making a more pleasant environment for students, faculty and staff, and prospective students visiting the campus. Clarifying the direct connection between the success of critical processes and overall institutional success can help create greater employee awareness and commitment to LHE solutions and future LHE efforts.

8.2.3 Provide Job Security

Regardless of the large-scale change initiatives embraced by the university's senior leadership, employee support is likely to co-vary strongly with perceptions of job security. Universities that use the gains from employee-centered LHE efforts to lay off employees or change the terms of their contracts (e.g., from full-time to part-time) will find that remaining employees are less willing to participate in future LHE initiatives. LHE should not be used to improve a process for the purpose of downsizing; fear of job loss weakens commitment and involvement by employees, who now fear that their own job is one LHE initiative away from being lost. Every effort should be made, in both words and actions, to provide job security to employees. This includes not only employees who are actively engaged in the LHE initiative, but also employees who are likely to be asked to participate in other future LHE initiatives. If downsizing is critical to the university's success, it should be accomplished prior to implementing LHE, and remaining employees should be told that job security will be respected moving forward with the introduction of LHE.

8.2.4 Standardize and Document How Steps and Activities Should Be Done

Standardizing the steps or activities employees perform as their part in the process, and clearly documenting how to complete them, can help prevent regression to the abandoned steps or activities. By standardizing work, expectations are established for the job: how to do it, when to do it, and how well to do it. Standardization would be more detailed for tasks that are highly repetitive with short cycles of performance (e.g., preparing a contract for a part-time instructor) and less so for a less repetitive and more variable task (e.g., a general template for a customer service call to the Information Technology Services help desk). The established standard, supported by the required support materials found in defined locations, provides clear direction that reinforces the correct completion of assigned steps or activities.

Documentation of work standards should be simple and clear, and provide a ready reference for the steps and activities completed by every university employee along the entire process. Where appropriate, this documentation should be posted in the workplace (e.g., the specific steps required when accessing, modifying, and saving a shared database) and provide an exemplar of correctly completed work (e.g., a completed purchase order form highlighting essential information and attachments required). Because continuous improvement practices by those doing the job will introduce improvements in how steps and activities are completed, the design of all documentation should allow for easy updating.

8.2.5 Train Employees to Consistently Complete All Steps and Activities to Expected Standards

All employees should receive training to ensure that they complete all steps and activities as required by the improved process. Employee training should closely follow the documented work standards for each step and activity, and employees should have the opportunity to observe and then demonstrate their ability to perform the steps and activities as expected. Training that supports LHE initiatives should also include a clear rationale for why adherence to the new work standards is necessary; this will help employees not only know how to complete their work, but also why it needs to be done this way. For example, a new graduate program secretary can be required to obtain peer training from a current graduate secretary (rather than a manager or human resource staff) in another academic unit who is proficient in the steps or activities on key processes critical to the job. This hands-on, on-the-job training provides the opportunity to ask specific questions and get detailed feedback from an expert, and this expert can determine when the new employee has attained a level of proficiency to perform tasks and activities to standard. In addition, LHE recommends cross-training employees on the steps and activities completed by other employees immediately upstream or downstream of their responsibilities. This deepens their understanding of the process and reinforces the expectation that others are depending on them to perform to established work standards.[13]

8.2.6 Monitor Performance and Solve Problems to Prevent Recidivism

Recognizing and addressing current (or imminent) threats to the newly implemented steps and activities of a process can help prevent the natural inclination to revert to the former familiar way of doing things (replete with its sources of waste and impediments to flow). As a first step, LHE practice recommends the measurement and posting of key performance metrics to track the performance of the improved process. The data for these key metrics should be obtained directly from employees at the place where the work is done (i.e., quality or information systems run by specialists who are removed from the workplace are of questionable accuracy and lag current performance), visually charted, and posted where they can be seen by all employees (e.g., whiteboards in the workplace and conference rooms). In addition, Six Sigma methods (i.e., defining acceptable levels of variation in performance) can be coupled with LHE to quickly identify the first sign of actionable deviations in performance.[14] Brief daily workgroup meetings at the beginning of the day can focus attention on performance concerns from the previous day, and be used to initiate efforts that day to understand and resolve the problem using LHE practices. For example, college academic advisors can post their own levels of performance on key metrics (e.g., the number of advisees seen) in comparison to the expected levels of performance (i.e., established by calculating the number of advisee appointments expected each semester by the number of available advisor hours). Significant deviations from expectations are brought to the group's attention, which then initiates an immediate LHE review into its cause.

A university can implement a number of problem-solving strategies to address concerns quickly and defuse suggestions that the process revert to the old way of doing things. The PDCA cycle (Plan, Do, Check, Act) provides a formal approach that incorporates automatic monitoring and problem solving following unanticipated consequences from the new process.[15] When a problem is identified (Plan), solutions are implemented (Do), observed to ensure they are working as expected (Check), and then incorporated into the standardized work (Act). For example, the purchasing office would closely monitor purchase order submissions after implementing changes to the process, paying careful attention to levels of performance on key metrics (e.g., errors in completing POs, processing time for approval of POs). If this performance check indicated any problems with the new process, employees would be required to initiate the PDCA cycle:

■ *Plan:* identify the specific problem (failure to include necessary second signature for POs over $5,000).

- *Do:* propose and implement a solution (revise the PO form to include a simplified flowchart depicting paths for POs under or over $5,000).
- *Check:* pilot the revised form for the next 5 to 10 POs to confirm that the problem is rectified.
- *Act:* Immediately implement the new PO form.

A university can also use the more elaborated process for problem solving developed by the Toyota Motor Company:[16]

Step 1: Initial perception of a large and complicated problem.

Step 2: Clarify the "real" problem (using a "Pareto diagram" analysis to show which problems are most important based on their severity, frequency, etc.).

Step 3: Locate the precise area or point of cause of the problem by visiting the workplace.

Step 4: Investigate the root cause of the problem (using the Five Why technique).

Step 5: Identify and implement countermeasures to eliminate the problem.

Step 6: Evaluate the impact of the problem solution.

Step 7: Standardize the new process.

The A3 Report can also provide an easy- and simple-to-use framework (e.g., current situation, underlying cause of problem, planned solution, implementation strategy and timeline, measuring and monitoring success) for working through problems and their solutions. As a final recommendation, formalized suggestion programs that allow employees to raise a concern about the revised process and submit a suggested change (with anticipated improvement) may bring unknown problems to the forefront for evaluation and, if necessary, action. This tool, which can be part of a larger suggestion program effort at the university, must ensure that those responsible for overseeing the revised process have quick access to the suggestions and solutions. These and other formalized problem-solving methods can address problems as they occur (and they will occur). In addition to having a formal system that resolves problems that might normally have caused backsliding to the old way of doing things, problem solving is a key component of LHE's core principle of ongoing continuous improvement.

8.2.7 Reinvent Leadership to Reduce LHE's Threat to Middle Management

Providing university employees with more autonomy and responsibility over their own jobs and a greater role in improving university processes (e.g., self-directed work teams, developing work standards, quality control or problem-solving groups) are some of the positive consequences of introducing LHE. This shifting of power and control to employees from university supervisors can cause considerable anxiety, apprehension, and (potentially) resistance among supervisors. Institutionalizing middle management support for LHE in general, as well as after the completion of an LHE initiative, requires the university to explore new roles for supervisors and managers that are equally valued at the university. With less need for direct supervision, top-down communication, and decision making, supervisors and managers can shift their focus to employee coaching and development. For example, supervisors can provide training and support on such topics as 5S, PDCA, A3, "Five Why," Six Sigma, and more. In addition, supervisors and managers can develop their personal LHE skills to the point that they can model LHE knowledge and skills during their daily interactions with their employees. Developing employees and promoting bottom-up problem solving when a process falls out of control, rather than top-down monitoring and directing employees, becomes the real work of supervisors and managers. One particularly helpful responsibility for the supervisor or manager is to provide visual management of critical processes using the Five M technique:[17]

- *Manpower.* Establish and monitor visual indicators that employees involved in the process have high morale, have the skills needed to do their jobs, and know how to do their jobs correctly. For example, absenteeism might be a reasonable indicator of morale.
- *Machines.* Establish and monitor visual indicators that critical equipment is functioning properly and adequately maintained. For example, a posted log sheet by the office photocopy machine can track the types of errors throughout the week to determine whether deteriorating performance requires a service call.
- *Materials.* Establish and monitor visual indicators that the process is not producing more than is needed. For example, cabinet space for stocking office supplies can be restricted to show when more supplies than needed are on hand.

- *Methods.* Establish and monitor visual indicators that employees are doing their jobs correctly. For example, posted documentation of work standards can be used to confirm that employees are following the right sequence of steps or activities as they do their jobs.
- *Measurements.* Establish and monitor visual indicators that individuals or materials are flowing smoothly through the process without bottlenecks. For example, a separate transparent, wall-mounted inbox at every workstation can show bottlenecks in each process.

The Five M technique offers new ways for supervisors and managers to add value to every university process. Overall, supervisors and managers who embrace and develop these new skill sets can help sustain processes improved through LHE. However, those unwilling or unable to do so may need to find other opportunities within or outside the university. Job security will be an issue for supervisors and managers as well, and attrition and reassignment are the best options for handling any reduction in mid-level managers due to expanded autonomy and self-directed work teams.

8.2.8 Additional Actions to Help Sustain Gains Following LHE

The list of possibilities that can help sustain gains following the implementation of LHE solutions is not limited to those detailed above. For example, the institution's performance review and compensation systems can motivate and incentivize employee behaviors that support and sustain LHE initiatives. A "Balanced Scorecard" appraisal method can recognize and reward an individual's behaviors and results identified as important to both the short- and long-term success of LHE (e.g., submitting one suggestion per month to improve a key process, serving as an LHE Team Leader, initiating and completing three LHE projects per semester, implementing 5S in a key work area). Group recognition and rewards for work teams and their supervisors can also reinforce job behaviors and results consistent with LHE. As a second example, the university can make hiring and promotion decisions using new job descriptions that include position-relevant LHE knowledge, skills, and abilities. As a final example, a university can design professional development training programs that provide all employees with what they need to be successful at an LHE university. These and other ideas can be used as needed to increase the probability that gains achieved through the implementation of LHE solutions are sustained over time and are followed by additional continuous improvement efforts.

8.2.9 Summary

The real benefits of LHE to a university accrue from the sustained gains achieved following the implementation of LHE initiatives and continuation of specific LHE solutions that reduce waste and improve flow in key university processes. Experience, however, shows that it is common for employee behaviors to revert to the old and familiar, especially when the newly implemented process faces its first problems. University leaders can choose from a number of specific actions to prevent or reduce resistance to changes introduced by LHE, allowing the new steps and activities that are part of the revised process to take root and show evidence of improved performance. Their commitment to and support of LHE will help create fundamental changes in employee behaviors that are essential to maintain the reductions in waste and improvements in flow achieved through the implementation of LHE principles and practices. The long-term success of these projects, including additional continuous improvement efforts to further improve revised processes and support other new LHE initiatives, can bring significant benefits to the university and those it serves.

8.3 The Approval Process for New Courses: Identifying, Gaining, and Sustaining Support for LHE Initiatives

The approval process for new courses introduced in Chapter 6 provides a useful example of the application of the information and recommendations contained in Chapters 7 and 8. This hypothetical example demonstrates how the LHE Project Team can work from the "current state" visual map to identify LHE solutions that reduce waste and improve flow, gain support from university leadership to implement their recommendations, and recommend actions the university might take to sustain support for this LHE initiative.

8.3.1 LHE Team Review of the Visual Map of the Approval Process for New Courses

The visual map of the current approval process for new courses (see Figure 6.3 in Chapter 6), and personal insights obtained while creating the map, provide the LHE Team with a useful starting point for identifying waste and poor flow. The LHE Team's "current state" visual map includes clear depictions of the multiple incidences of the waste of waiting, because the mapping task uniquely highlights this particular ubiquitous form of waste (see Chapter 7). First, the triangle icons in Figure 6.3 represent time wasted due to the movement of the new course proposal from office to office using the campus mail system, with the average time required noted above each triangle. In addition, the listings of time associated with the specific steps in the process completed by each office or person shed light on additional instances of the waste of waiting embedded in the approval process. For example, while the actual time required by the library staff to confirm that its holdings are adequate to support the proposed new course is 4 hours, the proposal remains in the library an average of 10 days while the proposal is forwarded from office to office, waits in the collection specialist's in-basket for review and action, and so forth.

Identification of waste. LHE Team members, with a raised awareness of waste after familiarizing themselves with the framework and definitions of waste (see Chapter 7), identify additional specific examples of waste:

■ *Waste of unnecessary transport.* The LHE team identifies multiple instances in the approval process for new courses where an individual receives the proposal and simply forwards it to someone else. For example, the Library Dean's contribution to the process is to route the proposal to the collection specialist, adding an unnecessary movement of the proposal that provides no value. The LHE team identified similar examples of waste due to unnecessary transport throughout the process (e.g., the department chair forwarding the proposal to the departmental curriculum committee, the college dean forwarding the proposal to the associate dean, the provost forwarding the proposal to the Undergraduate Council secretary).

■ *Waste of missing information.* The LHE team notes that only 80% of the proposals reviewed by the college associate dean are complete and accurate; 20% require additional communication with the department chair and faculty sponsor and/or editing because of missing information. More egregiously, only 20% of the proposals are deemed complete and accurate by the Undergraduate Council at its first reading; four out of five proposals are returned to faculty sponsors for additional information.

■ *Waste of correcting errors.* The LHE team determined that significant amounts of time are wasted correcting errors in the proposal. The requirement of revisions and a second reading by the Undergraduate Council is the most visible example of the waste of correcting errors in the approval process for new courses. However, the department chair, the department curriculum committee, the college's associate dean, and others also may return the proposal to the faculty sponsor for corrections.

■ *Waste of unreliable processes.* The LHE team documented that a lack of clear criteria for course approval by the Undergraduate Council, coupled with the strong personal ideologies of some council members, contributes to the low percentage of proposals approved during their first reading at Undergraduate Council. The approval of proposals is hard to predict because of the idiosyncratic perspectives of well-intentioned council members.

■ *Waste of irrelevant information.* The LHE team discovers that the Undergraduate Council does not use several pieces of information they require faculty sponsors to include as part of the proposal.

■ *Waste of checking.* The large number of individuals or groups required to review new course proposals draws the attention of the LHE team. An LHE-designed process would have quality/accuracy automatically built into the process and regard additional checking or "quality control" as unnecessary waste.

■ *Waste of overburdening people.* The LHE team notes that faculty sponsors of courses are required to provide duplicate information in their proposal submission; that is, responses to several items that must be completed as part of the approval process also need to be entered on the routing sheet that accompanies the detailed course approval request.

■ *Waste of poor scheduling.* The LHE team found that if the review and approval of a proposal is not completed by the end of the spring semester, no progress is made during the summer because the Undergraduate Council does not meet. The proposal approval process will automatically resume in the fall semester after a 4- to 5-month delay.

■ *Waste of nonstrategic effort.* The LHE team concludes that the overall length and complexity of the course approval process, coupled with the summer hiatus for the Undergraduate Council, falls short of meeting the long-term needs of students and employers, that is, a dynamic curriculum for a globally competitive educational environment.

Impediments to process flow. The LHE team also identified a number of impediments to smooth and continuous flow in the current approval process for new courses:

■ The process continually stops to correct errors, requiring the return of the proposal form to the faculty sponsor for rework. As noted above, the Undergraduate Council requires corrections or additional information for 80% of proposals following their first review.

- The approval process is a serial process, such that the new course request is under review by no more than one office or individual at a time. This mandated sequential flow of steps and activities adds time to the process.
- There is an uneven flow of agenda items to the Undergraduate Council, and an unexpectedly heavy agenda sometimes requires the postponement of review and action on new course proposals until the next meeting.
- The summer hiatus by the Undergraduate Council halts the flow of the new course approval process. Without knowledge of the actual length of time required to complete the entire process, faculty sponsors lack the information necessary to initiate the process early enough to obtain a decision prior to the summer hiatus.
- The university updates its course catalog annually. New courses that are received by the registrar after the last date for inclusion in the upcoming course catalog delays the listing and offering of the course until the next annual course catalog.

The in-depth review of the current process for approving new courses by the LHE team identified a large number of incidences of waste and poor flow that add no value to the beneficiaries of the process (i.e., the faculty sponsors, their academic units, and prospective students desiring the new course). The LHE team decides to establish four LHE Specialist Teams, each focusing on a prioritized area of the new course approval process:

- Specialist Team 1: reducing the overall time required by the process.
- Specialist Team 2: reducing unnecessary "errors" in the process that require rework and interrupt the flow of the process.
- Specialist Team 3: redesigning the application materials to reduce duplicative and unnecessary information.
- Specialist Team 4: applying currently available technology to reduce the waste of waiting and improve flow.

8.3.2 Identifying LHE Solutions to Improve the Approval Process for New Courses

Each LHE Specialist Team includes members of the LHE Project Team, and invites additional faculty and staff with relevant interest in LHE and experience in the process to join the teams as well. After a brief training session to introduce LHE principles and practices to the new members and share information and results collected to this point, each LHE Specialist Team addresses its assigned areas for removing waste and improving flow. The LHE Specialist Teams "walk" the process together, asking questions and collecting additional data as needed for their assigned area of focus. Two teams contact other universities and community colleges recognized for their best practices, gaining additional insights for improving the new course approval process. Using all the information available to them, each LHE Specialist Team prepares a number of specific recommendations following their charge. The LHE Specialist Teams then convene under the umbrella of the original LHE Project Team to share and prioritize their proposed LHE solutions (based on ease of implementation, cost, impact on beneficiaries of the process, etc.) to create a revised process for approval of new courses with less waste and improved flow. The LHE Project Team then prepares a "future state" visual map of the approval process for new courses using an endorsed set of selected LHE solutions. The proposed visual map of the process, shown in Figure 8.1, includes a broad variety of LHE solutions:

- *Application form.* A streamlined electronic application form (with electronic signatures) eliminates missing information, reduces mistakes, and simplifies routing. The form requires essential information only (confirmed by the Undergraduate Council, deans, and provost). The form organizes information around the needs of each individual and office with no duplicative materials required of the faculty sponsor. Each application section addresses a single issue (i.e., reviewers do not need to read long narratives to find responses to specific questions).
- *Total time.* Applications are routed directly to assigned decision makers with copies to their administrative assistants (if the decision maker is unavailable due to travel, vacation, or other obligations, the administrative assistant will forward the application to the approved [and cross-trained] alternate decision maker). Review times for each step are established in collaboration with all decision makers based on the level of review required at that step. Automatic notification of the status of the application is provided to the Undergraduate Council secretary (and made available to faculty sponsors) as it moves through the process steps to surface any unexpected delays in review that will then trigger an appropriate follow-up response. The proposed process completes several steps in a parallel (as opposed to serial) fashion to

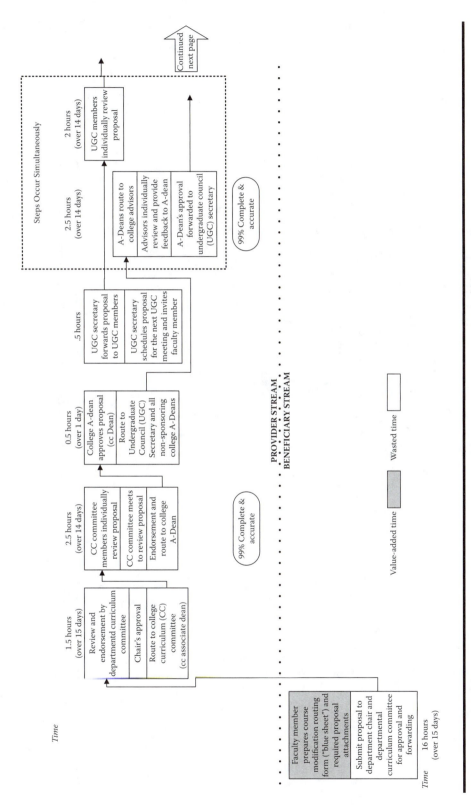

Figure 8.1a   Visual map of proposed approval process for new courses: combined perspectives.

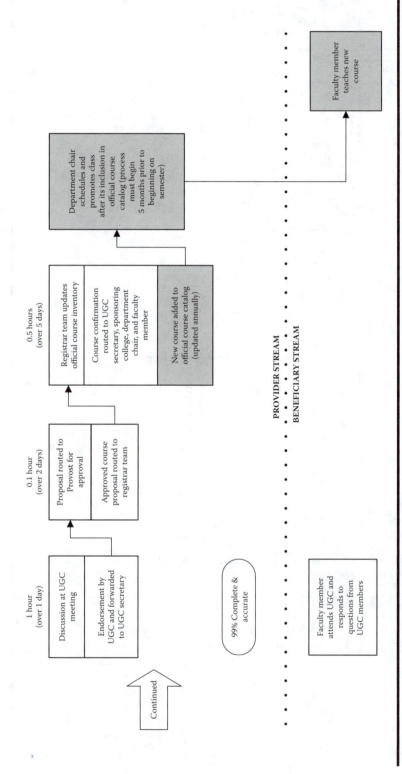

Figure 8.1b Visual map of proposed approval process for new courses: combined perspectives.

reduce the total time required. The availability and widespread use of statewide electronic holdings eliminates the need for approval by the library dean.

■ *Mistake proofing.* Enhanced instructions provide clear directions on what the faculty sponsor must include in the proposal, and exemplars of correct responses are available. Undergraduate Council members and deans use the agreed-upon standards provided for their roles in the approval process. Any future error is flagged and shared with the LHE Project Team (or, if after their disbandment, an identified "process owner" such as the Undergraduate Council secretary) for review and resolution, consistent with a commitment to continuous improvement.

■ *Publicized deadlines.* With an understanding of the expected total time required by the proposed approval process, and the critical March 1st deadline for including new courses in the upcoming university course catalog, critical time periods for faculty sponsors to initiate the process can be identified and communicated. The Undergraduate Council secretary earmarks agenda time at the point in the semester when proposal submissions are expected to be heavy (i.e., in response to the course catalog deadline).

The LHE Project Team considered and rejected as impractical and cost prohibitive a number of additional LHE solutions. For example, they held off on recommending that the university shift from an annual course catalog to a quarterly catalog (thus leveling out the number of completed applications flowing through the process across the year), or having a subcommittee of the Undergraduate Council provide a 3-day expedited review for simple and straightforward proposals.

Overall, the proposed visual map of the approval process for new courses will reduce the "Total Time" from 144 days to approximately half that number (i.e., 69 days, including 15 days for the faculty member to prepare the proposal). This significant reduction in Total Time, coupled with greater publication of deadlines, will increase the "on-time delivery" of new courses into the undergraduate curriculum (i.e., proposals initiated before the end of the fall semester can be included in the undergraduate course catalog for the following academic year). Finally, the LHE Project Team and the LHE Specialist Teams also expect the revised application form to improve the "Percent Complete and Accurate" to 99% at key review steps during the approval process.

8.3.3 Gaining Support for and Implementing LHE Solutions to Improve the Approval Process for New Courses

Members of both the LHE Project Teams and LHE Specialist Teams use the A3 Report format to present their findings to senior university leaders from areas that oversee the approval process and representatives from the office that provides oversight for LHE activities. The LHE Project Team members address questions and concerns raised during the meeting, communicating to their audience the beneficial impact of the proposed LHE solutions on key performance metrics for the approval process for new courses. Shortly after the meeting, the LHE Project Team learns that university leaders endorse all of their proposed changes as well as the timetable for implementing them.

The LHE Project Team leader and the team's representative from the LHE Steering Committee quickly establish an LHE Implementation Team, which includes individuals from both teams as well as some additional university employees with critical expertise (e.g., an ITS employee with specialized skills in online forms and signatures). The LHE Implementation Team fleshes out a detailed written implementation plan with clearly assigned responsibilities and expected dates of completion for all critical implementation steps. Working closely with university employees who are part of the approval process for new courses, LHE Implementation Team members finalize their changes and begin a widely publicized rollout of the revised approval process for new undergraduate courses.

8.3.4 Sustaining Support for LHE Improvements to the Approval Process for New Courses

The university's centralized support office for LHE initiated a comprehensive communication plan describing the recently introduced LHE solutions to improve the approval process for new courses, including a strong message of thanks and support from the provost whose office oversees this critical process. The LHE Implementation Team also collaborated with the provost to establish a monitoring system that provided performance levels on key performance metrics identified for the course approval process as well as comparing the actual versus expected time required for key steps in the process. Data from the first two proposals reviewed under the new process indicated that the Undergraduate Council (UGC) required additional information for these proposals (requiring additional effort by the faculty member sponsoring the proposal, and delaying any decision until the next UGC meeting approximately 2 weeks after the faculty member returned the revised proposal). A discussion between members of the LHE Implementation Team and the UGC identified two sources of the problem: (1) a missing piece of information that the UGC had mistakenly forgotten to request, and (2) passive resistance by a few UGC members who felt that the previous multiple readings of a proposal provided better quality assurance for the process. The LHE Implementation Team easily alleviated the former concern through a quick modification of the application used by the process. The team addressed the latter problem by presenting data that showed that the second reading surfaced no additional relevant information beyond that contained in the revised application form. In addition, they underscored for UGC members that this additional review wasted their committee's valuable time and was counter to the university's strategic priority of maintaining an up-to-date and competitive (i.e., for attracting new students) curriculum. The number of requests by the UGC for second readings dropped from one out of two to one out of twenty, and the university adopted the updated application form as the new standard for approving new undergraduate courses.

In the future, monitoring of the course approval process, and responding to unforeseen problems or new suggestions for continuous improvement, will shift to employees involved in the process who served on one or more of the LHE teams. These employees will use the formal problem-solving process developed by Toyota to resolve problems and evaluate suggestions to improve the approval process for new courses.

8.3.5 Summary

Overall, the LHE implementation to improve the hypothetical approval process for new courses suggests that significant improvements are possible. LHE solutions introduced to eliminate waste and improve flow provide a more timely review of new undergraduate courses. This allows the university to provide a curriculum responsive to both changing academic disciplines and the global, dynamic workplace of the future. The up-to-date curriculum meets the expectations of key beneficiaries: faculty sponsors, prospective and existing students, and employers of university graduates. Furthermore, employee participation in the LHE process has expanded the capabilities and interest of applying LHE principles and practices to other key processes and services more broadly throughout the university.

Endnotes

1. Tapping, D., and Shuker, T. 2003. *Value stream management for the lean office: Eight steps to planning, mapping, and sustaining lean improvements in administrative areas.* New York: Productivity Press. p. 25.

2. Adapted from Tapping, D., and Shuker, T. 2003. *Value stream management for the lean office: Eight steps to planning, mapping, and sustaining lean improvements in administrative areas.* New York: Productivity Press. p. 135.

3. While it is often possible or appropriate for the established LHE Project Team to address the prioritized incidences of waste and poor flow themselves, the benefits of new perspectives, additional resources, and expanded understanding and support for LHE provide a strong case for forming LHE Specialist Teams whenever feasible.

4. Based on Hirano, H. 1989. *JIT factory revolution: A pictorial guide to factory design of the future.* New York: Productivity Press; and Laraia, A., Moody, P., and Hall, R. 1999. *The kaizen blitz: Accelerating breakthroughs in productivity and performance.* New York: John Wiley & Sons. Chapter 1.

5. Based on Keyte, B., and Locher, D. 2004. *The complete lean enterprise: Value stream mapping for administrative and office processes.* New York: Productivity Press. Chapter 8.

6. From Liker, J.K. 2004. *The Toyota Way: 14 management principles from the world's greatest manufacturer.* New York: McGraw-Hill.

7. The A3 Report is named after the larger international size paper. For an example of an A3 Report, see Liker, J.K. 2004. *The Toyota Way: 14 management principles from the world's greatest manufacturer.* New York: McGraw-Hill. Chapter 19.

8. The following two books provide overviews of 2-day and 5-day schedules for Lean implementation teams, respectively: Imai, M. 1997. *Gemba kaizen: A commonsense, low-cost approach to management.* New York: McGraw-Hill. Chapter 13; and Laraia, A., Moody, P., and Hall, R. 1999. *The kaizen blitz: Accelerating breakthroughs in productivity and performance.* New York: John Wiley & Sons. Chapter 1.

9. The use of distinct subteams working on different pieces of a process under the coordination of the team leader is possible because all team members are thoroughly familiar with the entire process and have both technical skills and a conceptual understanding of LHE to work in a parallel and coordinated fashion.

10. Based on Tapping, D., and Shuker, T. 2003. *Value stream management for the lean office: Eight steps to planning, mapping, and sustaining lean improvements in administrative areas.* New York: Productivity Press. pp. 143–145.

11. Wiremold company executive Arnold Sargis, quoted in Laraia, A., Moody, P., and Hall, R. 1999. *The kaizen blitz: Accelerating breakthroughs in productivity and performance.* New York: John Wiley & Sons. pp. 224–225. Wiremold Company is a world leader in Lean manufacturing. http://www.wiremold.com/www/commercial/press_room/overview.asp.
12. Laraia, A., Moody, P., and Hall, R. *The kaizen blitz: Accelerating breakthroughs in productivity and performance.* New York: John Wiley & Sons. p. 226.
13. Cross-training also broadens the skills of those in the process or service, who are then able to perform other activities and steps if needed, that is, when other employees are absent or to help level out an unexpected high demand for the process.
14. The combination of Lean (i.e., an emphasis on eliminating waste and improving flow) and Six Sigma (defect-free performance) has become increasingly popular in recent years. An excellent source is George, M.L. 2003. *Lean Six Sigma for service: How to use Lean Speed & Six Sigma quality to improve services and transactions.* New York: McGraw-Hill.
15. While there are many references available for PDCA, a good example is Dennis, P. 2002. *Lean production simplified a plain-language guide to the world's most powerful production system.* New York: Productivity Press.
16. Liker, J.K. 2004. *The Toyota Way: 14 management principles from the world's greatest manufacturer.* New York: McGraw-Hill. pp. 254–257.
17. Imai, M. 1997. *Gemba kaizen: A commonsense, low-cost approach to management.* New York: McGraw-Hill. Chapter 8.

Chapter 9

Realizing the Promise of LHE
Current Challenges, Future Directions, and Next Steps

LHE holds great promise for universities confronting increasingly resource-constrained environments and greater expectations from those served by higher education. The application of LHE principles and practices described in this book provides a conceptual framework and set of strategies and tools for improving the efficiency and effectiveness of critical university processes. Figure 9.1 lists some of the benefits of LHE. The successful implementation of LHE provides the beneficiaries of the university—students, faculty, parents, employers, alumni, legislators, and others—with higher quality, more timely, less costly, and more convenient processes. The clear focus on meeting or exceeding the expectations of the different beneficiaries is a central tenet of LHE. Redesigning a process to deliver what a beneficiary values by removing waste and improving flow is fundamental to the application of LHE.

The university directly and indirectly benefits from the application of LHE. The enhanced efficiency of processes following LHE implementation will improve performance on common performance metrics (e.g., number of applications processed, cost per unit of service). The resources (e.g., employee time) freed up through improved efficiency in completing processes and delivering services can be reallocated to other processes and services that currently fall short of meeting the expectations of beneficiaries. Indirectly, LHE efforts can improve student and faculty recruitment and retention through processes that meet or exceed their needs. In addition, the

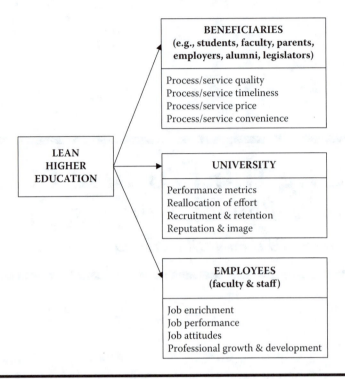

Figure 9.1   The benefits of Lean Higher Education (LHE).

successful implementation of LHE can enhance a university's reputation and image as an exemplar of efficiency and effectiveness, serving as a model of best practice to emulate.

Figure 9.1 also identifies significant benefits for employees who work at a university that embraces LHE principles and practices. A key concept in the development of the Lean philosophy is employee empowerment, which recognizes that respecting, developing, and challenging employees is a foundational element of success.[1] Employees' jobs are enriched through their active involvement in eliminating waste and improving flow in processes; their participation gives them greater input both as individuals and teams, and provides more meaningful work (i.e., eliminating steps in their jobs that add no value or being part of a process that is free of errors). Job performance improves through processes that are more efficient, and fulfilling work that is appreciated by those served contributes to increases in job attitudes (e.g., job satisfaction). Finally, LHE training and participation on LHE Project Teams offer expanded opportunities for professional growth and development.[2] Overall, the application of LHE directly benefits those served by the university, the faculty and staff of the university, and the efficiency and effectiveness of the university.

Results from the successful applications of LHE described in Chapter 3, along with findings from the introduction of Lean systems in a wide range of organizations outside of higher education, demonstrate its great potential for helping universities succeed in a competitive environment with expanding needs and diminishing resources. Chapters 4 through 8 presented a comprehensive framework for successfully launching, implementing, and sustaining LHE initiatives within and across all areas of a university. This final chapter reflects on current challenges to the broader adoption of LHE, and future directions that may hold significant promise for LHE going forward.

9.1 Challenges to the Broader Adoption of LHE

9.1.1 University-Wide Adoption

LHE is conceptualized as an institution-wide philosophy. As such, it has a central role in a university's strategic plan (e.g., eliminating waste is a strategic priority, adopting goals and timetables for implementing LHE in a planned fashion), organizational design (e.g., institutional leadership and oversight of LHE initiatives, cross-functional oversight of key processes), and the structuring of work (e.g., team-based work cells, established performance standards). For example, a strategic plan priority to "position the university to hold fiscal and market competitive advantages by reducing costs while improving services to students" may call for goals that create new cross-functional systems of operation, new performance metrics that emphasize service quality and cost effectiveness, new professional development standards for employees, and a centralized office of LHE to coordinate and implement change. The coordinated alignment of these university-wide goals, along with a comprehensive communication plan led by senior leaders and administrators, provide the broad operational support required to reach this priority. Furthermore, these university-wide changes in priorities and goals, operating systems, job expectations, communication content, and so on can begin to influence and shape the climate and workplace practices of the university.

As discussed in Chapter 4, the greatest gain will come from the university-wide adoption of LHE principles and practices. Many processes cut across vice-presidential divisions, requiring support from multiple leaders before implementing LHE. Without institution-wide support, key processes most in need of improvement that fall under the responsibility of a vice-president or director resistant or ambivalent to LHE will not be pursued. Finally, inconsistent support for LHE from the senior leadership team sends a mixed message to the university community, potentially weakening the ongoing commitment of mid-level supervisors and managers to shift more autonomy and responsibility to their subordinates in accordance with LHE practices. While the local implementation of LHE can have significant benefits to the university, its faculty and staff, and those they serve, its impact will be less far-reaching and unlikely to change the "DNA" of the university as it moves forward.

Overall, university-wide adoption of LHE will bring greater benefits to the university community and foster a workplace climate that fosters respect for employees and a commitment to continuous improvement for the benefit of those served. But not every university is ready to endorse, implement, and sustain LHE, which will require major organizational change. Chapter 4 discusses how both current workplace climate and existing leadership practices are important factors that point to the level of readiness for implementing LHE university-wide. In addition, honest responses to the following set of critical questions will help guide a thoughtful review of both the benefits and costs of a decision to launch, delay, or defer the introduction of LHE:[3]

- *Will the adoption of LHE result in improvements on what the university now accomplishes?* Pilot projects introducing LHE locally may be preferred to first demonstrate the effectiveness of LHE at the university prior to full-scale adoption.
- *Is the change expected from LHE really worth the time and money required and the disruption and challenges expected?* Carefully review what is proposed to make sure that costs are not underestimated and benefits are not overstated.
- *Would it be better to implement symbolic changes with less risk and less benefit rather than a core change with significant risk and significant benefit?* If the goal is to look good to the outside, there may not be enough support for the extensive changes required when adopting LHE.
- *Is the decision to adopt LHE influenced by a personal career agenda or the best interests of the university?* University leaders should recognize that university incentive systems and career ladders might exert an inappropriate influence on decisions to introduce or reject LHE.
- *Will the adoption of LHE have the needed resources and levels of power and support to implement and sustain change?* Leaders often have less power than they think and more confidence than they should in their abilities to implement and sustain large-scale change.

■ *Are faculty and staff and other constituencies already overwhelmed by too many changes at the university to embrace LHE?* The successive introduction of new programs and initiatives can overwhelm even the best followers and cause resistance to implementing what may come to be perceived as "flavor-of-the-month" changes.

■ *Will faculty and staff and other constituencies be able to learn and adapt in response to new circumstances following the introduction of LHE?* The inability to learn from experiences and make changes as needed after implementing LHE raises concerns regarding its overall level of success.

■ *If necessary, would the university be able to reverse course if the adoption of LHE did not work?* Risk is lower if the university can scale back or abandon LHE if it was determined to be ineffective.

9.1.2 Presidential Commitment, Advocacy, and Support

The role of the university president is critical to the successful adoption, implementation, and sustainability of LHE. The office of the president offers a unique "bully pulpit" for raising awareness, acceptance, and endorsement of LHE principles and practices throughout the university community as well as the authority and power to set strategic priorities, allocate resources, change organizational structure, and establish goals and objectives for senior leaders essential to any large-scale initiative. In addition, the personal qualities of the president and the community's respect for this individual provide additional sources of influence that contribute to the success of LHE. The level of presidential commitment, advocacy, and support for LHE will help shape the perceptions, attitudes, and behaviors of faculty and staff toward this new initiative. And recognizing that high levels of presidential commitment, advocacy, and support for LHE alone will not be sufficient to guarantee its success, they do create a positive context during adoption and implementation. Conversely, the lack of—or lukewarm—public commitment, advocacy, and support for LHE by the university president may unintentionally signal that LHE is unimportant and not a strategic priority of the president and his or her senior leadership team. Thus, it may be best to defer or abandon university-wide LHE efforts if the president is not ready or willing to nurture and encourage its success.

Presidents must recognize that embracing LHE university-wide is a commitment to cultural change, a significant undertaking that requires their personal involvement and effort as well as that of their senior leadership team.

Before embarking on LHE, the president (and the governing board) should affirm the following leadership commitment:[4]

■ Is the senior leadership at the university committed to transforming the institution's culture to embrace the core philosophy of LHE?

■ Is the senior leadership team at the university willing to make a long-term commitment to the professional development and involvement of faculty and staff in LHE efforts?

■ Is the president (and governing board) committed to providing continuity in the hiring and support of top leaders who continue to embrace the core philosophy of LHE?

Affirmative answers to all three questions indicate a sustained senior leadership commitment to LHE. Under the president's guidance, senior leaders can develop a multi-year action plan with specific accomplishments and a timetable that align with the LHE priority identified in the institution's strategic plan. In addition, presidents (and their senior teams) can use their power and influence to help ensure the success of LHE through a variety of methods, including their personal engagement and public support for LHE initiatives, active promotion of the philosophy of LHE, redesigning the university to better support LHE, and allocating the necessary resources to help ensure success.[5] In all areas, the president regularly and consistently models the commitment, advocacy, and support necessary to implement and sustain LHE university-wide.

9.1.3 Leadership Waste[6]

In addition to the four general categories of waste (i.e., People, Process, Information, and Asset) discussed previously in Chapter 6, a fifth is added: *Leadership Waste*. Leadership Waste is a "higher-order" level of waste that allows other forms of waste to remain hidden or continue (e.g., failure to share with workgroup members feedback from the individuals they serve). Leadership Waste also includes new incidences of People, Process, Information, and Asset Waste that are added to a process through the actions—or inactions—of university leaders (e.g., failure to provide employees with clear, measureable performance objectives to help them focus their time and energy). Leadership Waste is found at all levels of leadership and management at a university, making it a more insidious form of waste that is not reflected in the visual mapping of the steps or activities of a process, yet its presence permits other forms of waste to take root and stay hidden. University leaders need to understand how their leadership behaviors contribute waste to processes, and use LHE principles and practices to eliminate this form of waste. Four specific types of Leadership Waste have been identified, each following from a key responsibility of university leaders: focus, structure, discipline, and ownership.

Waste of focus. Leadership focus is clarity on the most important goal(s) of an institution and a focused commitment of energy to reach them. The *waste of focus* occurs when these critical objectives are unclear or are lost in translation as they filter down from the president and vice presidents through all levels of the university. In the absence of clarity, first-level supervisors and workgroups will decide what they think is important to the university and use this to guide how they do their jobs. For example, all employees may hear public statements that "student success" is a critical goal for their university. But different interpretations of success (e.g., faculty may define success as classroom performance, residence life may interpret success as adjustment to campus life, the career services office may define success as employment after graduation) or a belief that their position (e.g., admissions staff, food service workers) plays no role in student success can cause different priorities to be set by managers and workgroups, diffusing the university's commitment of energy and resources to what is most important. A university will eliminate the waste of focus when leaders communicate to help every employee understand how his or her job contributes to what is critically important to the university.

Waste of structure. Leadership-defined structure includes the physical design of the university (e.g., job titles, office names, reporting relationships) and other sources of influence (e.g., role expectations, communication patterns) that guide the day-to-day activities of the university. The *waste of structure* occurs when the combination of these influences fail to result in employee behaviors consistent with LHE. For example, if the university does not provide employees with standards for work performance, daily updates on key metrics that provide feedback on performance, or a mechanism to receive assistance from colleagues to help solve problems, they will be unable to recognize and address waste and poor flow in university processes. Leaders can help reduce the waste of structure by providing all employees and workgroups with an appropriately structured workplace (e.g., cross-functional workgroups, regular two-way communication with their supervisor) for accomplishing their responsibilities in support of the critical objectives of the university.

Waste of discipline. Leadership discipline is enacted through the university's motivational system and a process of checks and balances to ensure that employees provide ongoing contributions to the university's critical objectives. The *waste of discipline* occurs when employee goals and behaviors drift over time or when pressures at the university make it difficult for employees to support critical objectives. For example, if the university uses an unstructured end-of-year employee evaluation system (e.g., a narrative of strengths and weaknesses prepared by the immediate supervisor), the employee's contribution to the university's most important goals may not be addressed. As a second example, managers introduce waste of discipline when they continually provide employees with assignments that distract them from completing other parts of their job that are directly related to the critical objectives of the university—and employees may be uncomfortable speaking up. Leaders can help minimize waste of discipline by meeting regularly with employees to review performance relative to established goals that tie directly to the university's critical objectives and helping remove barriers to support employee success.

Waste of ownership. Leadership that allows employees to exercise ownership over their work, their work areas, and processes realizes the full engagement and talents of employees. The *waste of ownership* occurs when managers exert inappropriate control over employees, restricting their autonomy and stifling employees' opportunities to identify and resolve problems (i.e., waste and poor flow) that affect their performance and goal accomplishments. This type of waste is manifested in a workplace where decision making is delegated solely to supervisors and managers, requiring employees to bring problems to them and wait (a pernicious form of waste) for the supervisor or manager to provide a solution. Supervisors would fail to benefit from the insights of employees with direct involvement in the process, and miss an opportunity to enhance the professional development and growth of their employees. Leaders can reduce waste of ownership by creating an environment where employees are encouraged or required to assume greater responsibility and accountability for their contributions to critical university processes and services.

Overall, university leaders must recognize the impact their actions and behaviors can have on the amount of waste found in university processes. Individually or in combination, the four types of leadership waste contribute to, or hide, other forms of waste that add no value to the process. As part of their commitment to the successful implementation of LHE, university leaders should embrace the reduction of leadership waste as a strategic priority.

9.1.4 Conflating "Lean" with "Mean"

As conceptualized in its historical roots, Lean principles and practices refer to an organization-wide philosophy or system designed to improve business performance as well as working conditions for employees.[7] Unfortunately, the term "Lean," which was adopted as a simple label for a comprehensive set of operating practices for eliminating waste from processes and operations, is often used to describe a business practice whose primary goal is to reduce the number of employees. Thus, university communication announcing the decision to implement LHE must clearly distinguish the adoption of these new principles and practices from the more colloquial and pejorative, "Lean = Fewer employees." Under LHE, eliminating waste and increasing flow will reduce the amount of time and effort required in the improved processes, and then reinvesting these savings in other processes that provide more value to the beneficiaries served by the university. The goal of LHE is *not* to reduce the size of the university's workforce and should *not* be used as a pretext for doing so.[8] While staff reductions might occur over time with natural attrition (i.e., retirements and resignations), because the continuous improvement efforts of LHE allow more processes to be completed more efficiently, this is a secondary consequence of LHE rather than its intended goal. Overall, LHE is not designed to cut personnel budgets, but rather to help a university exceed the expectations that its beneficiaries value and desire. This, in turn, will result in greater support and growth for the university, providing greater—not less—job security.

A second potential challenge during the adoption of LHE is the misperception that Lean principle and practices are "mean" principles and practices. A fundamental principle of LHE (and Lean) is respect for employees. Employees are important partners in the success of LHE. They assume key roles in LHE initiatives, participating on LHE teams (i.e., LHE Project Teams, LHE Specialist Teams, LHE Implementation Teams) to radically improve university processes. They contribute to ongoing continuous improvement efforts that further reduce waste and improve flow. The revised steps and activities employees are required to complete reflect a commitment to providing work that is safe, meaningful, and satisfying. As a critical partner in the success of LHE, the university invests in the professional growth and development of employees. This investment helps prepare employees to assume greater responsibility for improving the processes in which they are involved, and offers job security both to reinforce this respected partnership and protect its significant investment in people. Some writers, however, describe the Lean workplace as one that is fast-paced and inflexible, where employees have limited autonomy and work under stressful conditions that affect their health and well-being. In addition, employee layoffs and firings following other organization-wide interventions that are antithetical to Lean's philosophy of respecting employees (e.g., business process improvement programs), or have misappropriated the Lean name when introducing a program that is inconsistent with Lean's philosophy, create suspicion and resistance to Lean (and, by extension, LHE). Conducting rigorous field experiments that conclusively demonstrate the positive benefits of Lean and LHE is difficult, resulting in conflicting research findings, testimonials, and anecdotal reports by both proponents and opponents of Lean and LHE.[9]

Overall, colloquial usage and misperceptions of the term "Lean" may create some initial concern and resistance when adopting LHE. The extent of these concerns and resistance may depend on the university's climate and past experiences with university-wide change. University leaders can help defuse strong resistance to implementing LHE by visibly promoting the benefits of LHE while acknowledging potential concerns through early and direct communication. Including an ongoing formal assessment of LHE's effect on employee perceptions, attitudes, and performance would provide a more comprehensive evaluation of LHE's overall impact on the university community.

9.2 Opportunities for the Broader Adoption of LHE

9.2.1 Expanding LHE's Impact through Process Families

LHE initiatives typically focus on a single process, identifying its sources of waste and poor flow and using LHE methods and tools to implement improvements. Even with a strong commitment to implementing LHE initiatives, addressing the large number of university processes would take some time, and any individual process would likely wait before an LHE initiative can begin. Fortunately, a university can expand the benefits it receives from LHE by identifying "families" of similar processes and establishing an LHE initiative that focuses on improving this group of processes simultaneously. For example, most graduate programs are likely to include an applicant credential review process as part of graduate admissions, where a set of materials (e.g., application form, GRE scores, letters of reference) is compiled for a graduate admissions committee to review and make admission recommendations. While there are likely to be disciplinary differences in what information is collected, criteria used for selection, and so forth, there will be a number of steps and activities completed that are common to all: tracking when an application is complete, communication with applicants, routing of completed applications to committee members for review, and so on. The LHE team can sample and develop visual maps for several of these individual application processes, uncover examples of waste and poor flow, and use LHE tools and practices to identify improvements to these processes (e.g., visual cues that show the completion status of any applicant's file, eliminate duplication of effort by graduate college staff, standard templates for communication with applicants, scanning materials to allow simultaneous review of completed credentials by all committee members, standardized format of application credentials consistent with the importance of the material to the admission decision). The LHE team, with the support of the graduate dean, can share the recommendations broadly with all graduate programs at the university, broadening the benefits of the LHE initiative throughout the university. Every university will have a number of process families among decentralized academic units (e.g., summer class scheduling), residence halls (e.g., room repairs), plant operations (e.g., restocking custodial supplies), budget officers (e.g., approval for "no bid" purchase), and other areas that can benefit from the generalized findings and recommendations from these LHE initiatives.

9.2.2 Expanding LHE's Impact across a Beneficiary's Total Experience

Beneficiaries typically encounter a large number of processes that comprise their total university experience. LHE initiatives conducted by the university may have improved a number of these processes, offering beneficiaries more of what they value and expect. However, it is likely that LHE has not comprehensively removed waste and improved flow from all of the common or consecutive processes a beneficiary encounters, providing them with an inconsistent university experience. Universities can expand LHE's impact by broadening LHE efforts to address a common set of processes that the beneficiary typically encounters. For example, new students experience a series of university processes in rapid succession during their first week: residence hall move-in, ID card processing, adding and dropping classes, purchasing textbooks, finding campus employment, and so on.

Prioritizing LHE efforts on the processes that comprise this first-week experience can address both the waste and poor flow within each process as well as the waste and poor flow that occurs between them (e.g., processes can be co-located or arranged in a way that minimizes the amount of walking required). Similarly, the university can focus LHE efforts on improving the amalgamation of processes that faculty members experience when seeking external funding for their scholarship (e.g., grant writing assistance, budget development, institutional review board approval, obtaining cost-share commitments, proposal routing for approval). This approach can be expanded to encompass an even longer time period or a larger set of typical processes. For example, LHE efforts can target all processes commonly experienced during the freshman year (and ultimately the entire undergraduate experience). Overall, a university can provide a singularly positive experience for beneficiaries when LHE initiatives are prioritized to remove waste and improve flow as they move through a linked set of typical processes.

9.2.3 Expanding LHE's Impact beyond University Boundaries

The previous section discusses the strategy for expanding the impact of LHE efforts to a series of processes *within* the boundaries of the organization. A university can further expand LHE's impact by partnering with other institutions and organizations *outside* its boundaries that play a prominent role in the "higher education supply chain." At the simplest level, this might include helping key university vendors embrace Lean principles and practices in their own companies.[10] Their adoption of Lean would help them improve their internal business processes to provide the value in their products and services expected by their beneficiaries, one of whom is the university. For example, improving their ordering/purchasing process, shipment process (i.e., creating just-in-time shipments), service call process, product returns, and so forth will have a positive impact on those university processes that directly interface with the vendor. Similarly, the university may play a vendor role to some beneficiaries of higher education, presenting an opportunity to share the process improvements gained through the application of LHE with them. For example, community organizations that sponsor student co-op and internship opportunities may decide to introduce Lean principles and practices to reduce waste and improve flow across the comprehensive recruitment and hiring process that span both university and sponsor organizations. In either case, LHE teams drawing visual maps of the steps and activities of critical university processes can expand their beginning and/or endpoints to include activities and steps that occur outside the university's boundaries, creating more integrated processes with university partners.

At a more fundamental level, university leaders can expand the impact of LHE principles and practices outside their institutional boundaries with other educational institutions through K–16 partnerships. This more encompassing enterprisewide "education supply chain" could address significant waste and poor flow that are all too common: enrolled high school students in college courses, incomplete sequences of high-school courses that result in extra college requirements, the need for remedial coursework in college, nonstandard applications to college, concurrent enrollments at two or more institutions, transferring academic credits among institutions, fulfilling academic major and graduation requirements, advisors knowledgeable about majors and degree requirements at multiple institutions, purchasing consortia, merging "backroom" business operations, inter-institutional grant proposals, and more. Conceptualizing K–16 education as an extended set of common processes across partnering institutions presents a tremendous opportunity to reinvent these processes to meet student—not institutional—needs. While many public higher education systems and student-centered private institutions have made some progress in these areas (e.g., articulation agreements, mandated course transferability standards, in-residence academic advisors from other institutions), these efforts are not guided by the core LHE principles. Thus, these new processes may work, but they will include both waste and poor flow and fall short of expectations held by multiple beneficiaries (e.g., students, parents, boards of regents, state legislators). The enterprisewide application of LHE, involving employees from multiple institutions who are intimately familiar with existing processes who receive training in LHE principles and practices, offers great promise.

9.2.4 Expanding LHE's Impact to the Student Learning Process

The astute reader will recognize that the vast majority of examples of university processes discussed to this point as benefiting from LHE have focused on business operations and support services, not the core process of higher education: student learning. These examples represent areas that are certainly critical to the experience of the beneficiaries of a university, and reductions in waste and improvements in flow made possible through the application of LHE will result in university processes that better meet their expectations and use limited university resources more efficiently and effectively. Current LHE efforts have focused on business operations and support services because they are common to virtually all organizations; they have been studied and improved through the implementation of Lean principles and practices in the fields of manufacturing, healthcare, and other business sectors that were early adopters of Lean. But just as manufacturing organizations use Lean to address their core manufacturing processes, and healthcare organizations use Lean to improve the delivery of medical services, LHE has the potential to alter the way universities fulfill the educational needs of the students they serve.[11]

Given the relatively recent extension of the application of Lean principles and practices in higher education, only two examples demonstrating the impact of LHE on student learning were found, both at Rensselaer Polytechnic Institute (see Chapter 3). In the redesign of a graduate business course on leadership, the faculty member made specific changes to seven discrete course elements (e.g., course syllabus, required readings, assignments, examinations) to reduce waste and improve flow in the student learning process based on the expectations of value identified by both students and future employers (see Table 3.9). For example, required readings were selected that were both shorter and clearly focused on the planned learning outcomes for the course, rather than simply continuing to assign long readings that required unnecessary time and effort and never clearly demonstrated the scientific method that was identified by employers as a key learning outcome. These changes, introduced over time as part of the faculty member's continuous improvement efforts for the course, were recognized and appreciated by students as assessed through their end-of-course evaluations. In the second application of LHE, the faculty member led rapid improvement workshops for each of the ten courses in the executive management program. Cross-functional teams led by a trained facilitator used Lean tools to identify opportunities to eliminate waste and poor flow in each course. Improvements included the standardization of materials (e.g., written learning objectives for each class session and course assignment), reordering of topics to improve the flow of course materials, eliminating duplicative materials across the ten courses, and adding value desired by both students and employers (e.g., non-U.S. business case studies and comparative analyses). Self-report scores provided by both course instructors and Lean team members agreed that the workshops led to positive course improvements. Unfortunately, neither LHE project included direct measures of their effect on classroom learning or transfer to performance in the workplace.

Despite limited results from only two examples at a single institution where LHE was used to improve the student learning process, LHE holds real promise for removing waste and improving flow from the student learning process, whether at the level of a single course or throughout the totality of the undergraduate experience. Table 9.1 uses the general framework for identifying what value beneficiaries expect (see Chapter 4) to propose some solutions that might follow LHE initiatives to reduce waste and improve flow in the student learning process. Some universities have implemented one or more of these changes, most likely in an effort to increase enrollment and not as part of a set of solutions designed to remove waste and improve flow from the extended learning process in higher education. Thus, the uniqueness of LHE is not in the particular solutions that it chooses, but rather the rationale for choosing among many different solutions: a prioritized commitment to continuous improvement of the learning process for the ultimate benefit of the beneficiary.

Overall, LHE principles and practices can help an LHE Project Team recognize examples of waste and poor flow in the current learning process at a university that add no value from the perspective of the beneficiary. This can help the LHE Project Team identify a combination of common and/or unique solutions to propose a future process that dramatically improves learning from the perspective of the student and other beneficiaries (e.g., employers) and use the university's limited resources more effectively. Universities can apply LHE to improve all core processes in higher education, including student learning, faculty scholarship and grantsmanship, and service learning and community outreach, all to the ultimate benefit of those they serve.

9.3 Next Steps

Chapter 4 discussed workplace climate and leadership practices as two critical factors to consider before making the decision to become an LHE university. If both offer consistently high support, university-wide implementation of LHE may be relatively easy. Changing the workplace climate of a university to embrace LHE, and gaining unconditional support for LHE across all levels of university leaders as a prelude to implementing LHE, is doable—but very difficult. However, LHE can be implemented locally (i.e., within a single vice-presidential division, college, or administrative area), providing some benefits to the university until circumstances are more broadly supportive of LHE principles and practices. This section briefly lists some simple recommendations for getting LHE started locally with limited support, followed by some additional recommendations to facilitate a university-wide transition to LHE.[12]

Table 9.1 Potential LHE Solutions to Enhance Student Learning

Value Expected by Beneficiaries	Potential LHE Solutions to Enhance Value
Providing exactly what is wanted adds value	Design professionally developed multimedia course/program material that supports unique learning styles and established learning objectives
	Modularize course/program to allow students to selectively enroll in course component(s) relevant to their learning needs or objectives
	Update course/program curriculum regularly to reflect developments in discipline and needs of employers
Delivering services where it is wanted adds value	Offer course/program at remote locations convenient for students
	Develop asynchronous Web-based course/program that permits students to complete their work at any location and at any time
	Promote seamless access to other universities providing required courses at more convenient times and locations (with guaranteed transferability)
Offering service when it is wanted adds value	Allow students to enroll at any time and begin course/program immediately or at a large number of times throughout the year
	Offer self-paced courses that allow students to complete requirements on a personalized timeframe
Not wasting the beneficiary's time adds value	Tailor course/program requirements based on each student's educational background, professional experiences, and learning objectives
	Reduce waiting by compressing course/program schedules (e.g., classes held throughout the year including weekends)
	Standardize formats of syllabus, online course materials, class exercises, Web sites, etc.
	Incorporate regular testing and feedback to demonstrate mastery of learning outcomes and/or target areas requiring additional review

Table 9.1   (continued) Potential LHE Solutions to Enhance Student Learning

Value Expected by Beneficiaries	*Potential LHE Solutions to Enhance Value*
Solving the beneficiary's problem completely adds value	Consolidate all course/program material into a single, searchable, easily accessible location
	Design course/program materials consistent with established learning principles for long-term retention and transfer to the workplace
	Provide continuing access to faculty following course/program completion to reinforce learning outcomes in the workplace
Solving the beneficiary's problem forever adds value	Create online portfolio that documents course/program success and which can be regularly updated by alumni throughout their careers
	Provide "lifelong learning" modules and other educational options that are directly integrated into previously learned course/program material to keep alumni professionally up-to-date

9.3.1 Getting LHE Started Locally

Identify one or more LHE change agents. Find or recruit the right person(s) to help spearhead LHE at your university. Faculty or staff who have earned the respect of others, who are willing to lead the LHE initiative through to completion, and who can inspire others to participate in the LHE journey are excellent candidates for taking on the role of LHE change agent. If this person does not exist at your university, become that person yourself.

Learn about LHE. Gather information about LHE (and more broadly, Lean). Call or visit other universities to learn about their LHE initiatives. Attend an LHE or Lean webinar or conference, or enroll in a noncredit LHE or Lean certificate program. Visit LHE and Lean Web sites (e.g., the Lean Enterprise Institute at www.lean.org; Lean in Higher Education at www.st-andrews.ac.uk/lean/ResourcesforChange/LeaninHigherEducation/).

Find an LHE teacher. Identify any faculty members with expertise in LHE or Lean and ask them to advise the LHE initiative. Barter their services by agreeing to have your project provide data for their research program. Check with local organizations that have implemented Lean and request their voluntary assistance in implementing LHE at your institution. Seek university, foundation, or corporate funding to hire an LHE or Lean trainer.

Invite broad participation. Openly solicit volunteers to participate in the LHE initiative. While not everyone can serve on the LHE Project Team, the LHE Specialist Team, or the LHE Implementation Team, project leaders can identify additional roles and activities that expose more faculty and staff to LHE principles and practices.

Identify pilot projects to demonstrate the benefits of LHE. Identify an important but manageable process as a pilot project for the LHE initiative. If possible, select a process that has the potential for creating a significant improvement for those served, significant savings in resources (people, financial, or space), or both.

Make LHE a hands-on experience and not a classroom experience. Let faculty and staff learn about LHE through their immediate participation on the LHE initiative. More will be learned about creating a visual map or identifying waste and poor flow through experiential learning. Limit classroom training, and always try to follow classroom training with an opportunity to put what was learned into practice.

Conduct rapid improvement workshops to make rapid changes in processes. Establish an aggressive timetable to complete the LHE initiative. When possible, complete the project within 2- to 5 days. Implement LHE solutions quickly and fine-tune as needed. It is not essential to create a perfectly revised process; additional continuous improvement efforts should follow all LHE initiatives to provide ongoing, incremental improvements.

Publicize your demonstration project to create more LHE change agents. Create opportunities to share LHE successes with the broader university community. Invite university leaders to attend a LHE Project Team wrap-up meeting that summarizes the project and demonstrates the improvements achieved in the targeted process or service. Solicit invitations to share the results from the LHE initiative at standing meetings (e.g., president's cabinet, university senate, vice-president senior staff meeting). Share your results at regional conferences, and consider writing up your results for publication.

9.3.2 Facilitating a University-Wide Transition to LHE

Seize a crisis to promote LHE. Use existing challenges and threats (e.g., external demands for efficiency and accountability, enrollment or budget declines) to provide a clear rationale for radical change. Promote the benefits of LHE to the university's beneficiaries (e.g., dramatic improvements in critical processes that serve students, competitive marketing advantage to prospective students and faculty) and employees (e.g., job security, greater autonomy and accountability, meaningful work).

Establish an office that oversees and promotes LHE. Create a high-level administrative structure (preferably reporting to the university president) with the budget and authority to ensure LHE success. Appoint an individual to serve as the university's LHE leader, with responsibilities for promoting, approving, supporting, and monitoring LHE initiatives. Include the LHE leader as a peer in senior-level policy discussions.

Hire, train, and promote LHE leaders. Recruit staff and faculty with expertise in LHE or Lean, and establish performance expectations related to LHE responsibilities and activities. Provide in-depth training opportunities and mentored experiences to develop on-campus expertise in LHE. Implement an LHE succession planning system that provides progressively increasing responsibilities on LHE projects to maintain and expand LHE expertise.

Include LHE in strategic planning, policy deployment, and goal setting. Seek support for LHE from the university's board of trustees. Priorities of the institution's strategic plan, operational objectives developed and deployed to implement the strategic plan, and individual and unit goals should reflect the core role of LHE in the overall effectiveness and success of the university. Establish and closely monitor quantitative metrics of individual, unit, and university performance that flow from strategic plan priorities and operational objectives that flow from the adoption of LHE.

Reorganize the university by processes or service streams. Shift the responsibilities of university leaders from the traditional oversight of specific business functions to ownership and accountability for critical "value streams" (i.e., broader level processes and service streams) that ensure that beneficiaries receive the value they expect from the university. Provide each leader with complete responsibility over the value stream, and monitor performance with metrics that reflect what beneficiaries of the process value.

Shift from top-down leadership to bottom-up initiatives. Empower all employees to play an active role in managing and improving the processes in which they are involved. Create opportunities for sharing employee ideas to improve processes and recognizing these contributions. Teach leaders to serve as mentors and advisors to employees.

Make LHE mandatory. Require all academic and nonacademic units to use LHE principles and practices. Use established unit goals and objectives (e.g., complete four LHE initiatives annually) to evaluate individual and team performance. Include performance on these metrics when making personnel decisions.

Ask vendors and K-16 partners to adopt LHE principles and practices. Share LHE experiences and expertise with the leaders of other organizations that also contribute to the value expected by your beneficiaries. Collaborate on LHE initiatives. Establish performance metrics for the extended process, and provide feedback on each metric to all partners on a regular basis.

Overall, LHE proponents can pursue a number of tactics to bring LHE principles and practices to their university. Whether initiated locally, creating small pockets of success and interest in expanding LHE, or initiated university-wide, with the strong support of senior leaders and a complementary workplace climate, the critical first step on the path to becoming an LHE university has been taken.

9.4 Summary

LHE, the extension of Lean principles and practices to higher education, holds great promise for all colleges and universities seeking academic and operational excellence through an intentional and disciplined approach that builds on the expertise and commitment of faculty and staff. While challenges exist that may potentially limit the acceptance and impact of LHE, there are enormous benefits to the university, its faculty and staff, and those it serves, made possible through its broader adoption. Universities have much to gain:[13]

- LHE can make universities distinctive and competitive in the increasingly cluttered landscape of higher education.
- LHE allows universities to use their limited resources (human, financial, space) more effectively, providing cost savings or the reallocation of these resources to deliver more value to those they serve.
- LHE takes advantage of the expertise and ideas of all employees, who are encouraged to play an active role in improving university processes.

Getting started on the LHE journey is easy, and the payoffs significant. Begin the journey today.

Endnotes

1. See, for example, Liker, J.K. 2004. *The Toyota Way: 14 management principles from the world's greatest manufacturer.* New York: McGraw-Hill. Chapter 16.

2. While proponents of Lean provide evidence for these positive benefits to employees, opponents of Lean suggest that its implementation results in fast-paced and inflexible work practices that negatively impact worker health and well-being. Data supporting either side are largely anecdotal or fall short of conventional standards for reaching firm conclusions. Thus, any conclusions regarding the benefits of LHE on employees are tentative and require further study. For a review, see Balzer, W.K., Alexander, K., and Smith, E.N. 2009. What do we know about the psychology of lean? In *24th Annual Conference of the Society for Industrial and Organizational Psychology*. New Orleans, LA.

3. These questions are adapted from Pfeffer, J., and Sutton, R.I. 2006. *Hard facts, dangerous half-truths & total nonsense: Profiting from evidence-based management*. Boston: Harvard Business School Press. Chapter 7.

4. These minimum levels of leadership commitment are adapted from Liker, J.K. 2004. *The Toyota Way: 14 management principles from the world's greatest manufacturer*. New York: McGraw-Hill. Chapter 22.

5. These suggestions are drawn from a longer list developed from interviews with healthcare leaders and reported in Joint Commission Resources (2005). *Overcoming Performance Management Challenges in Hospitals*. Oakbrook Terrace, IL: Joint Commission on Accreditation of Healthcare Organizations. Cited in Joint Commission Resources (2006). *Doing More with Less: Lean Thinking and Patient Safety in Health Care*. Oakbrook Terrace, IL: Joint Commission on Accreditation of Healthcare Organizations. Table 3.2.

6. Based on Lareau, W. 2003. *Office kaizen: Transforming office operations into a strategic competitive advantage*. Milwaukee, WI: ASQ Quality Press. Chapter 4.

7. For a review of the historical development of Lean, see Womack, J.P., Jones, D.T., and Roost, D. 1991. *The machine that changed the world: The story of lean production*. New York: Harper Perennials. Chapter 3.

8. If a university is in an extreme financial situation and cost cutting and personnel reductions are required, these actions should be taken prior to implementing LHE. The subsequent introduction of LHE can then be coupled with a sincere commitment to job security moving forward.

9. To many Lean and LHE proponents, the immediate and significant improvement in critical performance metrics following its intervention provide conclusive evidence of its effectiveness, making the need for more rigorous field experiments moot. However, these results are usually focused on improvements to processes and services and to a much lesser extent on employee attitudes and outcomes. For a review, see Balzer, W.K., Alexander, K., and Smith, E.N. 2009. What do we know about the psychology of lean? In *24th Annual Conference of the Society for Industrial and Organizational Psychology*. New Orleans, LA.

10. In fact, some university vendors may have already adopted Lean principles and practices. In these cases, they may be willing to share their expertise and "loan" Lean experts to guide and support the university's efforts to adopt LHE.

11. The scholarship process (i.e., the creation, integration, and dissemination of ideas and creative works), while recognized as important to the mission of many universities, is not discussed here. However, LHE principles and practices can certainly reduce waste and improve flow in this critical area, as demonstrated in earlier applications of Lean principles and practices. For example, the research and development process at Toyota embraces the Lean philosophy, and its application is given credit for the development and success of Toyota's luxury Lexus brand and the rapid development and production of its Prius hybrid vehicle. See Liker, J.K. 2004. *The Toyota Way: 14 management principles from the world's greatest manufacturer.* New York: McGraw-Hill. Chapters 5 and 6.

12. Recommendations are adapted from Liker, J.K. 2004. *The Toyota Way: 14 management principles from the world's greatest manufacturer.* New York: McGraw-Hill. Chapter 22; and Womack J.P., and Jones, D.T. 2003. *Lean Thinking: Banish Waste and Create Wealth in Your Corporation.* New York: Free Press. Chapter 15.

13. See Tapping, D., and Shuker, T. 2003. *Value stream management for the lean office: Eight steps to planning, mapping, and sustaining lean improvements in administrative areas.* New York: Productivity Press. p. 15.

About the Author

Bill Balzer has over 25 years of experience working in higher education. He is a professor of industrial-organizational psychology at Bowling Green State University, and currently serves as Dean of BGSU Firelands College. He has served in a number of leadership roles including program director of the nationally ranked doctoral program in I-O psychology, chair of the Department of Psychology, and Dean of Continuing and Extended Education. In 1996–97, he was a fellow of the American Council on Education and spent his fellowship year working in the office of the president at Wayne State University.

Dr. Balzer's research interests include understanding the effects of Lean principles and practices on individual job attitudes and behaviors, evidence-based organizational diagnosis and intervention, the assessment of job satisfaction, and understanding, measuring, and improving job performance. He has participated in numerous university initiatives to improve university processes and effectiveness. He has consulted with profit and non-profit organizations including Owens-Illinois, Citibank, the Pennsylvania State Police, Merrill Lynch & Company, and Procter & Gamble.

For more information, visit http://leanhighereducation.com or contact Dr. Balzer at wbalzer@leanhighereducation.com.

Index